LITTLE ENCYCLOPEDIA

OF

Card

& Magic

Tricks

THE LITTLE GIANT ENCYCLOPEDIA

OF

Card & Magic Tricks

THE DIAGRAM GROUP

Sterling Publishing Co., Inc.   New York

Many thanks for Isabella Percy and Toby Gee for testing
the tricks.

Library of Congress Cataloging-in-Publication Data
The little giant encyclopedia of card & magic tricks / the
  Diagram Group.
        p.   cm.
  Includes index.
  ISBN 0-8069-9347-2
  1. Card tricks—Encyclopedias.   2. Conjuring—
Encyclopedias.   I. Diagram Group.
GV1549.L48   1996
795.4'38'03—dc20   96–25432
                                                    CIP

17   16   15   14   13   12   11

Published 1996 by Sterling Publishing Co., Inc.
387 Park Avenue South, New York, N.Y. 10016
© 1996 by Diagram Visual Information Ltd
Distributed in Canada by Sterling Publishing
C/o Canadian Manda Group, 165 Dufferin Street
Toronto, Ontario, Canada M6K 3H6
Manufactured in China
All rights reserved

Sterling ISBN-13:978-0-8069-9347-8
        ISBN-10:0-8069-9347-2

For information about custom editions, special sales, premium and
coporate purchases, please contact Sterling Special Sales
Department at 800-805-5489 or specialsales@sterlingpub.com

Foreword

Performing tricks has been a popular pastime among young and old for thousands of years. Historically, magicians have commanded great power and influence because of the magical effects they have created. Today, the most popular magic performers are TV stars who have achieved international fame.

This illustrated encyclopedia brings together over 150 tricks. It is divided into two sections. Section 1 contains over 80 card tricks and includes essential information on card handling and performing. Many tricks can be performed with just an ordinary pack of cards – and you can take a pack of cards anywhere.

Section 2 gives a brief history of magic, types of magic performance, what you will need and advice on performing. Over 60 tricks are included; they require the minimum of equipment – in many cases, just coins, handkerchiefs, and so on, without the need for specialist and expensive apparatus.

Each trick is described with step-by-step instructions, complemented with clear explanatory diagrams. The tricks are arranged by type and in roughly ascending order of difficulty. Information on finding a suitable trick – easy, moderately easy, or those requiring skill and practice – is given at the end of the book, together with a glossary of important terms and an index.

Contents

SECTION 1 CARD TRICKS

SECTION 2 MAGIC TRICKS

CONTENTS

Section 1
CARD TRICKS

Props

Some tricks require special props. You can usually find these around the house – a handkerchief, for example, is used in several tricks. You might also need a particular item of clothing. Some tricks require the performer to wear a jacket with deep side pockets big enough to hide two packs of cards.

CARD HANDLING

The tricks in this book are all easy to perform, but they do require practice at handling the cards. You will develop your card-handling skills gradually as you learn new tricks. Most tricks work better with nearly new or little-worn cards. Being able to handle cards well has many advantages. Your presentation looks much more professional and your audience takes you more seriously. Slick card handling is part of the entertainment – it can mesmerize your audience. Finally, and most importantly, good card handling is essential for the effective performance of many card tricks.

The overhand shuffle

This is the most common way to mix up the cards. Modifying the way this is done is the basis of many card tricks.

1

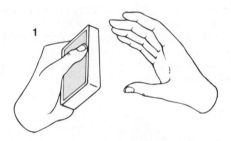

● Hold the deck in the left hand gently between thumb and fingers, with the backs of the cards facing to your left (**1**).
● With the right hand, pick up a block of cards from the lower half of the pack (**2**).

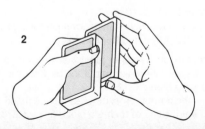

● Bring this block of cards back over the top half of the pack.

● With the thumb of your left hand scrape a few cards off the block and onto the pack, raising your right hand slightly as you do so (**3**). Repeat this action several times until you have shuffled all the bottom cards on to the top of the pack.

● Repeat the above procedure three or four times so that you have shuffled the entire pack.

● Practice this shuffle technique until you can do it smoothly, comfortably and without looking. You are then ready to modify the technique to perform some useful sleights of hand.

False overhand shuffles
There are several ways of performing a false overhand shuffle. They achieve different effects.

Keeping bottom cards in place Use this method when you have cards at the bottom of the pack which you want to keep there.

● Follow the normal procedure for the overhand shuffle, but instead of taking a block of cards from the bottom of the pack, take a block of cards from the top of the pack.

● Scrape cards from the block onto the top of the pack, as with an overhand shuffle. Continue shuffling this top block while leaving the lower cards untouched.

Keeping bottom cards in place

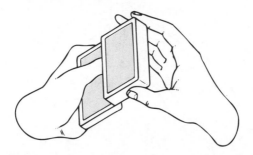

Keeping top cards in place Use this method when you have cards at the top of the pack which you want to keep there.

● Follow the procedure above for keeping bottom cards in place, but turn the pack around so that the cards are facing to your left, with their backs to your right.

● Shuffle as above while keeping the top cards (which are now at the bottom) in place.

Bringing top card to bottom This method brings the top card to the bottom of the pack – it can be later brought to the top again if needed (see below).

● Hold the pack in the normal position for an overhand

shuffle. With the left thumb pull the top card off the pack and into the left hand.
● Now shuffle the rest of the cards on top of the first card in the normal way.

Bringing top card to bottom

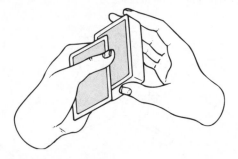

Bringing bottom card to top This method brings the bottom card to the top of the pack – later it can be brought to the bottom again if needed (see above).
● Shuffle in the normal way as for an overhand shuffle, bringing a block of cards from the bottom of the pack and shuffling these on top of the pack.
● As you shuffle to the end of the cards, scrape them off singly. This is made easier by applying pressure between the thumb and fingers of the right hand and so bending the cards.
● The final card is then dropped on top of the pack.

Bringing bottom card to top

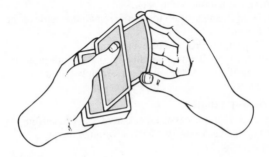

Keeping the order of the pack You can give the impression of shuffling the pack while keeping the order of cards the same. This is particularly useful for tricks employing a stacked deck.

Keeping the order of the pack

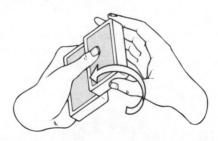

● Hold the pack in the left hand in the normal position for an overhand shuffle.

- With the right hand pick up about half of the cards from the bottom of the pack.
- Drop these cards on top of the remaining cards in the left hand.
- Repeat this procedure several times.
- Done quickly and smoothly, it gives the appearance of shuffling, when really you are simply cutting the pack several times in quick succession.

The riffle shuffle

This is an impressive and effective way of shuffling.
- Cut the pack into two halves, with the top stack to your right (**1**).

- Place the two stacks together and at an angle so that when you riffle the two nearside inner corners with your thumbs, the two stacks interweave (**2**).

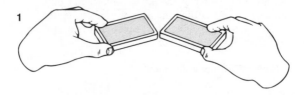

● When you finish riffling the cards, straighten them and square up the pack (**3**).

3

The false riffle shuffle
Like the overhand shuffle, the riffle shuffle can be modified to perform various sleights of hand.

Keeping bottom cards in place For a false riffle shuffle, you will need to adopt a more crowded finger position than with the normal riffle shuffle, so that onlookers can't see what is going on.

● Follow the normal procedure for the riffle shuffle, but release a block of cards with your left thumb before releasing any cards with your right thumb.

Keeping bottom cards in place

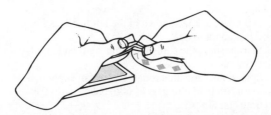

Keeping top cards in place The procedure is the same as that for the false riffle keeping bottom cards in place. The only difference is the order in which you release the cards.
- Start by interweaving right and left piles as normal.
- Finish by riffling with your left thumb while holding back the top of the right stack, and only letting this group of cards fall at the end.

Keeping top cards in place

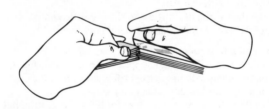

Card spread
Most card tricks are of the "pick a card" variety. One of the best ways to present cards to a spectator is to spread the cards in the hand, either in a straight line or in a fan shape.
- Hold the pack face down in the left hand, as if you are just about to deal.
- Start pushing the cards into your right hand with your left thumb.
- Spread the cards in a rough line or fan supported underneath by the fingers of both hands, with the thumbs on top.

Card spread

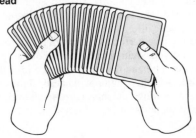

Ribbon spread

This is an on-the-table spread of cards. It is much easier to perform on a cloth-covered table than on a smooth, polished surface.

● Hold the squared-up pack face down between the thumb and fingers of your right hand.

● Place the pack on the table and sweep your hand from left to right, keeping your thumb and fingers in position and dragging your index finger across the top of the cards.

Done smoothly, the cards will spread out neatly and evenly in a line.

Ribbon spread

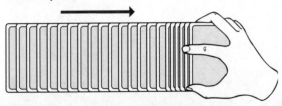

Flourish

This is a quick and elegant way of exposing all the cards face up.
- After you have performed a neat ribbon spread (see above), rest your right hand at the end of the spread.
- With your left hand flip over the left side of the left-hand card. A chain reaction will cause all the cards to turn over in a wave-like motion from left to right. Your right hand supports the last few cards to turn over.

Flourish

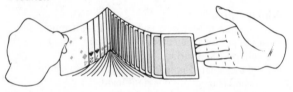

Cutting the cards

Cutting involves dividing the pack into two and putting the bottom half on the top. It alters the start and end point of the pack, but it does not alter the order or sequence of the cards.
The easiest way to cut cards is on a table top.

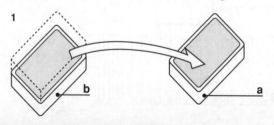

● Simply lift the top half of the pack (**a**) and place it to one side (**1**).
● Then place the bottom half (**b**) on top (**2**).

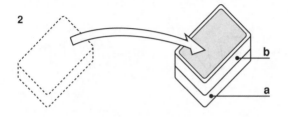

Swing cut This is a much more elegant method than the basic cut (above). It is done in the hand.
● Hold the pack face down by its short edges with your right thumb at the bottom left corner and your right index finger at the top left corner (**1**).
● With your index finger, lift and swivel the top half of the pack to the left, using your thumb as a pivot (**2**).

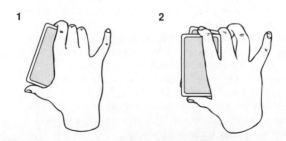

● Take the top stack in your left hand (**3**) and with your right hand bring the bottom stack over the top to rest on it (**4**). You have completed the cut.

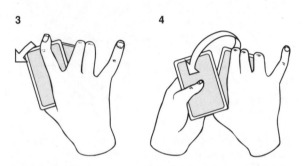

3   **4**

False cut This keeps the bottom card in place while the pack appears to be cut normally.

● Hold the pack lengthways between the fingers and thumb of the left hand.

● For a normal cut, grasp the lower half of the pack with the right hand, withdraw this bottom stack and bring it to the top.

● To make this into a false cut in order to keep the bottom card in place, follow the above procedure but squeeze the pack gently with your left hand as you withdraw the lower stack. This keeps the bottom card in place while the stack is withdrawn.

● Carefully shield the cards with your hands while you carry out this maneuver. This prevents the audience seeing exactly what is happening.

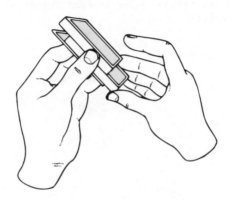

Glide

This sleight enables you to keep a selected card – one that you have already identified, for example – at the bottom of the pack so that you can produce it at any time.

● Transfer the selected card to the bottom of the pack using a false shuffle or some other technique.

● Hold the pack in your left hand, face down, with your fingers over and around the cards.

● With your little finger, draw back the bottom card about an inch. Now when you take cards from the bottom of the pack, you will avoid the selected card, which will remain on the bottom.

● Whenever you wish to take out the selected card, simply move the card forward into position with your

little finger (**1**), then withdraw it from the pack as
normal (**2**).

1 (bottom view)

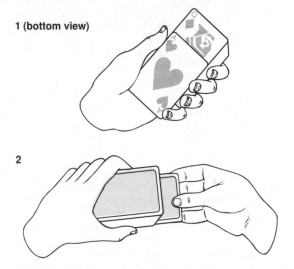

2

Glimpse
There are two effective ways of glimpsing the bottom
card of the pack.
• In one case, simply take the pack in your right hand
and square it against the table with the cards facing left
(**1**). A quick downward glance is all that is needed to
glimpse the bottom card.
• In the other case, grasp the pack in your right hand,
with thumb underneath and fingers on top.

● As you transfer the pack from right to left hand, tilt the pack just enough to catch a glimpse of the bottom card (**2**).

Both techniques work well when you are taking the pack from a spectator just after she has shuffled it.

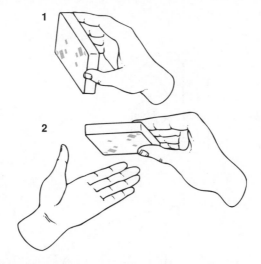

The double lift

Here, you take two cards from the top of the pack but give the appearance of taking only one. This has to be done cleanly, without fumbling, if it is to fool the audience.

● While you are talking and looking at the audience, square the deck with the fingers of your right hand.

● As you do so, bend your index finger and press it down on the top of the pack, and then lift the near ends of the two top cards with the ball of your right thumb.

● Move these two top cards very slightly to the right, and leave them there with your right thumb in place (**1**).

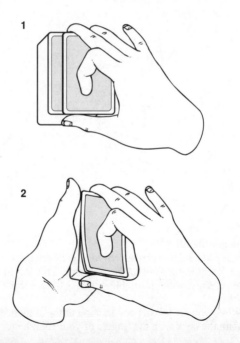

● Later, when you show the top card it is easy to pick up the top two cards as one. Simply bend them up at the back as you did before and lift them cleanly off the top (**2**) and show them to the audience (**3**).

When you normally pick up a single top card, make sure your moves look the same. From the spectator's point of view, taking one or two cards from the top should look exactly the same.

3

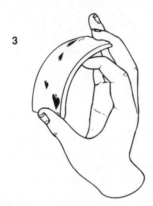

The slip force

The success of some tricks depends on you being able to "force" an unsuspecting spectator to pick a card you have already selected. Here is one force involving a simple sleight of hand, which "forces" the spectator to choose the top card of the pack.

● Stand with your right side to the audience with the cards in your left hand, furthest from the audience. The

card you wish the spectator to have is on top of the
pack.
● Riffle through the pack with your left thumb and ask
a spectator to say "stop" when she chooses.
● When stopped, tilt up the top cards using the right
hand (**1**).

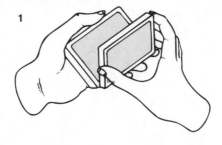

● Explain to the spectator that she has freely chosen a
card. While you are doing this, press on the edge of the
top card with your left fingers and in a sweeping
motion remove the top pile with your right hand. The
top card – trapped by your left fingers – will drop down
onto the lower pile (**2**). Done correctly, the sleight, in
particular the sweeping right hand, both misdirects the
audience and obscures the secret move.
● You now offer the spectator the lower pile and ask
her to take the "top" card. The card she has apparently
"chosen" from the middle of the pack is, of course, the
card from the top.

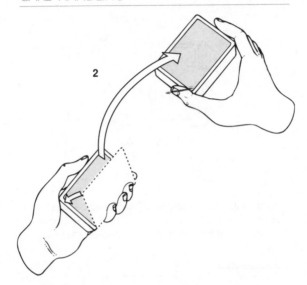

The palm

Palming is the process of hiding a card in the hand. It is quite hard to master at first, but is a very powerful technique. Here is one way to do it.

● With the chosen card on top of the pack, and with the pack in your left hand as though you are about to deal, bring your right hand over to take the pack. As you do so, misdirect the audience in some way – perhaps with a long-winded explanation – and use your left thumb to push the top card to the right (**1**).

● With the middle fingers of your left hand, push the

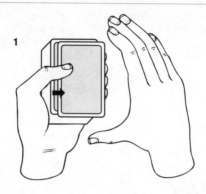

top card into your right palm. Providing you keep your right hand relaxed, you will find it folds easily around the card, and the move will not be conspicuous (**2**).

2 (bottom view)

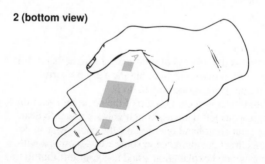

● You can now take the pack back into your left hand, as though you have just changed your mind. Your right

hand should hang naturally down by your side with the
card hidden.

● Some time later you can retrieve the card – perhaps
by appearing to pluck it from behind someone's ear.

Practice palming in front of the mirror to ensure that
your hand looks natural and no edges of the card can be
seen.

Switching packs

Many startling tricks can be performed by secretly
exchanging a pack that has been shuffled for one that
has been prearranged. To the onlooker, miraculous
tricks are performed with an apparently well-shuffled
deck.

Equipment

You will need to use two ordinary packs of playing
cards of identical design, and an elastic band. You will
also need a jacket with deep side pockets.

● Place an elastic band (**1**) (**a**) around one end of the
prearranged pack in order to hold the pack in place.

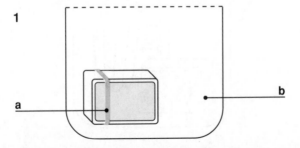

● Place this pack in the side pocket (**b**) of a jacket you
are wearing.

● Use the unarranged deck to perform tricks described
elsewhere in the book.

● When you are finished, have a spectator thoroughly
shuffle this pack.

● Put the pack in your pocket (next to the prearranged
pack) (**2**), pretending that you have finished with it and
are about to do something else.

● Grasp the second pack in your pocket and push the
elastic band off with your thumb. Suddenly pretend to
remember that you want to do another card trick.

● Bring out the prearranged deck. If you do this
casually, the spectators will not suspect that the
shuffled pack has been switched for another one.

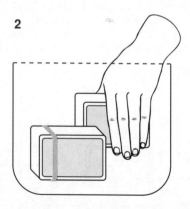

PREPARATION

Simply knowing how a trick is done and how to carry it out will not make you a successful performer. You are still only halfway there. You need to entertain the audience and convince them – by all your actions – that something exciting is happening. This takes practice – and a lot of it.

Here are the dos and don'ts of preparation for mastering each trick.

Dos
- Learn one trick at a time.
- Learn the trick thoroughly so that you are absolutely confident how to present it.
- Learn a few tricks well, rather than many tricks sloppily.
- Imagine what the trick will be like from the audience's point of view. Will it be interesting? Will they spot something they aren't meant to see? How can you distract them so they won't notice what you're doing with the cards? How can you finish the trick in a dramatic way?
- Continue working on a trick, and making adjustments, until you are completely happy with it. This may mean the trick is slightly different from the way it is described here – but you will have made the trick your own.

continued

- Adjust your finger positions if you find a particular move difficult or awkward – not everyone's hands are the same.
- Track down the weak spots in a trick and work out ways to get around them, using misdirection if necessary.
- Practice frequently but in small doses. You are more likely to overcome a problem when you come to it afresh.
- Practice in front of a mirror. It helps "fine-tune" your performance and allows you to see how it looks from the audience's point of view. It also encourages you to look away from your hands and at the audience.
- Try a new trick on friends or family and listen to their comments.
- Make the props yourself or buy them from a reputable dealer in magic equipment. You can then be sure you are buying reliable equipment which looks good, does the job, and will last.
- Remember, first and foremost, you are an entertainer – you must make your performance interesting and lively.

Don'ts

- Don't show any trick until you have practiced it thoroughly.
- Don't perform a trick until you can do it so well that you don't have to worry about "what comes next."
- Don't tell anyone how the trick is done. There is a saying among magic-trick performers: "Practice. Practice again. Practice until you can do it perfectly. Then practice some more."

PERFORMING

A performance of card-trick magic – whether a single trick or a whole routine – is not merely a collection of bits cobbled together. You need to prepare your performance as a whole piece, with a start and finish. Think through your act carefully so that it is smooth and polished and so that one trick or part follows on naturally from another.

The structure of a performance

If you plan to do a performance, make your act last 10–15 minutes using six to eight tricks. Here are some suggestions as to what you might include:

- At the beginning do quick and easy tricks which allow you to relax and let the audience get to know you. Simple key card and mathematical tricks are suitable here.

• In the middle of the performance, when you and the audience are more relaxed, use longer, more complicated tricks which involve the spectators more. Tricks using arranged cards, sleights of hand or props are suitable here.

• Try to finish on a spectacular visual trick. The Fabulous Four Aces (see p. 142), Three Cards Across (see p. 137), and Finale (see p. 250) are good tricks with which to finish your act.

Here are the dos and don'ts in preparing and performing your act.

Dos – Preparing the performance

• Choose tricks which are suitable for the kind of audience you are expecting.

• Read about magic and magicians, and use every opportunity you can to look at magicians as they perform and to learn from them.

• Plan your performance in detail.

• Decide in which order you are going to do the tricks, and how one trick will lead on to the next.

• Inject variety into your act. To the performer, the tricks work in different ways. To the spectator, most tricks appear to be of the "spectator takes a card and the performer identifies it" type. Make sure you

continued

emphasize the differences among tricks and include a variety of tricks that involve more than one person, where cards are revealed in different ways, and where various props are used.

- Work out what to say from start to finish.
- Vary the pace of your performance; for example, intersperse slow tricks with fast ones.
- Be aware of your own strengths and weaknesses and tailor your performance to make the most of your strengths.
- Make sure your hands and fingernails are clean and that you are neat and well groomed.
- Make sure you have all your props in the right places at the start of a performance.
- Expect to get excited and anxious before a performance. Professionals do.
- Practice regularly and pay attention to detail. This increases confidence in your performance and reduces the chances of getting stage fright – an attack of nerves on stage.
- Take a dozen deep breaths before walking on stage. It calms your nerves and allows you to concentrate on entertaining your audience.

Dos – During the performance

- Choose a trick you can do well as your first number.
- Speak clearly and talk slowly.
- Tell a story, make a joke – above all, entertain – but do it naturally. Be yourself. Find your own style.
- Be prepared to make changes during the performance if things go wrong.
- Use your hands and eyes to direct the audience where you want them to look.
- Use explanations and patter to misdirect the audience from what you are actually doing.
- Handle props confidently and openly to allay the suspicions of the audience.
- Involve spectators in the trick. This helps to direct attention away from yourself and whatever you are doing.
- Ask a spectator to show the chosen card to someone else in the audience. This prevents the possible embarrassment of the spectator later forgetting the card, or even purposely naming another card to spoil the trick.
- Relax and smile. Look as though you are enjoying yourself.

continued

- React to your own tricks. Scratch your head, shrug your shoulders, and so on to help convey your feelings.
- Use words to create drama. Talk slowly to show concentration and build up suspense. Talk louder and faster at the climax of a trick.
- Think about your performance and constantly strive to improve your presentation.
- Aim to make the audience believe – by your words, movements and appearance – that you are truly a successful magician.
- Leave the audience wanting more.

Don'ts – During the performance
- Don't do two similar tricks in the same performance.
- Don't repeat a trick.
- Don't include too many "take-a-card" tricks.
- Don't try to do a trick if you are not confident about it – you are likely to give a poor performance.
- Don't speak too fast. This is easy to do if you are nervous. Slow down.

continued

- Don't state the obvious, such as "Here is a pack of cards."
- Don't say anything to arouse suspicions, eg "This is a pack of cards – look, there's nothing wrong with them."
- Don't spoil a surprise by stating what will happen before it does.
- Don't insult anyone – whether present or not.
- Don't take everything so seriously that if things go wrong your act falls apart. Laugh with everyone else and then get on with the next trick.

USING THIS BOOK

The tricks

Each trick is described as follows:

Effect – what the audience will see happen.

Equipment – all the materials you need to do the trick (it is assumed that a table or flat surface is available).

Preparation – techniques you need to practice and any card sorting or prop preparation required.

Performing – a step-by-step procedure (with illustrations) explaining how the trick is done.

1. Tricks using key cards

A "key" card is a known card which you can place next to or near an unknown card to identify the location of the unknown card. When you find the key card, you find the unknown card.

THE MAGIC TOUCH

This trick requires at least two spectators.

Effect

A spectator chooses a card from the pack. The card is returned to the pack and the pack is cut. The performer spreads the cards face up in a row and finds the card by apparently sensing reactions in the spectator.

Equipment

An ordinary pack of playing cards is needed.

Preparation

The trick depends on the use of the glimpse (see p. 24) with the top card as key.

Performing

● Ask for a volunteer. As the volunteer comes forward openly scan the cards. Say you are checking to make sure they are all there, but as you do so, glimpse the card at the top of the pack (**1**). This is the key card (**a**).

- Close the pack and place it face down on the table.
- Ask the volunteer to cut a small pile of cards (**2**) (**b**) from the top of the deck (**c**) and to memorize the bottom card (**d**).

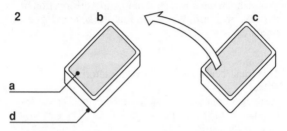

- Tell the volunteer to now cut this small pile of cards (**3**) (**b**) so that the chosen card (**d**) is in the middle – doing so brings the selected card above the key card (**a**).

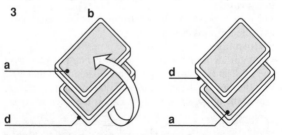

- Ask a second spectator to lift up some of the cards in the remaining pack (**c**). The volunteer then places the small pile (**b**) on top of this pack, and the spectator returns his cards to the top of the pile, so losing the chosen card in the center of the pack (**4**).

4

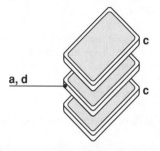

• Pick up the cards and turn them face up on the table, spreading them across the table so that most of them are seen. The selected card will be directly to the left of the key card.

5

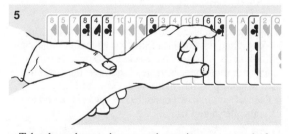

• Take the volunteer's arm and, starting at one end of the spread cards, pass the volunteer's index finger over the cards apparently sensing for small muscle reactions (**5**). Pass back and forth several times, and finally push the volunteer's hand forward so that the index finger touches the selected card. Say: "This is the one; I can sense your reaction."

GET TOGETHER

Effect

The pack is cut in two, and the spectator and performer each take half a pack. They both choose a card from their respective piles, look at them and return them. When the piles are combined the two selected cards mysteriously come together.

Equipment

An ordinary pack of playing cards is needed.

Preparation

The trick depends on the use of the glimpse (see p. 24) with the bottom card as key.

Performing

● Allow a spectator to shuffle the deck and cut it in half.

● Get the spectator to give you one half of the pack and to keep the other half.

● Each of you shuffles your pile of cards.

● Ask the spectator to remove any card from her pile, look at it and remember it. Say that you will do the same.

● Look at the card you have selected but make no attempt to remember it. Instead, glimpse the bottom card of your pile. This will be the key card (**c**).

● Each of you places your selected card (**1**) (**d**) on top of your pile (**a** and **b**).

1

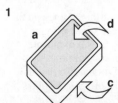

● Now place your pile (**2**) (**a**) on top of your spectator's (**b**). Doing so puts your key card (**c**) on top of her card (**d**).

2

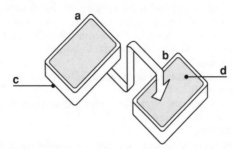

● Ask the spectator to cut the deck twice "to lose both cards in the deck."

● Now explain: "My card was [name the bottom key card]. Would you be surprised if my card had magically come to lie next to yours?"

● Hand the cards to the spectator. When the spectator sorts through them she will find her card next to yours.

TURN-AROUND CARD

Effect

A spectator selects a card from one of three piles. The
performer merges the piles, attempts to find the chosen
card and leads the spectator into thinking a mistake has
been made. The performer then turns the tables on the
spectator, suddenly exposing the right card.

Equipment

An ordinary pack of playing cards is needed.

Preparation

The trick depends on the use of the glimpse (see p. 24)
with the bottom card as key.

Performing

● Spread the cards face up to show the audience that the
cards are well sorted.

● Re-form and cut the pack.

● Square the pack, and as you do so glimpse and
memorize the bottom card. This is the key card.

● Place the pack face down.

● Ask a spectator to cut the deck into three even piles
and take a card from the middle of any pile. (You
should have followed which of the three piles has the
key card at the bottom.)

● The spectator should then replace the chosen card at
the top of any pile.

● If the spectator puts the chosen card (**1**) (**a**) on top of
the pile containing the key card (**b**), ask him to cut that
pile and replace the cut. This will put the key card on
top of the selected card. Then put the piles together.

1

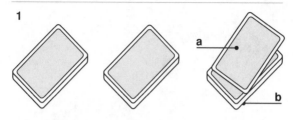

● If the spectator places the chosen card (**2**) (**a**) on a pile other than the one containing the key (**b**), put the piles together so that the key card goes on top of the selected card.

2

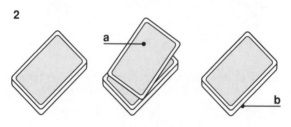

● Turn the pack face up and cut it into three piles.
● Spread each pile to show the spectator all the cards (**3**, see over).
● Ask the spectator to pick out the pile containing the selected card.

3

● Pick up this pile (**4**). By this time you will have seen the key card (**b**) and know that the card next to it is the selected one (**a**).

4

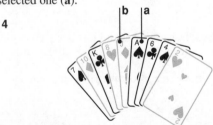

● Hold the pile face down and start to deal the cards slowly face up on the table, overlapping each card.

● When you deal the key card (**5**) (**b**), note the card that
follows it – this is the chosen card (**a**). Deal a few more
cards.

5

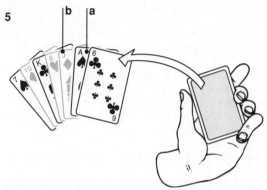

● Now say that the next card you turn over will be the
chosen one. Since the spectator saw you deal his card
already, he will assume that you missed it.
● Pick up his card (**a**) and turn it face down (**6**).

6

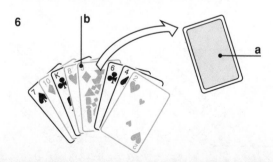

IN BETWEEN

You will need three or more spectators.

Effect

Two spectators each select a card from the pack. A
volunteer then selects a card. They return the cards to
the pack and the performer then extracts the volunteer's
card sandwiched between the two spectators' cards.

Equipment

An ordinary pack of playing cards is needed.

Preparation

This trick relies on the use of the glimpse (see p. 24)
and the bottom card as key. It also requires the ability to
cut cards with precision.

Performing

● Ask two spectators each to select a card from a
shuffled pack.

● Get them to replace the two cards on top of the pack.

● Square the pack and as you do so glimpse and
remember the bottom card. This is the key card.

● Cut and replace the pack (**1**) so that the key card (**a**) is
now on top of the two chosen cards (**b** and **c**).

1

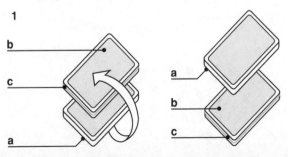

● Ask a volunteer to name a card (not one of the
spectators' chosen cards).
● Ask the volunteer to help you find that card. Get her
to turn the pack face up and look for the card (**2**). You
are looking for your key card (**a**). The spectators' cards
(**b** and **c**) are next to it. The volunteer now takes out her
card (**d**).

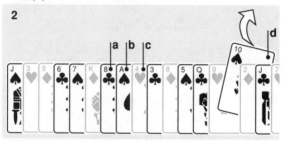

● As you bring the cards together to re-form the pack
(**3**), slip your right little finger between the spectators'
cards (**b** and **c**). Turn the cards face down and in the
same movement cut the pack at the break where your
little finger is inserted. One card (**b**) goes to the bottom
of the pack and the other (**c**) goes to the top.

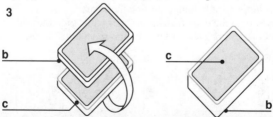

● Ask the volunteer to put her card (**d**) on top of the pack (**4**).

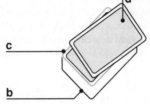

● Now cut and re-form the pack (**5**) so that the bottom card (**b**) rests on top of the volunteer's card (**d**), sandwiching it between the spectators' cards (**b** and **c**).

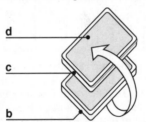

● Ask the spectators to name their cards. Thank the volunteer for helping you find their cards.
● Spread the deck face up (**6**). The cards on either side of the volunteer's card will be the spectators' cards.

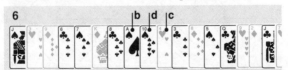

THE TWO DETECTIVES

This trick can be used to tell a story.

Effect

A spectator chooses a card and returns it to the top of the pack. The performer takes out the two black Js from the pack – the "detectives." By quickly manipulating the pack behind the back, the performer miraculously sandwiches the chosen card between the two Js – the detectives have found the card.

Equipment

An ordinary pack of playing cards is needed.

Preparation

The trick depends on the use of the glimpse (see p. 24) and the bottom card as key. You will need to practice manipulating the cards behind your back.

Performing

● Ask a spectator to shuffle the pack.
● Take back the pack and square it, glancing at the bottom card as you do so.
● Ask the spectator to choose a card and place it on the top of the pack.
● Cut and re-form the pack (**1**), bringing the bottom card – the key card (**a**) – on top of the chosen card (**b**).

1

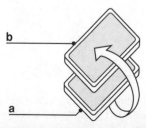

● Turn the deck of cards over and spread them out (**2**).
Explain that you are looking for the two detectives –
the black Js – who will help you find the card. In fact
you are looking for your key card (**a**) which is to the
left of the chosen card (**b**).

● Take out the two black Js and put them to one side.

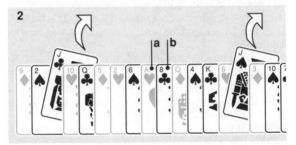

● Now cut and re-form the pack (**3**) so that the key card
(**a**) goes to the bottom of the pack. The selected card
will now be at the top of the pack (**b**).

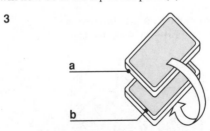

● Tell the spectator: "I'll let the detectives find the
card." With one hand place the deck behind your back.

With the other hand, take one of the black Js and place it face up under the top card (**b**) of the deck. Then take the other black J and place it face up on top of the deck (**4**).

4

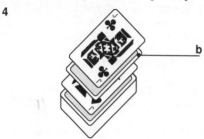

● Cut and re-form the deck to hide the cards in the middle.
● Bring the deck round to the front and ask the spectator for the name of the chosen card.
● Place the deck on the table and with a flourish spread the cards face down (**5**). The two black Js will be face up on either side of a card. The card sandwiched between the two is the spectator's card (**b**). Hold it up and say: "The detectives have found the card!"

5

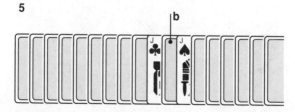

PERFORMER'S MISTAKE

This is a simple key card trick with a twist.

Effect

The performer appears to make a mistake, but just as the spectators are about to enjoy a laugh at the performer's expense, the tables are turned.

Equipment

An ordinary pack of playing cards is needed.

Preparation

The trick uses the glimpse (see p. 24) and false overhand shuffle (see p. 12) techniques.

Performing

● Begin by squaring the pack and glimpsing the bottom card. This is the key card.

● Shuffle the pack using a false overhand shuffle which keeps the bottom card in place.

● Give the pack face down to one spectator and ask her to cut the pack into three piles (**1**). Keep track of which pile contains the key card (**a**).

1

● Ask the spectator to look at and remember the top card of any pile, show it to the audience, and replace it on any pile.

● Your job is to ensure that the key card goes on top of the spectator's card. If she puts her chosen card (**b**) back on the pile that contains the key card, tell her to cut the pile (**2**). This puts your key card (**a**) on her card (**b**). Then ask her to put this pile on either of the other piles, and put the third pile on top.

2

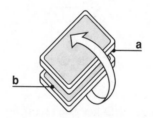

● If she puts her card on one of the other piles, point to the pile containing the key card and say: "Put this pile on your card, and the last pile on both." Again, your key card is on the chosen card.

● Ask the spectator to cut the pack twice; the chances of separating the key card from the spectator's are small.

● Now take the pack and deal the cards one at a time, face up, in a column of overlapping cards.

● As you deal, continue talking: "Don't say anything. Let me find the card. I'll tell you when I see it."

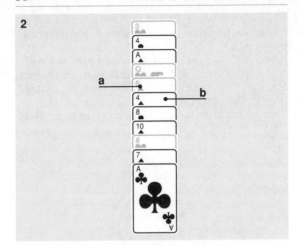

● When you get to the key card (**2**) (**a**), deal the next card – the chosen one (**b**) – and keep going. Deal out four or five more cards.

● By this time, the audience will think you have missed the card. Prepare to deal out the next card and say: "The next card I will turn over will be the chosen card. Anyone care to take a bet?" You should get some takers.

● Now, instead of turning over the next card as the audience is expecting, reach out to the column and flip over the chosen card (**b**). It is time to call in your bet.

There are many ways of inconspicuously marking a
card to identify it as a key card. Here are two examples.
Several tricks using marked cards appear later.

IMPOSSIBLE LOCATION

This highly effective trick uses a card with a bent
corner as a temporarily marked key.

Effect

A spectator removes a card from the pack, remembers
it, and returns it anywhere in the pack. The performer
then takes the pack and hands it back to the spectator to
shuffle. Afterwards, the performer cuts the pack and
reveals the chosen card.

Equipment

A new or nearly new pack of playing cards is needed.

Preparation

Practice the moves – particularly bending and
unbending the corner of the card – and accompanying
patter so that you can do it flawlessly every time.

Performing

● Hand the pack to a spectator and ask him to shuffle it.

● Take back the pack, fan the cards with faces down
and ask a spectator to remove a card, look at it and
remember it.

● Close up the pack and ask the spectator to return the
card to any location within the pack. As he does so,
hold the pack tightly so that it is difficult to insert the
card all the way.

● With a twist of your wrist, turn the pack (**1**) so that
the chosen card (**a**) protrudes slightly toward you.

● Say "Thank you" and confirm that the spectator has freely chosen where to replace the card. As you talk, use a hidden finger (**b**) to bend over one corner (**c**) of the protruding card.

1

● Now square up the pack and hand it back to the spectator to shuffle.
● Take back the pack. If you have bent the card correctly, it will form a slight break (**d**) in the pack (**2**). Cut the cards at the break and locate the chosen card (you can even do this behind your back).

2

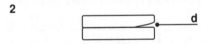

● As you remove the chosen card from the pack run your fingers over the corner to straighten out the bend. The audience will now have no clue as to how you carried out the trick.

THE DENTED CARD

This sophisticated trick uses a dented card as the temporarily marked key.

Effect

The trick produces two effects. The performer is able to guess how many cards a spectator keeps in her pocket, and then correctly predicts one card she has chosen.

Equipment

A new or nearly new pack of playing cards and a sharp fingernail are needed.

Preparation

Practice denting cards with your fingernail. When practicing, mark the sides, not the top and bottom, of the cards.

Performing

● Allow the spectator to remove any 12 cards from the pack. Ask her to shuffle these.

● As she is shuffling these, take the rest of the deck and nick the top edge of the top card with your fingernail. Turn the deck around and nick the bottom edge of the top card in the same way (**1**).

1

● Place the pack on the table. Your key card is on top.

● Ask the spectator to place some of the 12 cards in her pocket.

● Ask her to shuffle the cards remaining in her hand and look at and remember the bottom card. Then ask her to place the cards on top of the rest of the pack. Her chosen card is now on top of the key card.

● Hand the pack to her and ask her to deal face down a row of six overlapping cards.

● Ask her to deal face down a second row of six cards below the first (**2**).

● Look for the key card (**a**). This card is number one. Now count the cards from this one to the card at the far right of the second row. This number is the number of cards in her pocket. (Note: If the key card is in the first row, the number will be greater than six; if it is in the second row, the number will be six or less.)

● Now tell the spectator how many cards she has in her pocket and get her to take them out and confirm this.

● Then, ask her to put a finger on one of the cards in the second row. There is a chance it is the card she originally chose (**b**) – the one just before the key card – in which case the trick is over. Ask her to turn over the card, and everyone will be amazed.

● If she places her finger on another card, scoop up all the other cards, making sure her original chosen card (**b**) is on the bottom. Glimpse this card as you add the pile to the rest of the pack.

● Now ask the spectator to turn over her card. Say: "Ah, lovely" and pretend to go through a complicated calculation. Finally, identify the original chosen card.

2

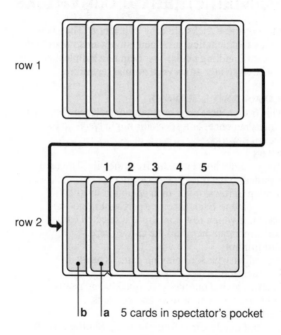

row 1

1 2 3 4 5

row 2

b a 5 cards in spectator's pocket

2. Mathematical card tricks

Most of these tricks are easy to perform. They depend on the mathematical arrangement of cards rather than on card-handling skills. Try them as a simple and effective change from your normal repertoire.

ROWS AND COLUMNS

This trick is best used on a young audience. Don't use it more than once, or a spectator might catch on to how the trick works.

Effect

A spectator chooses a card from the pile. The card is returned to the pile. The performer spreads the cards face up in rows of six, then again but in a new arrangement. Each time, the performer asks the spectator which row contains the selected card. The performer can then find the chosen card.

Equipment

An ordinary pack of playing cards is needed.

Preparation

Practice laying out the cards quickly and neatly into a tight arrangement of rows and columns.

Performing

● Count out 36 cards from the pack. Shuffle this pile using an overhand shuffle.

● Ask a spectator to choose a card from the pile, put the card back, and then shuffle the pile.

● Take the pile and lay the cards face up in six rows of six cards each (**1**), proceeding from left to right in a row, and then starting on the next row underneath. The cards must be arranged precisely as shown, so that the cards in each row are touching one another but there is a space between one row and the next. Thus the rows will be noticeable, but the columns will not.

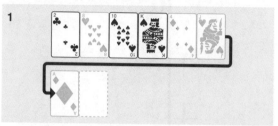

● Ask the spectator to point out which row contains the chosen card (for example, row 3).

● Now pick up the cards in the same order in which you put them down. Make sure you remember in which row (from the top) the chosen card is found.

● Arrange the cards in six rows again, but lay them out as columns (**2**, see over). Instead of proceeding from one row to the next, proceed from one column to the next. When you finish one column start the next one to the right. Just as before, let the cards in the same row touch each other, but leave spaces between one row and the next.

● Once again, ask the spectator which row contains the chosen card (for example, row 4) (**3**, see over). At this point, you can name the card. How? If the spectator said the card was in row 3 first time round, and in row 4 second time round, then the card is located in the third column of the fourth row (**a**). Because of the way you have arranged the cards, rows the first time round become columns the second time round. Where the column and row intersect is where the chosen card is found.

2

3

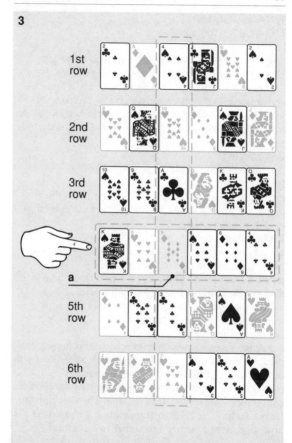

1st row

2nd row

3rd row

a

5th row

6th row

THREE COLUMNS

This trick is a foolproof one.

Effect

A spectator chooses a card and returns it to the pile. The performer spreads the cards face up in three columns of seven, three separate times. Each time, the performer asks the spectator which row contains the selected card. The performer is then able to pick out the card, which is always the middle card of the final arrangement.

Equipment

An ordinary pack of playing cards is needed.

Preparation

Practice laying out the cards in three columns three times in a row, so as to consistently find the chosen card as the center one.

Performing

● Count out 21 cards from the pack. Shuffle this pile using an overhand shuffle (see p. 12).

● Ask a spectator to first choose a card from the pile, then put the card back and shuffle the pile.

● Take the pile, and openly lay the cards face up in three columns of seven cards, proceeding from top to bottom and from left to right (**1**).

● Ask the spectator which column contains his selected card. Now pick up the cards in each column from top to bottom (**2**), starting with the first column and continuing with the column which contains the chosen card – for example, the third column. Then pick up the final column. The column containing the chosen card is now sandwiched between the other two columns.

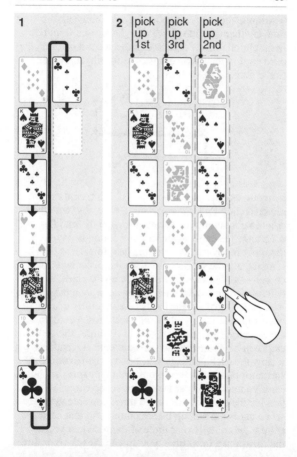

● Arrange the cards again in three columns but this time lay them out in rows. Place the first card in the first column, the second card in the second column, the third card in the third column, the fourth card in the first column and so on (**3**).

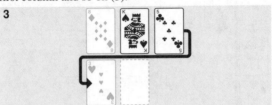

3

● Again, ask the spectator which column contains the selected card. Pick the cards up in columns, with the column containing the selected card in the middle.
● Arrange the cards again in three columns, laying them out in rows as you did the last time.
● Again, ask the spectator which column contains the chosen card. For the final time pick up the cards, as before in columns, with the chosen column in the middle.
● To finish, deal out the cards face up either in a single pile or in columns (**4**). In a pile, the chosen card will be the eleventh card you deal out. In columns, the chosen card will be in the middle (**a**) – also the eleventh card.
● How the trick works is as follows: The first time the spectator points out the column that contains the chosen card, you know the card is one of seven cards. When you lay the cards out a second time, you spread these seven cards out among three columns, so that each column has only two or three of them. When you lay the cards out a third time, you spread these two or three

cards out so that each column contains only one of
them, and always in the middle of the column. By
putting the chosen column in the middle the last time
you pick up the cards, you automatically make the
chosen card the middle card – the eleventh.

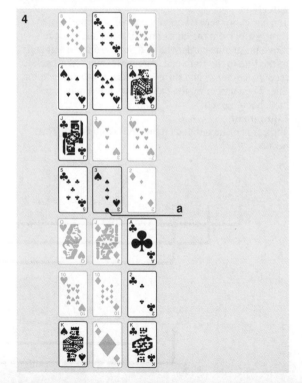

TEN IN A LINE

This trick is best used on a young audience. Providing the order of cards is not disturbed, the trick can be repeated successfully several times in a row, to the increasing bewilderment of the audience.

Effect

Ten cards lie face down on the table. The performer turns away from the cards and asks the audience to move up to nine cards, one at a time, from the left end of the line to the right end. The performer turns back to face the audience and turns over one of the cards in the line. The number on the card shows how many cards have been moved.

Equipment

Ten cards of mixed suits numbered from A to 10 are needed.

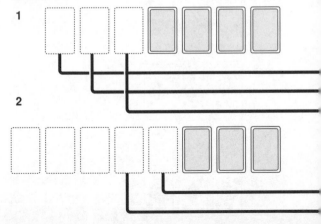

Preparation

Practice the trick several times with the cards face up to see how it works. Before performing the trick, prepare the ten cards so that they are in order, from A to 10.

Performing

● Lay the cards face down in a row so that they are in order, from A to 10, going from left to right.

● Tell the audience that, while your back is turned, they should move some cards from the left end of the row to the right end of the row, one card at a time. They may move up to nine cards, and you will guess how many cards they moved.

● Before you turn your back, move some, say three, of the cards yourself to show how they should be moved (**1**).

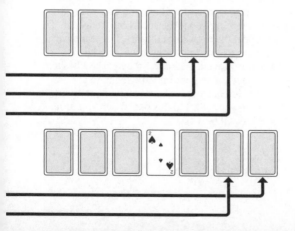

● Now, turn your back and let the audience move the cards.

● Turn back to face the audience. If in your initial demonstration you moved three cards, count three cards from the right-hand end of the row, and turn over the fourth card. The number of the card will tell you how many cards were moved. If, for example, the audience moved two cards (**2**), the number on the card you turn over will be a 2.

● You can repeat this method several times, but each time you must add the moved number of cards to the previous score, and this will tell you which card to turn over. In our example, if you do the trick a second time, you need to add the three you moved to the two moved by the audience. This gives you five, the number of cards to count from the right-hand end of the row. Turning over the sixth card will tell you how many cards the audience moved the second time round.

● You can repeat the trick several times, but you have to keep a running score in your head of the total number of cards moved. Whenever the total reaches ten or more, subtract ten and use only the remainder.

Note: If your audience tries to fool you by not moving any cards at all, you will find this out. When you turn over the card it will be a 10.

TIME WILL TELL

This trick uses cards displayed as the hours on a clock face as a way of finding a chosen card.

Effect

A spectator is given a pile of cards and asked to pocket several and shuffle the rest. She memorizes the bottom card and then returns the pile to the top of the pack. The performer then deals out 12 cards in a circle to form the hours on a clock face, and asks the spectator to count the cards in her pocket. That number gives the hour on the clock face where her chosen card will be.

Equipment

An ordinary pack of playing cards is needed.

Preparation

Practice spreading cards between your hands so that you can quickly and easily count out 13 cards without your audience noticing.

Performing

● Ask a spectator to shuffle the deck.

● Take the pack and casually spread the cards between your fingers. As you do so, silently count off 13 cards and hand them to a spectator saying, "Here, take these."

● Place the remainder of the pack face down on the table.

● Turn your back to the audience and explain to the spectator with the cards: "While my back is turned, put some of your cards in your pocket. Shuffle the remainder. Now look at the bottom card and memorize it. Put those cards back on the deck on the table."

● When the spectator has done this, turn back around. Pick up the deck and explain: "I will deal out the cards to represent a clock face."

● Begin to deal out 12 cards in an anticlockwise direction. The first card is placed at the 12 o'clock position, the next card at 11, and so on, until you have dealt a circle of cards on the table. Place the rest of the pack below the 12 o'clock card (**1**).

● Explain to the audience which card position represents each hour on the clock face.

● Ask the spectator to remove the cards she placed in her pocket earlier. Ask her: "How many cards do you have?" For this example, let us assume she has six cards.

● Explain: "You have six cards. Please look at the clock and point to the card that lies in the six o'clock position."

● Ask: "What was the name of the card you memorized?" When she names the card, ask her to turn over the card she is pointing to. It will be her card.

Note: The trick works because the number of cards the spectator returned to the deck is always equal to 13 minus the number of cards she pocketed. If she pockets five, there are eight of her cards on top of the deck, and the eighth card is the one she memorized. Starting at 12 o'clock and moving anticlockwise, the memorized card will always be found at the hour indicated by the number of cards in the spectator's pocket.

1

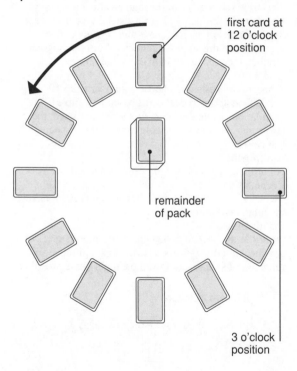

first card at
12 o'clock
position

remainder
of pack

3 o'clock
position

THE NINTH CARD

This trick relies on a simple mathematical principle. Numbers 10 through 19 have a special property; when the two digits of each of these numbers are added together, and this total is subtracted from the original number, then the result will always be nine.

Effect

A spectator is asked to choose a number from 10 to 19, and is then asked to deal cards based on simple calculations using this number. Once completed, the performer will always be able to predict the spectator's last card.

Equipment

An ordinary pack of playing cards is needed.

Preparation

The trick is straightforward. Practice quickly glimpsing the ninth card of the pack.

Performing

● Shuffle the pack and then glance through it as if you are checking it for jokers. As you do so, glimpse and remember the ninth card from the top. (Remember that

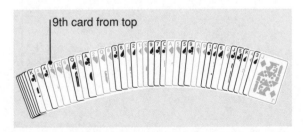

9th card from top

because the cards are face up, the top of the deck becomes the bottom.)

● Set the deck face down on the table in front of a spectator.

● Ask the spectator to choose a number from 10 to 19.

● Now ask him: "Do you have that number? Good." Hand him the pack and say: "Now please deal that many cards face down onto the table."

● Ask him to pick up the cards he now has on the table. Say: "In your head, please total the digits of your original number to arrive at a single digit. For example, if you chose 13 you would add the 1 and the 3 together, giving you 4. Have you got that?" You may have to repeat your explanation.

● Say: "You now have the new number. Deal that many cards back onto the deck from the pile in your hand."

● When he has done this, say: "Please look at the top card of the pile you now hold. This card was arrived at strictly by chance. Remember it." Providing he has done his calculations correctly, the spectator will now be looking at the card that was originally the ninth card in the deck – the one you glimpsed and remembered.

● Ask the spectator to bury the card in the middle of the pack, re-form the deck and shuffle it.

● Spread the cards face up, and then run your finger along the cards as though sensing for the right card, until you stop and pick the chosen card.

THE PIANO TRICK

This is an old but reliable trick. It dates back to about 1900 and gets its name from the position of the spectator's hands – similar to that when playing the piano. Don't do the trick more than once, or someone might catch on to how it works.

Effect

The performer apparently makes a card move from one pile to another.

Equipment

Fifteen cards from an ordinary playing pack are needed.

Preparation

Slick presentation is needed for this trick to be successful. Practice doing the moves quickly with the right accompanying patter.

Performing

● Ask to look at the hands of your spectators, and after doing so, pick out one person to be your assistant, saying: "You have nice hands. Help me do the piano trick. Please put your hands on the table as though you were sitting at the piano keys. Let me take some cards and set them between your fingers."

● Insert two cards, as shown, between adjacent fingers and between finger and thumb. Do this for both hands, starting with the spectator's right hand. When you get to the final position, between the third and fourth fingers of the left hand, place only a single card (**1**).

● Explain what you have done: "We have placed two cards, an even number, between each of your fingers, and a single odd card here." Show the position of the last card.

1

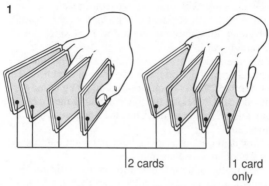

|2 cards |1 card only

• Now remove the first two cards from between the fingers, and lay them side by side on the table (**2**).

2

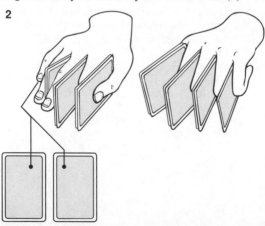

● Do the same with the next two cards, placing one card in each pile. Repeat this with all the cards, forming two equal piles, until you are left with the single remaining card.

● Ask the audience: "On which pile shall I put the remaining card?" Add it to whichever pile is chosen.

● Continue: "Now watch closely. I'm going to move the odd card." Pick up the pile containing the extra card and, with a grand gesture, click the fingers of your other hand.

● Now deal out the cards in pairs and point out that the "odd card" has disappeared.

● Pick up the other pile and deal out the cards in pairs. You will have a single card left over. Exclaim: "Ah, here it is!"

Note: The trick works because each pile contains seven cards. Adding the extra card to one pile makes it eight, an even number. The spectators don't catch on to this because you have misdirected them.

YOUR DEAL

Effect

The spectator cuts the pack and chooses and replaces a card. By dealing the cards into piles, discarding some, the spectator miraculously holds the chosen card.

Equipment

An ordinary pack of playing cards in fairly new condition is needed.

Preparation

Practice your patter so that you can quickly and clearly give instructions to a spectator. Check that you can cut the pack reliably into two equal or near equal halves.

Performing

● Ask a spectator to shuffle the pack and then get her to "cut the pack exactly in half." This may be difficult to do, so after the cut has been made, try to even up the two piles by moving a few cards from the higher pile to the lower one. For the trick to work, the cut must be within four cards of the center.

● Now ask her: "Take a card from anywhere in one of the piles. Please remember the card and place it on top of its pile. Now cover it with the other pile so that it is lost in the middle of the deck."

● Point to the table top and say: "Deal the top four cards face down in a row here. Keep dealing the cards in this way until you have four heaps" (**1**).

1

● After she has dealt the cards, turn over and spread out each pile so that the cards can been seen.
● Get her to indicate which pile contains the chosen card. Turn that pile face down and discard all the other piles (**2**). This remaining pile should now contain 13 cards.

2

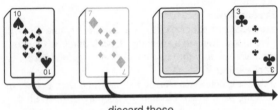

discard these

● Ask the spectator to deal this pile into four new piles.
● When this is done, the last card dealt should be on the first pile. Explain: "This pile isn't even so we'll discard it."
● That will leave three piles, each containing three cards. In fact, the middle card of the middle pile will be the chosen one.
● Ask the spectator to discard the top and bottom card of each pile. Three single cards now remain on the table.
● Pick up the three cards from left to right and hand them to the spectator. Get her to discard the top and bottom card and ask her to state her chosen card. The card remaining in her hand is the one she originally chose.

DUCK ONE, DROP TWO

This trick provides an effective change of pace in a routine. It is very easy to learn. Perform it just once, and then move on to the next trick.

Effect

The performer appears to mix up the order of cards according to the spectator's instructions. The cards, however, always stay in the same order.

Equipment

An ordinary pack of playing cards is needed.

Preparation

Try the trick out once for yourself to see how it works.

Performing

● Openly remove from the pack ten cards of one suit, A through to 10.

● Arrange them face down in a pile in sequence, with the A on top and the 10 at the bottom.

● Explain to a spectator: "This is a simple demonstration. I will deal the cards onto the table, one at a time. As I lift each card tell me whether to deal or duck the card. Each time I duck a card I will drop it on the table with the next card. I'll show you how it works. Are you ready? Here goes."

● Start to deal the cards, one at a time (**1**).

1

● When you are told to "duck," take the card you would have dealt and slip it directly under the very next top card. Lift both of them off the deck and drop them together onto the cards on the table (**2**).

2

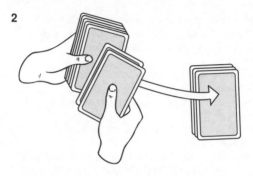

● Continue to deal or "duck one, drop two" as the spectator requests.
● When finished, pick up the cards on the table and go through the procedure again.
● When you have done this twice, ask "Shall we do it once more, or are you happy that they're all mixed up?" Whatever the reply, announce: "Well, let's see."
● Turn all the cards face up. They will still be in their original order. Act surprised and say: "Well I never!"

A PROCESS OF ELIMINATION

Effect

The performer spreads the cards and a spectator takes one and returns it to the pack. The performer then sorts the cards into two piles – one face up, the other face down. The spectator is asked to say when the card appears in the face-up pile. It never does. The performer repeats the procedure over and over again until left with one card – the spectator's card.

Equipment

An ordinary pack of playing cards is needed.

Preparation

Practice spreading the cards with ease and precision so that you can reliably count out 21 cards in one hand.

Performing

● Spread the deck of cards face down between your hands so that your spectator can choose a card (**1**).

1

● Close the pack, and then spread the deck again, silently counting the cards as you go, until you have 21 cards in one hand.

● Ask the spectator to place his card (**a**) on top of the pile in your other hand, and then replace the pile of 21 cards on top. The selected card is now twenty-second from the top (**2**).

2

a

21 cards

● Now explain: "I'll deal some cards face up and some face down. Watch the face-up group. Look for your card, but don't tell me when I pass it."

● Start to deal the cards. The first card is placed face up in front of your spectator; the next card face down near you; the third card face up near him; the fourth card face down near you. Continue in this way until you have two piles of cards, one face up and one face down (**3**).

● When all the cards have been dealt ask the spectator whether he has seen his card. The answer should be "no."

3

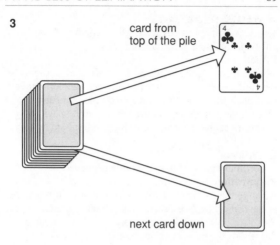

card from
top of the pile

next card down

● Push the face-up pile of cards to one side, and pick up the face-down pile of cards. Deal these cards as before: first face up, second face down, and so on.

● When you have finished dealing, again ask your spectator whether he has seen his card. He should still answer "no."

● Keep repeating this procedure until you have been through the entire pack without him seeing his card. The very last face-down card in your hand will be his card.

A MAGIC SEQUENCE

This is a simple novelty trick which can be performed only once using a prearranged pack.

Effect

The performer quickly shows 13 cards to an audience – the cards appear to be out of sequence. The performer then deals alternate cards face up on the table and places every other card at the bottom of the pack. Soon the entire sequence, from A to K, is assembled on the table as if by magic.

Equipment

An ordinary pack of playing cards is needed.

Preparation

Arrange the following cards, of mixed suit, in this order at the top of the face-down pack: 10 on top, then a 6, K, 5, 9, 4, J, 3, 8, 2, Q, A and finally a 7. The sequence of the rest of the pack does not matter.

Performing

● Pick up the pack and deal the top 13 cards face down in a pile on the table. Put the rest of the pack aside.

● Pick up the pile of 13 cards and briefly fan them face out towards the audience – do this quickly, so that the spectators have just enough time to see that the cards are not in a simple sequence (**1**). Explain: "You can see that the cards are not in order. But look what happens. . . ."

1

● Now keep the cards face down in one hand and deal them out in the following manner: take the top card and place it face down underneath the pile, then deal the next card face up on the table (**2**). Continue alternating the cards in this way until you have dealt out all the cards.

2

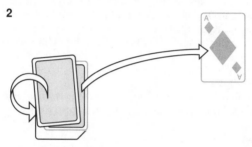

● You will finish with a line of cards in sequence, from A through to K (**3**).

3

3. Tricks using arranged stacks of cards

Knowing the exact position of some or all of the cards in a pack enables you to perform some startling tricks. To use a stacked deck – one in which the cards are arranged in a particular order – you need a system which is easy to remember but difficult for onlookers to spot.

SI STEBBINS

Si Stebbins was an American vaudeville performer who developed this system and kept it a secret for forty years.

Effect

The Si Stebbins system is used to perform a whole range of tricks. In its simplest form, as described here, a spectator can pick any card from the pack. With a cut of the pack, the performer immediately names the chosen card. Various ways of revealing the card make the performance more entertaining.

Equipment

An ordinary pack of playing cards is needed.

Preparation

The trick requires use of the glimpse (see p. 24). The cards need to be arranged beforehand in a specific sequence:

● Each card in the sequence has a value of three more than the preceding card. For example, if the first card in the pack is a 3, the second is a 6, and the third is a 9.

(Note: The J has a value of 11, the Q 12 and the K 13.
The A is always 1.)

• The order of suits is clubs, hearts, spades, diamonds.
For example, if the first card is the 3 of clubs, the
second is the 6 of hearts, the third is the 9 of spades and
the fourth is the Q of diamonds. The order is
remembered using the mnemonic CHaSeD.

• To arrange the pack, divide it first into four stacks of
13 cards (3 to K) ordered in the sequence described
above. The stacks are as shown below:

3-C	3-H	3-S	3-D
6-H	6-S	6-D	6-C
9-S	9-D	9-C	9-H
Q-D	Q-C	Q-H	Q-S
2-C	2-H	2-S	2-D
5-H	5-S	5-D	5-C
8-S	8-D	8-C	8-H
J-D	J-C	J-H	J-S
A-C	A-H	A-S	A-D
4-H	4-S	4-D	4-C
7-S	7-D	7-C	7-H
10-D	10-C	10-H	10-S
K-C	K-H	K-S	K-D

• Then put the stacks together, one on top of the other
left to right, to form the pack.
Note: Cutting the pack does not alter the sequence of
cards; it simply changes the starting point.

Performing
• Fan the cards face down towards a spectator and ask
her to remove a card of her choice.

- Cut the pack at the point where she removed the card.
- Glance at the bottom card, which was above the spectator's chosen card. Simply add three to the value of the bottom card and determine which suit follows that of the bottom card. Now you can name the spectator's chosen card. For example, if the bottom card is the 5 of diamonds, the chosen card is the 8 of clubs.

Note: If you intend to repeat the trick, make sure you return the spectator's card to the top of the pack so the sequence is unbroken. Use a riffle shuffle (see p. 16) when you wish to break up the stacked arrangement of cards.

THE JOKER KNOWS

This trick uses an entertaining method of revealing the spectator's card.

Effect

The spectator chooses a card and puts it in her pocket without looking at it. The performer uses a joker to help predict the chosen card.

Equipment

An ordinary pack of playing cards is needed, plus a single joker.

Preparation

The pack needs to be arranged according to the Si Stebbins system (see p. 92), with a joker placed at random. It requires the use of the glimpse technique (see p. 24).

Performing

● Fan the cards face up so you and the audience can see them.

● Openly remove the joker and place it face down on the table.

● Give the deck a few cuts and then spread the cards face down and ask the spectator to take one and put it in her pocket without looking at it.

● Cut the deck at the point where the card was removed, and glimpse the bottom card as you complete the cut.

● The bottom card will tell you the name of the spectator's chosen card. For example, if the 3 of diamonds is the bottom card, the top card is the 6 of clubs.

● Now pick up the joker and put it to your ear as though you are listening for something. To make the trick more dramatic pretend to get the information in stages. Say, for example: "It's a black card. It's a 6. Ah, it's the 6 of clubs."

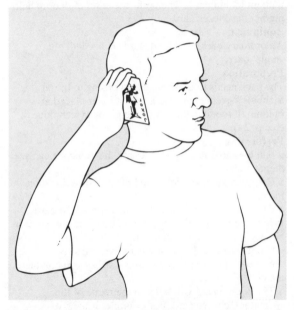

● Finish with: "Jokers are pretty useful sometimes!"

COUNTING THE CARDS

You need to be good at mental arithmetic to perform this trick.

Effect

The performer riffles through the pack, and the observer is invited to say "stop" at any time. The deck is broken at that point, and the spectator is handed the larger pile. Within seconds – without counting the cards – the performer tells the spectator how many cards she holds.

Equipment

An ordinary pack of playing cards is needed.

Preparation

The pack needs to be arranged using the Si Stebbins system (see p. 92). The trick uses the glimpse technique (see p. 24).

Performing

● Hold the pack vertically with one hand, facing away from you, and with the other hand riffle through the pack from back to front (**1**).

1

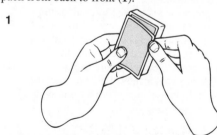

● Ask a spectator to call "stop" at any time.
● When the spectator calls "stop," break the deck at that

point and hand the spectator the pile with the largest number of cards. As you do this, make a show of weighing both piles face up in your hands (**2**). This gives you time to glimpse her bottom card and start to do a mental calculation.

2

● Note the bottom card of her pile (for example, the 5 of hearts) and the bottom card of your pile (for example, the J of clubs). Then give the spectator her pile.
● To work out the number of cards you and she are holding, perform the following mental calculations.
● First, you must determine the value of the nearest card in your pile which is of the same suit as the spectator's bottom card (in this case, hearts). (Note: If the spectator's bottom card is of the same suit as your bottom card, there is no need to calculate this.)
Using the mnemonic CHaSeD, work backwards from C (clubs) to H (hearts) to calculate how far away the nearest heart is. In this case, it is three cards away (**3**).

3

CHaSeDCHaSeD

Take the number of cards (in this case 3) and multiply it by 3 (the increase in value from one card to the next in the system): $3 \times 3 = 9$

Subtract this number from the value of your bottom card: $11 - 9 = 2$

You now know that the nearest card of the same suit is the 2 of hearts. Knowing this, you can do the rest of the calculations:

Of the two same-suit cards, subtract the lower number from the higher one. For example: $5 - 2 = 3$

Then multiply this number by 4: $3 \times 4 = 12$

Note: If the spectator's bottom card is of the same suit as your bottom card, then this is the number of cards in one pile. If the bottom cards are of different suits, do the next calculation.

Add on the number of cards between your bottom card and the nearest card in your pile which is of the same suit as the spectator's bottom card: $12 + 3 = 15$

This gives you the number of cards in *one* pile.

Subtract this number from 52
to give the number of cards
in the *other* hand:

$$52 - 15 = 37$$

● Announce the number of cards the spectator is
holding. Have her confirm your "guess" by counting
her pile of cards as she deals them face down.

● The above calculation will work in all cases but one.
If the spectator's bottom card has the same value as
yours, then you know that the two cards are multiples
of 13 away from one another – in other words, your pile
(the smaller one) has either 13 or 26 cards. Unless your
piles appear to be equal (and both thus have 26 cards),
her pile must have 39 cards (52 – 13 = 39).
Note: You can repeat the trick, but the spectator's stack
must be put back in the right place to maintain the order
of cards.

MULTIPLE IDENTIFICATION

This is an effective trick for use with three or more
spectators. It relies on spotting disruptions in the
sequence of cards.

Effect

Three spectators each choose a card from different parts
of the pack. The cards are then pushed back into the
pack at three different locations. The performer cuts the
pack several times and picks out the three cards.

Equipment

An ordinary pack of playing cards is needed.

Preparation

The pack needs to be arranged according to the Si
Stebbins system (see p. 92).

Performing

● Fan the cards face down and ask three spectators each
to remove one card from different parts of the pack (**1**).

1

● Ask the spectators to memorize their selected cards and then return them to the pack but at a different location.

● Cut the cards a few times and then fan them out so only you can see their faces.

● In the Si Stebbins system, each card should have a value three higher than the card to its left. If it does not, then you know a card has been added or removed from that position.

● You can now pick out the three selected cards (**2**) (**a**). They will be the ones out of sequence – but remember, their original locations will leave "gaps" (**b**) in the sequence.

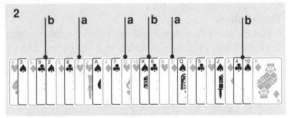

● Place the three selected cards face down on the table.

● Ask the spectators to name their cards. Turn the cards over and take your bow.

Note: You will have to put the cards back in their original locations if you want to use the stacked sequence in further tricks.

THE THREE PILES

This trick uses a stacked deck to identify one selected card. The performer uses this information to stay one step ahead of the audience and so identify two other cards.

Effect

The performer cuts the pack several times, and then divides the pack into three piles and correctly identifies the top cards of all three piles.

Equipment

An ordinary pack of playing cards is needed.

Preparation

The pack needs to be arranged according to the Si Stebbins system (see p. 92). You will need to practice the false overhand shuffle (p. 12) and glimpse technique (see p. 24), and you will probably need to practice this trick several times to get the order of moves right.

Performing

● Do a false shuffle, which keeps all the cards in the same order.

● Cut the cards, re-form the pack and then square the cards, glimpsing the bottom card as you do so.

● From the value and suit of the bottom card, calculate the value and suit of the top card, the next card in the stacked sequence. For example, under Si Stebbins, if the bottom card is the 2 of diamonds, the top card is the 5 of clubs.

● Now divide the pack into three piles (or get a spectator to do it for you). Keep your eye on the final position of the top pile. This is the pile whose top card you know. In the steps that follow, you will come to this pile last.

● Tap your finger on one of the other piles and say confidently: "This is the 5 of clubs" (**1**).

1

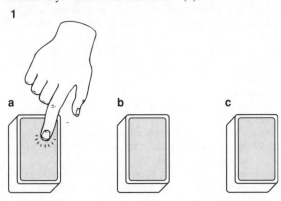

a   b   c

● Pick up the top card from that pile (**a**) and hold it facing you.

● Tap the other pile that was not the top pile (**b**) and state the top card to be the one you are actually holding. So, if you picked up the Q of hearts from the first pile, you tap the second pile and say: "This is the Q of hearts."

● Once again remove the top card and hold it facing you to the right of the first card.

● Now tap the third pile (**c**), which you know to be the top pile, and state the top card to be the one you picked from the second pile. For example, if you picked up the J of spades, call this as the top card of the third pile. (You know this card actually to be the 5 of clubs.)

● Remove the top card from the third pile and place it to the left of the two cards in your hand.

● Place the three cards face up on the table and show
that you have correctly identified them (**2**).

2

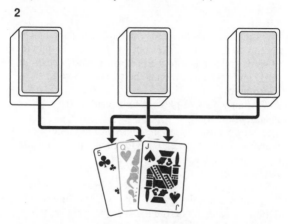

Note: If you are careful, you can place the cards back
on their original piles and retain the stacked sequence
to perform further tricks. Alternatively, riffle shuffle the
pack (see p. 16) to break up the sequence.

LISTEN TO THE QUEEN

This trick is a particularly effective last trick before breaking up a stacked deck.

Effect

The spectator cuts the cards three times and then takes the top card. He then takes out a Q from a face-up fan of cards and hands it to the performer, who "listens" to the Q and correctly predicts the spectator's card.

Equipment

An ordinary pack of playing cards is needed.

Preparation

The pack needs to be arranged according to the Si Stebbins system (see p. 92). This trick requires the use of the glimpse technique (see p. 24).

Performing

● Spread the deck face up on the table and announce: "As you can see, the deck is not stacked in any way." Scoop the cards up before the spectators realize this is not the case.

● Hand the deck to a spectator and ask him to cut the pack once, and then once again. Then add: "Just to be sure, cut it a third time."

● Instruct the spectator to take the top card and, without looking at it, to place it face down on the table.

● Ask for the pack, and then fan the cards face up and ask the spectator to choose a Q. As you do this, glimpse the bottom card. This will be the card that is directly before the chosen card in the arranged sequence. You can now identify the chosen card. For example, the 2 of clubs on the bottom of the pack will mean the spectator's card is the 5 of hearts.

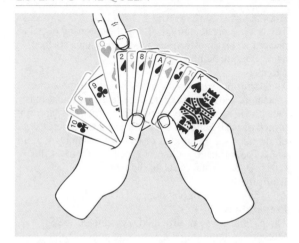

- Place the pack face down and take the Q from the spectator.
- Put the Q to your ear and pretend to be listening for information.
- Say to the spectator: "When you looked for the Q could you tell which card was missing? No? Neither could I. But the Q is very helpful. She tells me the card you took is the [for example, the 5 of hearts]."
- Ask the spectator to turn over the card and confirm that the Q is correct.
- Re-form the pack and riffle shuffle the cards (see p. 16) to break up the sequence.

A DREAM COME TRUE

This trick is particularly useful in the company of poker players and is an effective trick to break up a stacked deck. It requires three spectators.

Effect

The performer spreads the cards face up to show the spectators, cuts the pack and then deals out four hands face down, as though playing poker. When the cards are turned over all hands show a straight flush (five cards of the same suit in number order – for example, 4, 5, 6, 7, 8). The last hand – the performer's – is a royal flush (10, J, Q, K, A) and beats all the others!

Equipment

An ordinary pack of playing cards is needed.

Preparation

The pack needs to be arranged according to the Si Stebbins system (see p. 92).

Performing

● Spread the deck face up on the table. Announce: "As you can see, the deck is not stacked in any way." Scoop the cards up before the spectators realize this is not the case.

● As you scoop up the cards, look for a 2 and then cut the deck at that point, so the 2 is on the bottom.

● Say: "Let's play some poker, and I'll show you a dream come true."

● Deal out the cards face down as you would for four hands in a game of five-card poker – that is, one card to each player, and going round five times so that each player ends up with five cards. As the dealer, you get the fourth hand.

● Start with the first hand (**1**) and turn it over saying: "Let's see what you got." It will be a 5-high straight flush. Say: "Not bad."

● Repeat with the second (**2**) and third (**3**) hands; they will be progressively higher straight flushes.

● Finish with your hand (**4**) and say: "A royal flush. A dream come true."

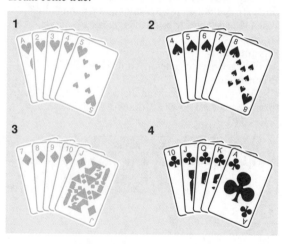

A SPECIAL ARRANGEMENT

This trick uses some stacked cards, but they are heavily disguised.

Effect

The performer extracts two suits of cards from the pack, seemingly at random, and gives one suit to a spectator and keeps the other. When the performer's cards are dealt, they form a straight run from A to K. When the spectator tries this, her cards are out of sequence.

Equipment

An ordinary pack of playing cards is needed.

Preparation

● Remove all the clubs from the deck and arrange them from the top card down as follows: A, Q, 2, 8, 3, J, 4, 9, 5, K, 6, 10, 7.

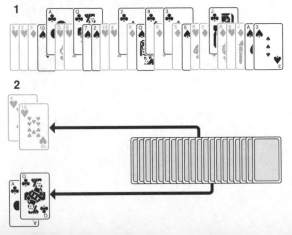

- Shuffle the remaining cards thoroughly.
- Turn the deck face up and replace the clubs at various points in the pack. It does not matter where you put them, but you must retain the order (**1**).
- Put the pack to one side ready for use.

Performing

- Spread the cards face up on the table.
- Begin by saying: "Here are 52 cards. We'll need two suits."
- Pick up the deck and say to a spectator: "You take the hearts and I'll take the clubs."
- Spread out the cards again, left to right and, starting at the left, pick out the cards of each suit. When you come to a heart, drop it face up in front of the spectator. When you come to a club, drop it face up near yourself (**2**). Make sure you keep your clubs in the original order.

● Pick up your pile and ask the spectator to do the same. Put the remaining cards to one side.

● Say to the spectator: "Follow me." Then lay down your top card face up on the table – it will be an A.

● Take the next card and place it at the bottom of the pack. Make sure the spectator is doing the same.

● Deal the next one face up – it will be a 2.

● Carry on in this way, ducking one and dealing one, until you have the whole sequence before you.

● The spectator, who has been doing everything you have done, will be surprised to find that her cards are not in sequence.

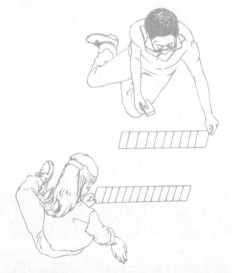

THE CARD IN THE MIDDLE

This trick requires no calculations to be performed. Use it only once or your audience might catch on.

Effect

The performer shuffles the pack and asks the spectator to cut the pack. The performer then picks up the pack and predicts which card is in the center (that is, which is 26th from the top). The performer then deals out the cards and shows the prediction to be correct.

Equipment

An ordinary pack of playing cards is needed.

Preparation

The pack needs to be arranged according to the Si Stebbins system (see p. 92). The trick uses the false overhand shuffle and glimpse techniques (see p. 12 and p. 24).

Performing

● Cut the deck several times rapidly to give the appearance of shuffling the deck. In reality, you are only cutting the deck. The order remains the same.

● Explain: "While I am shuffling the deck please call out 'stop' any time you like."

● When the spectator calls "stop," glimpse the bottom card.

● Say: "I'm getting better at predicting the middle card of the pack," and give your prediction. The 26th card will always be the same number as the bottom card and in the other suit of the same color. For example, if the bottom card is the 3 of spades, the 26th card will be the 3 of clubs.

● Pass the cards to the spectator and ask him to count down to the 26th card – it will be the predicted card.

CALLING THE CARDS

This is a powerful trick using a stacked deck and involving as many spectators as you can manage – a good trick for parties. You need a good memory!

Effect

A spectator picks a number of cards from the pack, keeps the top card, and distributes the other cards among the spectators. The performer proceeds to identify the first spectator's card, and then identifies all the other cards held by spectators.

Equipment

An ordinary pack of playing cards is needed.

Preparation

The pack needs to be arranged according to the Si Stebbins system (see p. 92).

Performing

● Fan the cards face down towards a spectator. Have him take a batch of cards from one location in the pack (you can specify the number or leave it up to the spectator: the number of cards taken should roughly correspond to the number of people in the audience or the number of cards you feel you can manage in the trick).

● As the spectator removes the cards, place your little finger at the break point in the pack. Cut the pack at this point.

● When the spectator has removed the cards, ask him to keep the cards face down, remove the top card and place it in his pocket without looking at it.

● Have the spectator shuffle his remaining cards and hand them, one at a time, to other spectators. The spectators are to look at their cards and keep them.

While all this is happening, glimpse the bottom card of
the pack. Knowing the stacked arrangement, you can
work out which card the first spectator has. The value is
three greater than the value of the bottom card, and the
suit is determined using the mnemonic CHaSeD. (If the
bottom card is the 5 of clubs, for example, the
spectator's card is the 8 of hearts.) From this, you can
identify all the cards distributed among the audience.

● At this point summarize what has happened so far:
"A number of cards have been removed from the deck,
shuffled, and then distributed among you. I will now try
to identify all the cards taken."

● Name the card the first spectator has in his pocket.
Get him to take it out and confirm your prediction.

● Now get the other spectators to concentrate on their
cards. Pretend you are engaged in a mind-reading
exercise and make a show of concentrating hard with
your eyes shut. To make it more interesting, let your
predictions trickle out slowly by saying, for example: "I
see a black picture card. . . . Yes, the queen of spades."

● If you look at people's reactions carefully, you may
well be able to work out who is holding which card. As
you predict each card, have the owner hand it back to
you, and then move on to the next card. Aim to give the
impression that you not only know what the cards are,
but also who has which card.

ACES AND KINGS

This is a quick and simple trick using a partially stacked deck.

Effect

The performer shuffles the cards and then demonstrates to the spectator how he wants her to deal the cards face down into four piles. When she has done this, she discovers an A at the top of each pile. When the performer turns over each pile, a K is revealed at the bottom of each.

Equipment

An ordinary pack of playing cards is needed.

Preparation

You will need to practice the false overhand shuffle (see p. 12). Prepare the deck by placing four As at the top of the deck followed by four Ks. The rest of the pack is in any order (**1**).

1

Performing

● Use a false overhand shuffle which keeps the top portion of the pack in place but gives the appearance of mixing all the cards.

● Set the deck face down in front of the spectator.

● Begin by saying: "Please cut a small number of cards from the top of the pack. I'll take them."

● Take the small pile and say: "What I want you to do is deal four piles onto the table." Demonstrate this by dealing the four top cards (the As) face down onto the table in four piles.

● Now place the remainder of the small pile (**2**) (**a**) back on top of the pack (**b**) and nonchalantly scoop up the four As (**c**) and place them at the bottom of the pack. All this should look relaxed as though you are simply demonstrating what the spectator has to do.

2

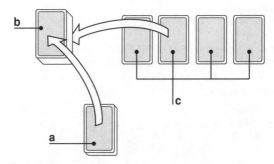

● Have the spectator deal out the four piles.

● When she has finished, ask: "What is your favorite ace?" Whatever she replies, ask her to turn over the top card of one of the piles. If she hits the right A first time, you will have an amazed spectator. Have her turn over the top card of all the piles and so reveal the four As.

● Finish with the throwaway line: "Personally, I prefer the kings." Reach out and turn over each pile to reveal the K at the bottom of each.

EVEN BETTER THAN KINGS

This is another quick and simple trick using a partially
stacked deck.

Effect

The performer shuffles the cards and gives them to a
spectator and directs him to deal the cards face down
into two piles. The spectator then deals each of these
piles into two more piles, making four piles in all. The
spectator discovers a K at the top of each pile. When he
discards the Ks he then discovers an A at the top of
each pile.

Equipment

An ordinary pack of playing cards is needed.

Preparation

You will need to practice the false overhand shuffle
(see p. 12). Prepare the deck by placing four Ks at the
top of the deck followed by four As. The rest of the
pack is in any order.

Performing

● Use a false overhand shuffle which keeps the top
portion of the pack in place but gives the appearance of
mixing all the cards.

● Set the deck face down in front of the spectator and
begin: "I just want to check that something that
happens when I deal will also happen when you deal.

Now, just deal the pack into two face-down piles, alternating the cards."

● Allow the spectator to deal out about half the pack and then add: "You can stop any time you wish."

● When he finishes (it does not matter if he deals the entire pack), take the remainder of the cards and continue: "Now pick up one of the two piles and deal that pile into two piles. Do the same with the other pile so that we now have four piles in all." Dealing out the piles in this way will bring the Ks back to the top with the As just below them.

● "I think you've just dealt me my favorite cards. Turn over the top card of a pile and see what we've got." He will now reveal a K.

● Ask: "What about the other piles?" The spectator should now discover a K at the top of every pile.

● Have the spectator discard the Ks and say: "Of course, we can go one better." Close your eyes and pass your hands over the four piles. Then add: "Let's see what we have now." Turn over the top cards to reveal the four As.

● Finish by saying: "Yes, it works for you too!"

4. Tricks using sleight of hand

These tricks depend on skillful sleight of hand and require good card-handling skills.

ABRACADABRA
Effect
A card is transformed into the spectator's chosen card.
Equipment
An ordinary pack of playing cards is needed.
Preparation
You will need to practice the false overhand shuffle (see p. 12) and the double lift (see p. 25).
Performing
● Hand the pack to a spectator and ask him to shuffle it.
● Take the pack back and fan the cards face down towards the audience.

● Ask the spectator to take a card and look at it. While you are shuffling the pack ask the spectator to return the card to the middle of the pack as you stop momentarily.

● Discreetly insert a little finger into the pack to form a break at the point where the card was returned. Then use a false overhand shuffle to get the chosen card to the top of the pack.
● Use shuffle control to get the chosen card to the top of the pack.
● Turn the pack so the bottom card faces out. Ask the spectator: "Is this your card?" He should say: "No."
● Do a double lift and show to the audience what looks like the top card but is really the second card. Ask: "Is this it?" Again, he should say: "No."
● Hand the pack to the spectator and ask him to tap lightly on the top card and say "Abracadabra." Then ask him to turn it over, revealing his chosen card.

CARDS CHANGE PLACES

Effect

Two cards taken at random apparently change places.

Equipment

An ordinary pack of playing cards is needed.

Preparation

You will need to practice the double lift (see p. 25).

Performing

● Hand the pack to a spectator and ask her to shuffle it.

● Take the pack back and, while squaring the cards, separate the top two cards from the others and push them a little to the side in readiness for the double lift.

● Remark that you will use the top card, whatever it may be, to conduct an experiment. Use the double lift and show the card to the audience; they think they are seeing the top card, but you are actually showing them the second card. For this example, it is the 3 of clubs.

● Return the cards to the top of the pack and then take the top card and place it face down on the table. The audience thinks this is the 3 of clubs; it is not – that card is still on top of the pack.

● Continue by saying: "Let us see what the next card is," as you square the deck and get ready for another double lift. Again, take two cards as one and reveal, for example, the 8 of hearts. Say: "Fine. That's a good contrast with our earlier card, the 3 of clubs."

● As before, return the two cards to the top of the pack, and take the top card and place it to one side face down on the table beside the first face-down card. The spectators think this is the 8 of hearts – it is actually the 3 of clubs. The 8 of hearts remains on top of the pack.

● Tell the audience: "Remember the two cards, the 3 of clubs here [point to the first card (**1**) (**a**)] and the 8 of hearts here [point to the second card (**b**)]."

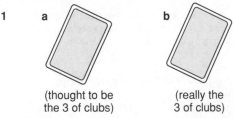

1 **a** **b**

(thought to be
the 3 of clubs)

(really the
3 of clubs)

● "I'll replace the 3 back on top of the pack." Pick up the first card, look at it, and put it on top of the pack (**2**) (**c**). Don't let anyone else see the card; the audience thinks this is the 3 of clubs.

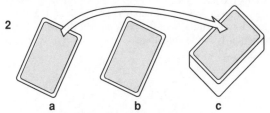

2

a **b** **c**

● Say: "Now comes the remarkable bit. I'm going to make the 3 and 8 change places." Tap the top of the pack, then pick up the deck and with a double lift show the second card from the top – the 8 of hearts.
● Ask a spectator to pick up the remaining card on the table – it will be the 3 of clubs.
● Finish by saying: "Don't ask me to do it again. That took effort," and continue with the next trick.

COUNTDOWN

This trick is particularly effective because the "magic" happens in the spectator's hands, not the performer's.

Effect

The performer fails to find the spectator's card and hands the pack to the spectator. The spectator then follows the performer's instructions and reveals the chosen card.

Equipment

An ordinary pack of playing cards is needed.

Preparation

You will need to practice the false overhand shuffle (see p. 12).

Performing

● Hand the pack to a spectator and ask him to shuffle.

● Take the pack back and fan the cards face down towards the audience.

● Ask another spectator to take a card, look at it, and return it to the middle of the pack as you stop momentarily while shuffling.

● Discreetly insert a little finger into the pack to form a break at the point where the card was returned. Then use a false overhand shuffle to get the chosen card to the top of the pack.

● Ask a spectator for a number between five and 15. Count out loud and deal that number of cards into a face-down pile (the chosen card will now be on the bottom of this pile).

● When you deal out the last card, turn it over as though you are expecting this to be the chosen card. When you ask the spectator, and discover it isn't his chosen card, pretend to be disappointed.

● Turn the top card face down, scoop up the pile and place it on top of the pack.

● Hold the pack and close your eyes for a moment, as though deep in concentration and waiting for inspiration.

● Suddenly "realize" what you have done wrong. Explain that you've been told what to do now.

● Pass the pack to the spectator and ask him to deal and count as you did before. This time, when the last card is turned over, it will be the correct one!

TWO OUT OF 52

Effect

Two spectators each remove a card from somewhere in the pack. They look at and return the cards. The performer shuffles the pack and then throws the cards into the air. As the cards fall to the ground the performer miraculously plucks out the two chosen cards from the falling shower of cards.

Equipment

An ordinary pack of playing cards is needed.

Preparation

You will need to practice the false overhand shuffle (see p. 12) to get two chosen cards to the top and bottom of the pack.

Performing

● Hand the pack to a spectator and ask him to shuffle.

● Take back the pack, fan the cards with faces down and ask two spectators each to remove a card and remember it.

● Close up the pack, and shuffle it. Then cut the deck and ask the two spectators to return their cards – one on top of the other – in the center of the pack where you have made the cut.

● Discreetly insert a little finger into the pack to form a break at the point where the cards were returned. Carry on shuffling and use a false overhand shuffle to get the two chosen cards to the top of the pack.

● Finally, with your last shuffle move, bring the top card to the bottom, so that the two chosen cards (**a** and **b**) are at the top and bottom of the pack.

● Explain that the next bit will be dramatic. Roll your sleeves up. This will emphasize the dramatic effect and also prove you don't have anything "up your sleeve."

● Lick the thumb and
fingers of your right hand.
This again increases the
dramatic effect, but is also
needed to perform the
trick.

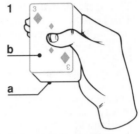

● Hold the pack tightly
between the thumb and
fingers of your right
hand (**1**).

● Turn your left side to the audience and throw the
cards into the air. As you do this, the top and bottom
cards will stay stuck to your fingers and thumb. Bring
your right hand quickly to your side after throwing the
pack (**2**).

● As the cards fall, plunge your right hand into the
middle of the shower of cards and pretend to pull out
the two cards (**3**).

● Show the spectators the two cards "you have caught"
– they are the two cards they chose!

THE CUT FORCE

This trick uses a simple yet powerful technique which ensures that the spectator takes a card predetermined by the performer.

Effect

The spectator appears to have a free choice as to which card to take. Whichever card is chosen, the performer can immediately identify it and can reveal it in a variety of ways.

Equipment

An ordinary pack of playing cards is needed.

Preparation

You will need to practice the glimpse technique (see p. 24).

Performing

● Shuffle the cards and discreetly glimpse and remember the bottom card. Control the shuffle and bring this card to the top; then glimpse and remember the new bottom card. You now know the top and bottom cards of the pack.

● Place the deck on the table in front of a spectator. Say to her: "Please cut the cards in half and place the bottom half crossways on the top half" (1).

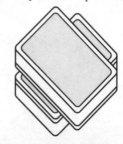

1

● Distract the audience for a moment or two by explaining the origins of card tricks. Say, for example, "Did you know that cards came to Europe in the fourteenth century . . . probably from Egypt? We're not sure where cards were invented in the first place . . . probably India or the Middle East."

● Then return to the pack. "You've cut the cards and chosen where to make the cut. Lift the cards at the cut and choose either the bottom or top card."

● Whichever card is chosen, you will know what it is. How you choose to reveal the card is up to you. One way is to ask the spectator to shuffle the pack and then slowly spread the cards face up on the table. Pretend to identify the chosen card by noticing her reaction when she uncovers it.

● Alternatively, you could pick out a bunch of cards and then, by "noting her reactions," home in on the right card.

ONE OUT OF FIVE

This trick relies on a good memory, acting ability and dexterity.

Effect

The performer is able to select which one of five cards the spectator is thinking about.

Equipment

An ordinary pack of playing cards is needed.

Preparation

Place any four cards in your jacket side pocket, lying horizontally with their backs facing outwards.

Performing

● Ask a spectator to shuffle the pack.

● Take back the pack and spread the cards face up on the table and allow the spectator to take out any five cards.

● Take the cards and arrange them in any sequence that is easy for you to remember; for example, you can group the numbers, or work out a relationship between them. Two examples are shown (**1**).

1

Remember as: 24 and 89 and Q

or as: 2 x 4 = 8 (+1Q) = 9.

● Now ask the spectator
to think of one of the five
cards. As she does this,
put the five cards (**2**) (**a**)
in your pocket, arranged
vertically and placed
behind the other four
cards (**b**).

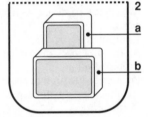

● Casually pick up the pack, close your eyes and
pretend to be concentrating. "Ah, I think I have it!"
● Put your hand into your pocket and one by one take
out each of the four horizontal cards, saying "It's not
this one, or this . . . ." Don't show these cards to the
audience but simply place them face down on top of the
pack.
● Put your hand back in your pocket and slip a finger
between each of the five cards. "There is only one card
left in my pocket. It should be the one you selected.
Which card did you choose?"
● When she names the card you can produce it from
your pocket easily. Leave the other four cards there and
put the pack in your pocket. If the audience asks to see
the pack, bring it out with the other four cards on top –
where they ought to be.

TURN-ABOUT

This trick has an impressive conclusion.

Effect

A spectator cuts the pack in half and takes the top half
while the performer takes the bottom half. Spectator
and performer each choose a card from their stack and
then place it in the other's pile. The performer
combines the two stacks into one, and miraculously the
two chosen cards are reversed with respect to all other
cards.

Equipment

An ordinary pack of playing cards is needed.

Preparation

Prearrange the pack by memorizing the bottom card
and reversing it with respect to the other cards.

Performing

● Fan the cards toward the audience so that the card
faces can be seen but the reversed card at the bottom is
not visible.

● Instruct one spectator: "Please cut off about half the
pack." Get him to shuffle the top pile of cards, while
you take the bottom pile.

● Ask him to take one card out of the center of his pile,
look at it and memorize it. You go through the motions
of doing the same with your pile, but don't bother to
remember your card.

● Tell the spectator: "I'll place my card in your half."
As you push your card into his pile, momentarily drop
your hand to your side so that your pile of cards is out
of sight for a moment. Turn your pile around so your
bottom card – the reversed one – is now on top.

● Take the spectator's card and push it into the middle of your pile. Make sure you put it face down. (Your pile is really face up with the exception of the top card.)

● "Now please give me half of your pile." Take these cards (**1**) (**a**) from the spectator, and place them face up on top of your pile (**b**).

● Take the other half of his pile (**c**) and place those face up on the bottom of your stack. Hold the three piles in your hand for a moment so that all three piles are visible. Your cards will appear to be face down, while the spectator's cards are face up.

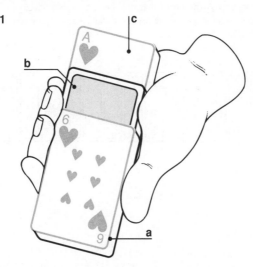

● Now push all the cards together into a single stack.

● "I will now achieve two things with one click of my fingers. Watch closely. I will make all the cards in the pack face in the same direction but with two exceptions – your card and my card. Here we go."

● Make a big show of clicking the fingers of one hand and as you do so turn the pack upside down, so that the top card is now face down.

● "My card was the [give the name of the card you reversed before starting the trick]. What was yours?"

● After he has named his card, spread all the cards in a ribbon across the table. All will be face down, except for the two cards – your reversed card and his chosen card (**2**).

2

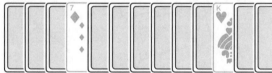

PICK A NUMBER

This trick is particularly effective because it combines the free choices of two spectators.

Effect

One spectator picks a card; another spectator picks a number. The performer then proceeds to find the chosen card at that number place in the pack.

Equipment

An ordinary pack of playing cards is needed.

Preparation

This trick uses the false overhand shuffle (see p. 12), false riffle shuffle (see p. 17) and glide (see p. 23).

Performing

● Ask a spectator to shuffle the pack.

● Take back the pack and spread the cards in a fan face down towards the audience.

● Ask a spectator to pick a card, look at it and remember it.

● In your hand, square up the cards and ask the spectator to place the chosen card on top of the pack.

● Make a show of rolling up your sleeves to convince the audience that nothing is hidden.

● Now with a false overhand shuffle, move the top card to the bottom of the pack. For good measure, do a riffle shuffle, making sure you keep the chosen card at the bottom of the pack.

● Now ask another spectator to choose a number from 1 to 26 and say what that number is.

● Explain what has happened so far: "I have asked one person to choose a card. I haven't even seen what that card is. I've shuffled the pack thoroughly and then I've asked another person to pick a number from 1 to 26.

I didn't know what that number was when I shuffled the pack. Now let's see what happens."

• Using the glide technique, slide the chosen card back (**1**) and slowly and deliberately deal out cards from the bottom of the pack, face up one at a time, counting them out as you do so.

1 (bottom view)

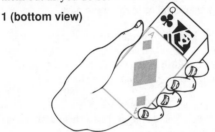

• If, for example, the chosen number was 21, count out 20 cards. When you get to the twenty-first card, look at the audience and say: "This is the moment of truth." As you are doing this, and the audience is momentarily distracted, slide the chosen card forward using your little finger (**2**). Pick up this card as the twenty-first card and place it face up. Say: "Hey presto – the chosen card!"

2

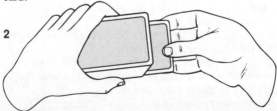

THREE CARDS ACROSS

This is a classic trick involving two spectators and some skillful sleight of hand.

Effect

One spectator counts out 15 cards into the performer's hand, then takes the cards and places them in her pocket. Another spectator does the same and places 15 cards in his pocket. The performer then makes three cards travel from one spectator's pocket to the other's. The spectators find that one has 12 cards and the other 18!

Equipment

A new or nearly new pack of playing cards is needed.

Preparation

This trick uses the palm technique (see p. 29).

Performing

● Ask two spectators to assist you. Get them to stand on either side of you, facing the audience.
● Have one of your assistants shuffle the pack.
● Take the pack and hold it in your left hand as if to deal.
● Explain to your assistants what you want them to do, and while you are doing this, move the top three cards to the right with your left thumb, and move your little finger under the third card (**1**).

● Move your right hand over the pack as though you are squaring the cards, and as you do so, push the cards up with your little finger and close your right hand around them (**2**).

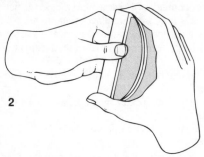

2

● Palm these three cards and keep them hidden in your relaxed right hand.
● Hand the pack to the spectator on your left.
● Offer her your hand palm up and ask her to count, out loud, 15 cards onto your left hand.
● As the fifteenth card is counted, turn to the other spectator and say: "I'll be with you in a moment." As you turn, bring both hands together and drop the palmed cards from the right hand onto the pile in the left.
● Make as if to square the cards, and then give the 15 cards (really 18) to the first spectator and get her to put them in her pocket.
● Take back the pack and hand it to the second spectator with the request that he, too, count 15 cards onto your left hand.

● As soon as he has counted 12 cards into your hand, move the tip of your little finger over the edge of the top card, so that the last three cards are placed on top, with a small break under them (**3**).

● Ask the second spectator whether he has a suitable pocket in which to put the cards, and as you do so, palm off the three cards into your right hand.
● Again, pretend to square the cards and then hand the cards (now only 12) to him and take back the remainder of the pack in your left hand.
● Bring the right hand across to pick up the pack, and as you do so, drop the palmed cards on top of the pack. Put the pack to one side or in your pocket.
● Now, announce that you are going to make three cards travel from the second spectator's pocket to the first spectator's pocket.
● With a big show, point across from one pocket to the other and say: "One, two, three!"
● Finish by asking the second spectator to take out his cards and count them onto your right hand – there will be only 12.
● Then ask the first spectator to count her cards onto your left hand – there will be 18!

MIDNIGHT FEAST

This is a trick with a storyline – change it to suit your audience.

Effect

One spectator picks a card; another spectator picks a number. The performer then proceeds to find the chosen card at that number place in the pack.

Equipment

A new or nearly new pack of playing cards is needed.

Preparation

Prearrange the pack with any three cards at the top followed by four Js or Qs. You will need to practice the double lift technique (see p. 25).

Performing

● Explain that this trick is one you learned one summer holiday when you were young. You and your friends were staying in a large old house, but you were in separate rooms and you wanted to meet up for a midnight feast.

● While you are explaining this, use the lift technique to lift off the four top cards as one (**1**).

● Hold the fourth card toward the audience and explain: "This card is me." The audience will think you are holding only one card in your hand.

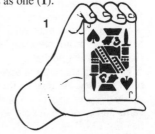

● Continue: "After lights out we all arranged to meet in an empty room at the top of the house. These are my friends." One by

one take the next three
cards from the top of the
pack and add them to the
displayed card so that all
four cards are visible (**2**).

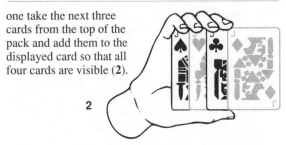

2

● "There we were at the top of the house, tucking into
our midnight feast, when we heard a noise outside the
door. We all scattered and sneaked back down to our
rooms through the fire escape." As you describe this,
take the four Js (or Qs) plus the three hidden cards,
square them up and place them face down on top of the
pack.

● As you continue with the story, take the top card and,
without showing its face, slip it into the pack near the
bottom. The next card goes about halfway into the pack
and the third card goes about two-thirds of the way
from the top. What you have appeared to do is to place
the three cards representing your friends randomly in
the pack, as if going back to their rooms. What you
have actually done is to place three ordinary cards into
the pack while leaving the four Js (your friends and
you) on top.

● For the finale, say that you waited about half an hour
until the coast was clear and then made your way up
again.

● At this point, turn over the top cards and show the
four Js (or Qs).

THE FABULOUS FOUR ACES

This is a classic card trick using a similar technique to that of the previous trick.

Effect

The four As are removed from the pack and a spectator chooses her favorite one. The four As are returned to the top of the pack and then dealt into four piles of four cards. Miraculously, all four As are in one pile – the pile the spectator chooses.

Equipment

A new or nearly new pack of playing cards is needed.

Preparation

You will need to practice the double lift (see p. 25) technique.

Performing

● Openly go through the pack and take out the four As, dropping them face up on the table in any order (**1**).

1

● Face a spectator and ask: "Which one of the aces is your favorite?" As the audience is momentarily distracted, maintain eye contact with the spectator and secretly push the top three cards of the pack slightly to the right, inserting your little finger underneath them to form a break (**2**).

● Pick up the spectator's favorite A – for example, the A of hearts – and place it face up on top of the pack.
● Place the other three As, also face up, on top of the favorite A.
● With your right hand bend and lift off the top seven cards (the four face-up As and the three face-down cards) (**3**).

● With the left thumb scrape the top A to the left, towards the pack in your left hand. The card will still be face up. Name the card and, as you do so, flip your right wrist and hit the back of the A with these cards, flipping the A face down onto the pack (**4**).

● Repeat this procedure with the next two As.
● In your right hand you now have the face-up A of hearts and below it three face-down cards.
● Drop the A of hearts (and cards underneath) onto the pack as though you are handling just one card.
● Pick up the A of hearts and turn it face down on top of the pack, saying: "And your favorite ace, the ace of hearts."
● The audience will think the four As are now face down on top of the pack. In reality, there are three other cards between the A of hearts and the other three As.
● Deal the top four cards face down in a row. The first card will be the A of hearts; the others will not be As (**5**).

5

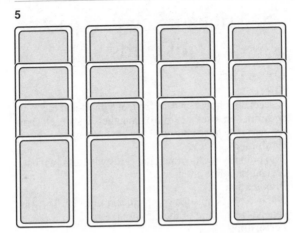

● Then deal three cards on top of each "A," making sure that the first three cards (the real As) go on top of the A of hearts.

● Now ask a spectator to pick one of the four piles. Use the technique described in The Magician Always Wins (see p. 236) to force the spectator to arrive at the pile which contains the four As.

● Pick up each of the other piles in turn and deal out the cards to reveal that the piles contain no As. Pause for dramatic effect with each pile before turning over the fourth card and showing it is not an A – the card the audience is expecting to see.

● Finally, deal out the four As in the "chosen" pile, pausing before dealing out the favorite A as the last card.

5. Tricks using two packs of cards

DO AS I DO
Effect
A spectator chooses a card from one pack, and the performer chooses a card from another. They each show the card they have chosen. They are the same!

Equipment
Two ordinary packs of playing cards with different back designs or colors are needed.

Preparation
The two packs must be complete and separate. The trick depends on the use of the glimpse (see p. 24).

Performing
● Have a spectator choose one pack; you keep the other.
● Tell the volunteer to copy exactly what you do.
● Shuffle your pack, and have the spectator shuffle hers.
● Exchange packs and shuffle the cards again.
● Once again exchange packs, but this time as you square the pack before passing it on, secretly glimpse and remember the bottom card (**1**).

1 (bottom view)

● Ask the spectator to remove any card from her pack, look at it, and remember it, and say that you will do the same. Look at the card you have selected but make no attempt to remember it.

● Each selected card (**2**) (**a**) is then placed on the top of its pack and the packs are then cut once. The selected cards are now "lost" in their packs. In fact, cutting the spectator's pack has brought the spectator's chosen card (**a**) beneath the card you have glimpsed (**b**).

2

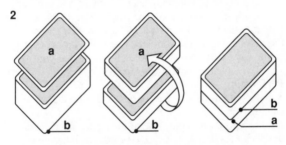

● Once again, exchange your packs.

● Now ask the spectator to sort through the pack and find the card she chose. Pretend you are doing the same to find the card you chose. In fact, you are hunting for the spectator's card which will be just to the right of the card you glimpsed.

● Remove the card, pretending it is yours, and place it face down. Have the spectator do the same.

● Now explain what you have both done and say: "Would you be surprised if we both chose the same card?"

● Turn your card over and ask the spectator to do the same. The cards are seen to be the same.

MIRACLE PREDICTION

Effect

A spectator freely chooses a card from one pack and discovers it matches the only reversed card in a second pack.

Equipment

Two ordinary packs of playing cards, in their cases, are needed.

Preparation

Arrange a card of your choice at the top of one pack. In the other pack, find the same card and turn it over and hide it in the pack. Put the packs back in their cases. If the cases are identical you need to ensure that there is some way to distinguish between them, so that you know which case contains the upside-down card.

Performing

• Place both decks of cards in their cases on the table side by side.

• Ask a spectator to pick one of the decks. If he picks the deck containing the reversed card, ask him to put the deck in his pocket. If he chooses the other deck, keep the deck and put the first deck to one side. Either way, you will be using the deck whose top card you know.

• Take the pack out of the case and ask a spectator to give you a number, somewhere between 1 and 52, adding: "It's best not to make it too high a number otherwise we could be here all day."

• Pick up the deck and deal out that number of cards, say 22, counting out loud as you do so (the known card is now on the bottom of the dealt pile).

● When you have finished, pretend to change your
mind. Say: "Wait a minute, it's better if you demonstrate
the trick."
● Put the pile of cards on top of the pack. The known
card is now twenty-second from the top.
● Hand the pack to the spectator, and ask him to repeat
what you did – to count down and deal to number 22.
Ask him to place the twenty-second card to one side.
● Continue by saying: "Now remember the other pack?
No one has touched it, is that right?" Ask the spectator
to take it out of his pocket or pick it up from the table.
"Open it up and you'll see all the cards are the same
way up, except for one. What is that card?"
● Then ask the spectator to turn over the twenty-second
card. The two cards match!

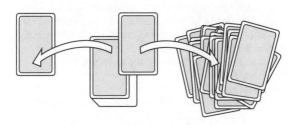

THE RED CARD

This is a novel trick using a stacked sequence of 10
cards from two packs.

Effect

The performer writes a prediction on a piece of paper.
A spectator then chooses a number from 1 to 10. The
performer deals out 10 cards. The spectator discloses
her chosen number, and the performer uses the 10 cards
to show how her chosen number fulfils the prediction.

Equipment

Two packs of playing cards – one with a red back
design, the other with a back design of a different color
– are needed, as are a piece of paper and a pencil.

Preparation

From the red-backed pack, take out any card from a
black suit. From the other pack, take out any eight
black cards and any red card. Arrange these cards in a
stack, alternating face up and face down, so that when
you deal them out in a line the third card from the left
(**a**) has a red back design and the fourth card (**b**) is of a
red suit. The actual values of the cards are not
important.

Performing

● Explain that you are going to write down a prediction.

On a piece of paper write: "You are going to choose a red card."

● Fold the paper and hand it to one of the spectators for safekeeping. Do not disclose what you have written.

● Ask a spectator to choose a number from 1 to 10. The number chosen will determine your next move.

● If the chosen number is 1, 2, 5, 6, 9 or 10, spell the number, tapping a card from left to right for each letter as you do so. (Numbers 1, 2, 6 and 10 have three letters and take you to the third card. Numbers 5 and 9 have four letters and so take you to the fourth card.)

● If the chosen number is 3 or 4, simply count along the row from left to right. If the chosen number is 7 or 8, count along the row from right to left.

● Either way, whatever number is chosen, you will end up on either the third or fourth card from the left. Now all you have to do is reveal your prediction.

● If it is the third card, turn all the face-up cards face down. Turn the third card over. It is the only card with a red back.

● If it is the fourth card, turn all the face-down cards face up. The fourth card will be the only red card.

● Ask the spectator to unfold the paper and read out your prediction!

A WORLD RECORD

This is a very impressive trick using a prearranged deck switched with a shuffled one. It requires at least four spectators.

Effect

Several spectators each choose a card and replace them anywhere in the pack. The performer promptly finds them all.

Equipment

Two ordinary packs of playing cards of identical design, and an elastic band, are needed.

Preparation

You will need to practice the false overhand shuffle (keeping the order of the pack, see p. 12) and switching packs (see p. 30). Prepare one pack with each suit in order, from A through to K. Place this prearranged pack in your pocket. When you have finished an earlier trick using the other pack, get a spectator to shuffle it well and then swap the two decks in your pocket (as described at switching packs) before performing this trick.

Performing

● Explain that this trick was once performed to break a world record.
● Fan the cards face down.
● Ask each spectator to come forward, take a card, remember it, and then return it anywhere in the pack.
● When all the spectators have done this, close the fan and do a false overhand shuffle to cut the cards once or twice, but maintain the order.
● Turn the pack to face yourself, and ask everyone to think hard of the card they chose. Explain how difficult the trick is, and how you need all the help you can get.

● Look through the cards. It should be easy to spot cards which are out of sequence (**a**). Don't forget there will be gaps where cards have been removed (**b**).

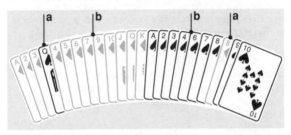

● As you come to each card out of sequence, take it out and throw it face down on the table, but leave one of the chosen cards in the pack. Remember this card.

● Explain that one of the spectators isn't concentrating properly, and say that you know who it is.

● Now riffle shuffle the pack two or three times to really mix up the arrangement.

● Look through the pack a final time and say: "That's better." Take out the final card and put it with the rest.

● Now pick up all the selected cards – there should be one for each spectator.

● Hold the cards toward you. Ask each spectator, in turn, to name her or his card. As each does so, throw it out face up on the table.

● When you have finished, say: "Back in the 18th century, [give the number of spectators] was a record for the number of cards identified in a single trick."

● Finish by spreading the pack face up to demonstrate that the cards are not in any order.

POCKET PREDICTION

Effect

The spectator takes one pack, the performer another, and both packs are well shuffled. The performer removes one card from her face-down pack and pushes it into the spectator's right-hand jacket pocket. The spectator selects a card from his face-down pack and puts it into the performer's right-hand jacket pocket. The performer summarizes what has happened so far and then removes the card from her pocket. The spectator removes the card from his. The cards are identical.

Equipment

Two ordinary packs of playing cards of different back design or color are needed. You will also need two jackets with deep side pockets – one for you and one for the spectator.

Preparation

From one pack remove a known card (**1**) (**a**) and place it in your jacket pocket lying horizontally with the back facing outwards.

1

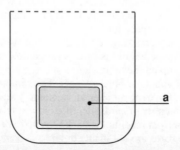

Place the identical card in the other pack at the top of that pack; it is the key card. You will need to practice the false overhand shuffle (see p. 12).

Performing

● Place the two packs face down on the table, side by side. Ask the spectator to pick a pack. If he picks the pack containing the key card, tell him to put that pack to one side. He should then pick up the remaining pack. If he picks the pack without the key card, let him keep it. Either way, he is left with the pack without the key card.

● Ask him to shuffle the pack thoroughly using an overhand shuffle. As he does this, say that you will do the same.

● Take the other pack and use a false overhand shuffle to keep the top card in place.

● Ask the spectator to take a card from his pack and, without looking at it, put the card in your right-hand jacket pocket. (Note: The card is bound to go in vertically rather than horizontally, and so you will not confuse it with your hidden card.) Say that you will do the same. At this point simply take your top card and without showing it to anyone put it in the spectator's pocket.

● Summarize what has happened so far and finish by saying: "I wonder what the chances are of us both choosing the same card – about 50 to 1, I suppose." With that, ask the spectator to take the card out of his pocket. You do the same, making sure you take out the horizontal card (**a**).

● You both place your cards face up on the table. They match!

6. Tricks using special cards

ONE-WAY

Effect

A spectator selects a card from the pack. She looks at the card and replaces it anywhere in the pack. The performer shuffles the pack, and then fans out the cards so they face the spectator. The performer then picks out the chosen card.

Equipment

You will need a pack of playing cards with a design on the back which has a recognizable top and bottom.

Preparation

Prepare the pack by placing all the cards with their back design the same way up.

Performing

● Ask a spectator to choose a card (**1**).

● While the spectator is looking at the card, turn the pack around so that she will replace the card with its pattern upside down. Shuffle the pack using an overhand shuffle.

● Hold up the pack and fan the cards to expose their faces to the onlookers (**2**).

● Ask the spectator to concentrate on her card when it appears.

● As you spread the cards, look for an upside-down back design (**a**). As soon as you come to this card, pull it out and exclaim: "It's this one!"

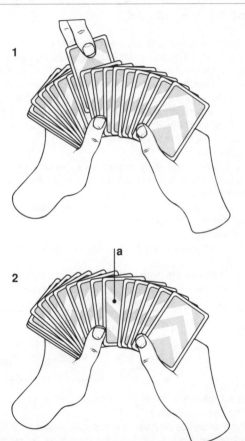

THE FOUR SPECIALS

Effect

A spectator is asked to say what his favorite card is – from A to K. The four cards of the chosen type – of each suit – are then removed from the pack, shown to the audience, and placed separately at intervals within the pack. Another spectator is invited to shuffle the pack. The performer then cuts the pack into four stacks and turns over the top card in each stack. Each top card is one of the chosen cards.

Equipment

You will need a slightly tapered deck of cards, called a stripper deck, available from a magic or trick shop.

Preparation

Make sure the cards are the correct way round, with all the narrow ends together.

Performing

● Ask a spectator what his favorite card is – from A to K.

● Sort through the pack with the cards face up and openly remove all four cards of the chosen type (**1**).

● Hold these four cards in your hand and turn the rest of the pack face down.

● Now place the four cards at separate locations in the pack, and as you do so, make sure you have turned the chosen cards around (**2**), so that the wide end of each card is at the narrow end of the deck.

● Have another spectator shuffle the pack and hand it to you.

● Holding the pack at the wide end (**3**) (**a**) between your thumb and two fingers, cut to the topmost chosen card. This will happen automatically when you cut, because the chosen cards are narrower than the rest (**b**). Discard the topmost stack (it does not contain a chosen card).

● Cut to the next chosen card and keep this stack. Continue in this way and you will be left with four stacks, each with a chosen card on top.

● To complete the trick, line up the four stacks, and turn over the top card in each stack to reveal the four chosen cards.

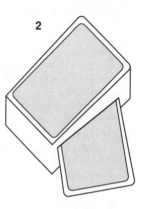

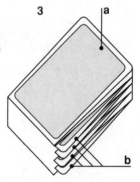

THE MARKED ONE-WAY PACK

Effect

An ordinary pack of cards can be marked to provide an
inconspicuous one-way pack (one in which the back
design has a recognizable top and bottom).

The marked one-way pack can be used to perform a
range of tricks. In one of the simplest, described here,
the performer deals out the cards face down and
separates all the spades from the other suits.

Equipment

An ordinary pack of playing cards and a sharp pin or
needle are needed.

Preparation

Use the pin or needle to scratch away some of the back
design at the top left of each card (**1**) (**a**). You now have
a one-way pack. (You can use this marked pack for
other tricks in this chapter.) Prepare the pack in advance
by making sure all the cards are the same way round.
Then remove all the spades, turn them around, and
insert them back in the pack.

1

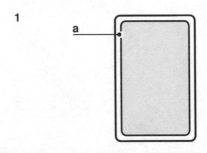

Performing

● Chat to the spectators as you shuffle the pack and deal the cards face down into two piles.

● Put all the spades in one pile (you can tell these because the back design will be upside down). Put all the non-spades into the other pile.

● When you have finished, ask the spectators what you have been doing. Listen to their answers. Then tell them that they are all wrong – in fact, you have been sorting out the spades because you thought one was missing. Say: "But you'll be glad to know they're all there."

● With this, turn over the smaller pile (**2**) (**a**); the spectators will be surprised to find it contains only spades. (You can show the second pile (**b**), containing a mixture of cards, to demonstrate that the pack is an ordinary pack.)

2

a   b

● To mix up the pack, and so avoid any chance of discovery, cut and turn each pile, and then riffle shuffle the piles together.

FOUR ACES

Effect

The performer magically extracts the four As by dealing from a face-down deck of cards.

Equipment

A marked one-way deck of playing cards is needed (see p. 160).

Preparation

Prepare the pack by placing all the cards with their backs the same way up (**1**) (**a**), except for the four As, which are reversed (**b**).

1

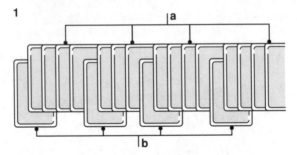

Performing

● Shuffle the pack using an overhand shuffle.

● Explain to onlookers: "Few people know that the As carry less printing ink than the other cards, and so weigh less. With practice you can feel this."

● Slowly deal out the cards face down. As you do so, make a show of pretending to weigh each card, but actually look for those cards which are upside down.

● Deal all the right-way-up cards into one pile (**2**) (**a**), and the four upside-down cards into a separate pile (**b**).

2

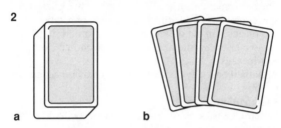

a   **b**

● When you have finished, pick up the four separate cards. Turn them right way up as you transfer them from one hand to the other, and then spread them out face up on the table to show the spectators that they are the four As (**3**).

3

● When you have finished, put them on top of the other cards. All the cards are now the right way up and the spectators will not notice how the trick was done.

FIND THE CARD

Effect

The performer cuts a shuffled pack into two piles. The
spectator chooses a card from one pile, remembers it
and places it in the other pile. The performer shuffles
the two piles together and extracts the chosen card.

Equipment

A marked one-way deck of playing cards is needed (see
p. 160).

Preparation

Prepare the pack by placing all the cards with their
backs the same way up (**1**).

1

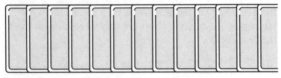

Performing

● Shuffle the pack using an overhand shuffle.

● Cut the pack into two equal piles, but reverse one pile
so that its back design is upside down (**2**).

2

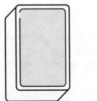
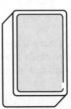

● Ask a spectator to select a card from one pile, look at it, and replace it in the other pile.

● Turn the first pile the right way up and riffle shuffle the two piles together.

● Spread the deck face down in a ribbon spread. The chosen card will be the one which is upside down (**3**) (**a**). Quickly remove it from the row of cards. Make a big show of finding the card, exclaiming "Here it is!" and engaging in lively patter as you show it to the spectators to confirm that it is the chosen card. By doing so, you distract the audience away from noticing that the card backs are marked.

3

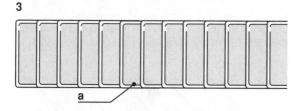

a

● When you are finished, return the card, right side up, to the row of cards. Quickly square the pack and begin a new trick with a different pack of cards.

THE SVENGALI DECK

Effect

The Svengali deck is a trick deck containing 26
different cards and 26 slightly shorter cards which are
all identical. The deck can be used to produce a variety
of effects: one of the most common is showing how, at
the click of a finger, the pack can be transformed from
a normal pack to one containing all identical cards.

Equipment

A Svengali deck of playing cards is needed.

Preparation

Prepare the pack by making sure that the shorter
identical cards alternate with the longer non-identical
cards (**1**), finishing with a non-identical card at the
bottom of the pack (**a**). You will need to practice cutting
the cards by holding their ends rather than their sides.

1

a

Performing

● Explain to the audience that you are using a normal
pack. Place the deck in a vertical position in one hand
with the bottom card facing towards the audience.

2

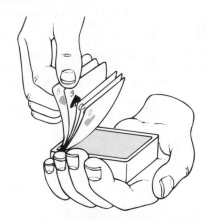

● With the thumb of one hand, release the cards so that they fall into the palm of the other hand (**2**). To the audience, the cards will all appear different.

● Now place the pack face down on the table and cut the pack, somewhere in the middle, holding the ends of the cards rather than the sides as you cut. Lift up the top pile and show the bottom card to the audience. Repeat this a couple more times to show that the cards are different.

● Continue by saying: "I like this trick because when I click my fingers – watch my fingers – a remarkable change happens."

● Click your fingers, and cut the cards as before, but do not show the bottom card of the top pile. Instead, show the top card of the bottom pile. In each case it will be one of the identical cards.

● Now pick up the pack and transfer the top card – one of the identical cards – to the bottom of the pack.
● Hold the deck in a vertical position in one hand with the back of the top card facing the audience. As you let the cards fall by releasing your thumb as before, the audience will now see the cards are all identical (**3**).

3

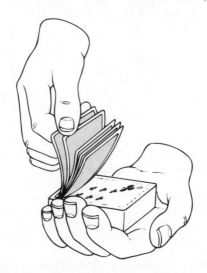

● To finish, say: "Luckily the change is reversible, otherwise I wouldn't be able to use the cards." Move the bottom card to the top, and with the new bottom card facing the audience, release the cards (as in figure 2) and show that they are all different.
● Then put the pack away for another day.

THE CHANGING CARD

This uses a single novelty card and is a good trick for
children. Perform it a few feet away from your audience.

Effect

A double-faced card changes miraculously from an A of
clubs on one side, to a 4 of diamonds on the other, then
to a 3 of clubs on one side, and a 6 of diamonds on the
other.

Equipment

You will need a double-sided card with five diamonds
on one side (**1**) (**a**) and two clubs on the other (**b**). (You
can get this from a joke or novelty shop or from a
magician's suppliers.)

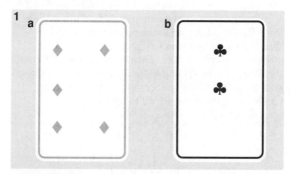

Preparation

Practice using the card with fast patter and slick
presentation – sure positioning of the fingers is needed
to do the trick well.

Performing

● Hold the card in the right hand with the diamonds

facing the audience and the tips of your first and second
fingers covering the center diamond (**2**).

● Continue by saying: "As you can see, I have the 4 of
diamonds on one side . . . and the A of clubs on the other."

● Turn the card so that the diamonds face towards the
floor. Transfer the card to your left hand with your
thumb forward and your first and second fingers
covering the bottom club. Then twist your wrist to turn
the card horizontally and bring the card into the vertical
position to face the audience (to position the card
correctly for the move which follows) (**3**).

• Use your right hand to grasp the card as before, with your fingertips covering the blank spot where the sixth diamond would normally be (**4**). Say: "And now we have the 6 of diamonds . . . and the 3 of clubs."

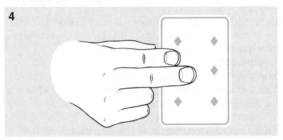

4

• Finally, use your left hand to take the card, covering the blank spot where the third club would normally be (**5**), and show it to the audience.

5

• Quickly turn the card with its edge towards the audience so they cannot see the faces of the card when you put it away.

HALF CUT

This is a self-working card trick using half cards. The pack, prepared in advance, can be carried easily in a pocket and used anytime, anywhere.

Effect

By a random process, two spectators each select a half card from a pack of half cards. It is later revealed that they have the two halves of the same card.

Equipment

You will need an ordinary pack of playing cards (an old pack, which you won't mind destroying), a metal rule, a modeling knife and cutting board, and a pencil.

Preparation

Take 17 cards from the pack. Choose cards of all four suits and of assorted values (**1**).

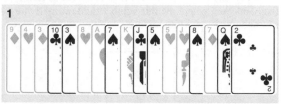

1

Take the metal rule and, with a pencil, lightly mark each card at the center of each long edge (**2**).

2

Carefully cut across the center of each of the 17 cards using the modeling knife on a cutting board. You will be left with 34 half cards.

Arrange these cards with their cut edges aligned.

Performing

- Shuffle the pack of half cards, making sure to keep the cut edges aligned. Offer the face-down pack to one spectator, explaining: "This pack was formed from ordinary cards which were cut in half. Check them if you like."
- Now have the spectator put the pack face down on the table and lift off and keep a portion of the cards.
- Have another spectator pick up the remaining cards.
- Ask the two spectators to silently count their cards while your back is turned and to memorize the number.
- Still with your back turned, ask the second spectator to give her cards to the first spectator, who then shuffles the two piles together.
- Turn around, take the cards, and deal them one at a time face up towards the first spectator. Ask him to mentally count the cards as they are shown and to remember the particular card that falls at the number he had earlier memorized. Tell him to give no visible indication – either to you or the other spectator – of his number or the card.
- The essence of the trick lies in the way you show the cards to the spectator. Hold the cards in your left hand, facing towards the first spectator.
- Push off the top card with your left thumb and take it in your right hand, with its face still towards the first spectator.

● Then push off the next card with your thumb and show it to the first spectator as you transfer it to your right hand behind the first card (**3**).

3

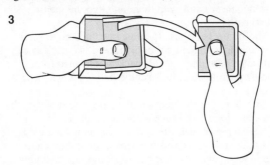

● Continue in this way with all the cards so that you reverse the order of the cards.
● When you get to the last card, show the card to the spectator but then keep the card face down in your left hand and place all the other cards on top of it (**4**).

4

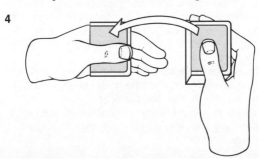

● Now turn to the second spectator. Ask her to mentally count the cards as you transfer them, face up and one at a time, from your left hand to your right, and ask her to remember the particular card that falls at the number she had earlier memorized. Tell her to give no visible indication of her number or the card.

● Hold the cards in your left hand, facing the spectator, as you did before.

● Proceed to show the second spectator all the cards, one at a time, as you transfer them to your right hand as before. This time, however, there is one important difference. When you get to the last card in your left hand put it on top of the face-down cards in your right hand (**5**).

5

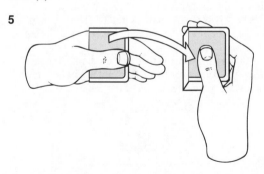

● When finished, hand the face-down pack to the first spectator, get him to shuffle them and then instruct him to find his particular card, which he is to place face down on the table.

● Ask the first spectator to hand the pack to the second, who now sorts through to find her card, which she places face down on the table.

● Place the two cut ends of the cards together (**6**) and quickly run through what has happened: "The pack was shuffled; you both had a random number of cards – only you knew how many; you used this number to later select a card."

6

● Look at the first spectator and, pointing to his half card, say: "This is your half, is it not?" Then look at the second spectator and, pointing to her half, say: "This is yours."

● "What is remarkable is that they are both from the same card!" Turn over the halves and it will be seen that they are matching halves of the same card (**7**)!

7

Note: The trick works on the simple premise that the two numbers must add up to 34. If one spectator's number is 16, for example, the other's must be 18. The rest is determined by the way the cards are shown to the spectators.

DOUBLE PREDICTION

Effect

The performer is able to predict the location of a card chosen "blind" by a spectator behind the spectator's back.

Equipment

You will need an ordinary pack of playing cards, a matching double-backed card (a card with the same back pattern on both sides), a pencil and paper.

Preparation

Reverse a card (**1**) (**a**) somewhere in the middle of the pack and remember the card that is on either side of it (**b** and **c**). At the top of the pack place the double-backed card (**d**).

1

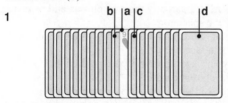

You will need to practice the false overhand shuffle (see p. 12) and the palm technique (see p. 29).

Performing

● Begin by using a false overhand shuffle which keeps the cards in the same order.

● Choose a spectator from the audience to assist you. Look intently at her and write down on a piece of paper: "The card will be placed between [name the two cards (**b** and **c**) that you remembered beforehand]." Explain to her: "I am writing down a prediction."

● Do not show what you have written to anyone. Fold the paper and place it to one side.

● Now, ask the spectator to join you. Give her the pack and ask her to put it face down behind her back so that neither she nor anyone else can see it.

● Instruct her: "Without looking, take off the top card, turn it over, and place it face up somewhere in the middle of the pack, and then square the pack."

● When she has done this, take back the pack and explain what has happened so far: "I have made a prediction. A card has then been taken from the top of the pack and inserted 'blind' into the pack. What I have actually predicted is the location of the chosen card."

● Spread the pack face down on the table. Reveal the reversed card – apparently the card chosen and placed "blind" by the spectator.

● Remove the cards above and below the reversed card and turn them face up.

● Unfold your paper to reveal your prediction. It matches the chosen cards!

● Return the cards right way up to the pack and casually sort through the cards, but without showing the faces to the spectators. As you do so, find the double-backed card and cut it to the bottom or top of the pack. Use the palm technique to remove this card from the pack.

7. Tricks using props

Props (short for "properties") refer to any gadgets or devices – other than cards – which you use in your performance.

SPOT THE THUMBPRINT

This trick requires a confident delivery.

Effect

A spectator shuffles the pack and then chooses a card. The card is returned to the pack and the pack is cut. The performer spreads the cards face up and apparently finds the card by identifying the spectator's thumbprint on it.

Equipment

An ordinary pack of playing cards and a magnifying lens or pair of spectacles are needed.

Preparation

The trick depends on the use of the glimpse (see p. 24) and the bottom card as key. To succeed you need to be convincing in explaining the use of fingerprints in detection.

Performing

● Ask a spectator to shuffle the pack.

● Tell the spectator to select and remove a card.

● Take the pack, turn your back to the spectator, and as you do so ask her to press the numbers or symbols on the top left and bottom right corners of her card (**1,** see over).

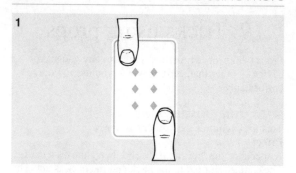

- While the spectator is doing this, take the opportunity to glance at the bottom card in the pack.
- Turn back and place the pack of cards face down on the table.
- Ask the spectator to place her card on top of the pack, and then cut the pack and replace the cut (**2**) so that her card (**a**) is at the center of the pack. Doing this brings the key card (**b**) from the bottom of the pack to lie on top of the chosen card.

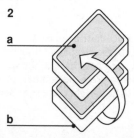

● Complete the trick by turning over the deck and spreading the cards in a ribbon spread so that they are all visible (**3**). The chosen card (**a**) will lie to the right of the key card (**b**).

● Make a show of using the magnifying lens or spectacles to study the thumbs of the spectator. Then use the lens or spectacles to study each card in turn as though you are looking for the thumbprint. When you arrive at the card just after the key card exclaim: "I can just about make out your thumbprint. This is the card!"

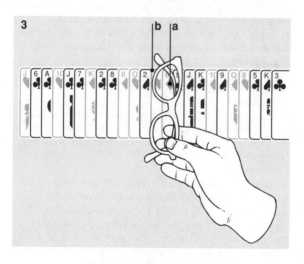

THE CLOCK TRICK

This is a rather novel mathematical trick where you appear to read a person's mind. You predict a chosen card by arranging cards to form the hour positions on a clock face.

Effect

The performer makes a prediction which is written on a piece of paper, folded over and put to one side. A spectator thinks of an hour in the day, and is directed to take that number of cards from a pile. Twelve cards from the remaining pile are dealt out and laid face up to form the hours on a clock face. Not only does the performer state which hour the spectator has chosen but the card at this location is the one predicted on paper.

Equipment

You will need an ordinary pack of playing cards, a pencil and paper, and a wristwatch.

Preparation

Practice this trick several times to ensure that you can give clear directions to the spectator. Before you start the trick you need to know the thirteenth card from the bottom.

Performing

● Make a mental note of the thirteenth card from the bottom of the deck – for example, the A of hearts.

● Take the pencil and paper and without disclosing what you are writing down, write "the selected card will be the ace of hearts." Fold the paper and put it to one side.

● Now, ask one of the spectators to think of an hour in the day – it can be in the morning or afternoon.

● Place the deck of cards face up on the table. Say to the spectator: "I will turn my back for a moment. As I do so, take from the top of the pack the number of cards which corresponds to the hour you thought of. For example, if you thought of six o'clock, take six cards; three o'clock, take three cards." Turn your back and let the spectator take the corresponding number of cards.

● Turn back to face the spectator. Pick up the pack and deal 12 cards face up onto the table, one at a time, to form a small pile. As you do so say: "I need 12 cards to show the hours on the clock face."

● Now pick up the small pile and lay the cards face up in a clockwise circle, beginning at the one o'clock position (**1**). Complete the circle and finish with "Now we have our clock face."

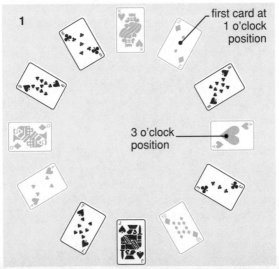

first card at
1 o'clock
position

3 o'clock
position

● Look for the A of hearts. This will lie at the position which corresponds to the spectator's chosen time. For example, if the card is at the three o'clock position, it means the spectator has three cards in his pocket.

● Make a point of looking at your wristwatch, as if to check the time. Then announce the spectator's chosen time: "I think the hour you chose was three o'clock. Is that right?" Ask him to remove the cards from his pocket and count them out on the table.

● At this point the trick will appear to be over. But the best part is still to come. Ask: "What is the card at the three o'clock position?" He will name the A of hearts. At this point unfold your piece of paper and show the audience your prediction.

THE ONE IN THE MIDDLE

This is a very simple trick which should be performed only once, before any of your audience catch on to how it works.

Effect

The performer makes a prediction which is written on a piece of paper, folded over and put to one side. A spectator then follows the performer's instructions and takes a card, then loses it in a pile, and then deals the cards out into five piles face up. The chosen card will always be the middle card in one of the piles. The spectator points to the correct pile. The performer then states the chosen card and shows his written prediction to be correct.

Equipment

You will need 15 playing cards from an ordinary pack, a pencil and paper.

Preparation

The trick is very straightforward and needs to be practiced only two or three times before performing it.

Performing

● Take the pencil and paper and without disclosing what you are writing down, write: "It is the middle card." Fold the paper and put it to one side.

● Ask a spectator to shuffle the cards and deal out three piles of five cards.

● Have the spectator pick up one of the piles and choose a card. He should then shuffle the pile and place this pile on top of one of the other piles. The last remaining pile should then be placed on top of the other two.

● Now ask the spectator to deal out five piles of three cards each, one card at a time to each pile, as though he were dealing out cards in a game with five players.

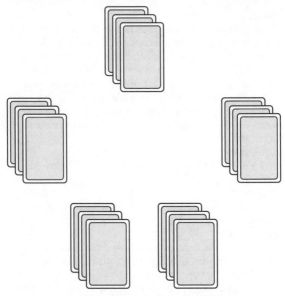

● Turn over the piles one at a time, and ask the spectator to point out which pile contains the chosen card.

● At this point you can say which is the chosen card – it will be the middle one in the pile the spectator has chosen. Unfold your piece of paper and show the audience your prediction.

BLINDFOLDED LOCATION

The trick uses a permanently marked key card.

Effect

The spectator selects a card and returns it to the pack. The performer locates the card while blindfolded.

Equipment

You will need an ordinary pack of playing cards, a pin or needle, and a scarf or handkerchief to use as a blindfold.

Preparation

Take the 10 of hearts from the pack and use the pin to prick a small hole at the top left corner of the card just above the 10. Turn the card around and repeat the procedure on the other end. You now have a card marked at top and bottom (**1**). Practice the trick blindfolded so that you can feel the marks you have made.

Place your marked card tenth from bottom of the deck.
Performing
● Spread the top two-thirds of the pack face down and
with your hand in place holding the lower cards (**2**).
Ask a spectator to take a card (**a**) and remember it.

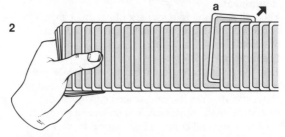

● Cut the pack at the point where the card was taken
and hold the bottom half in your left hand and the top
half in your right hand. Ask the spectator to replace the
chosen card on top of the pile in your right hand.
● Place the right-hand pile under the left-hand one (**3**),
and you will have placed the chosen card (**a**) ten cards
away from the marked card (**b**).

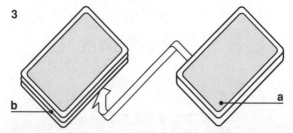

● Ask someone to blindfold you with a scarf or
handkerchief and explain: "I will now find your card
totally in the dark."
● Deal the cards face up one at a time (**4**).

4

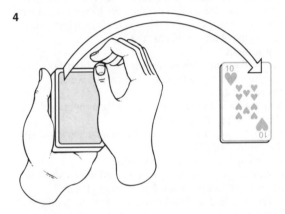

● When you reach the marked card you will feel it with
your right thumb. Deal out this card and ask: "Is this
your card?" The answer will be "No."
● Continue by saying "Of course not. What is the card
I've turned over?" When you get the reply say: "Oh
yes, that's my indicator."
● Count and deal ten more cards. The tenth card will be
the selected one. As you place it, say: "Here's your
card," and remove the blindfold.

FOLLOW ME

This is a novel trick using a marked card as key.

Effect

The pack is cut into two piles and performer and
spectator each select and initial a card from their pile.
They replace the card in the pile. Each then takes a card
from the other person's pile. By an amazing feat, each
selects the other's initialed card.

Equipment

You will need a pack of playing cards which has a back
design with a white border, and two soft pencils.

Preparation

You will need to practice a false riffle or overhand
shuffle (see p. 17 and p. 12).

● Surreptitiously take two cards from the pack and slip
them into your pocket.

● Find an excuse to leave the room.

● With no one looking, mark one card with a small dot
on the back in the top left-hand corner (**1**) (**a**).

● Turn the card upside down and repeat the procedure.
This key card is now marked at top (**a**) and bottom (**b**).

● Write your initials on the face of the other card (**2**) (**a**)
and remember the card.

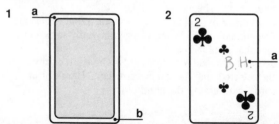

● Return to the room, and at a suitable moment return the two cards to the pack, with the dotted key card at the bottom and the initialed card just above it.

Performing

● Shuffle the pack with a false riffle shuffle or overhand shuffle so as not to disturb the two cards at the bottom.

● Place the pack face down and have a spectator cut off a pile from the top.

● Take this top pile and ask the spectator to take the bottom pile.

● Ask the spectator to turn his back to you and remove any card from the middle of his pile and place it face up at the top of the pile.

● Explain that you will do the same and that you and he must synchronize your actions and thoughts if the trick is to work.

● Instruct him to write his initials on the face of his card. You will pretend to write your initials on your card but will actually write nothing. Keep your card hidden from other people as you do this.

● Ask the spectator to turn his card face down on his pile as you do the same with yours.

● Finally, have him make one complete cut, as you also make a cut. His cut places his initialed card below the dotted key card.

● Explain to the spectator: "From now on you have to follow your intuition – your first impulse."

● Spread your own cards face down on the table and ask the spectator to remove one from the middle of the spread but not to look at the card.

● Instruct him to place this card anywhere in the middle of his pile.
● Now take his pack and spread it face down, from left to right.
● Run your finger over the cards as though deciding which one to take. Look for the dotted key card (**3**) (**a**). The card to its left will be the spectator's initialed card (**b**). Take this and place it in the middle of your own pile of cards.

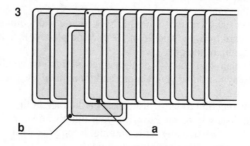

● Finish by saying: "If we have been following our intuition, and our minds are attuned, you will have taken my card name [the card you initialed before performing the trick] and I will have taken yours."
● Spread your cards face up and push out the card which he initialed.
● Have him spread his pile and he will find the card with your initials somewhere towards the middle of the pack!

THE MAGICIAN'S MESSAGE

This trick gives the appearance that it is the spectator –
not the performer – who makes the key choices.

Effect

The performer gives a spectator a sealed envelope.
Another spectator then shuffles the pack and deals and
discards cards until she has only one left. In the
envelope she finds a message which names this card.

Equipment

You will need an ordinary pack of used playing cards, a
piece of chalk, an envelope, a piece of paper and a
pencil.

Preparation

Choose a card from the pack, eg the Q of hearts. With
the chalk make a mark at the top and bottom edge of
this card (**1**) (**a**). When the card is placed in the pack
the mark will show in a used pack as a narrow white
line (**b**).

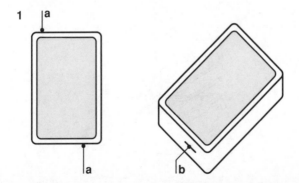

On a piece of paper write: "The card you have chosen is the Q of hearts." Seal the message in an envelope.

Performing

● Give the cards to a spectator to shuffle.

● Hand the sealed envelope to another spectator to look after.

● When the spectator has finished shuffling, take back the pack, glance at its end and look for the mark. If the card is near the top or bottom of the pack, cut the pack to bring the card nearer the center.

● Explain: "I am going to cut the pack into two." Cut off all the cards above the marked card. To do this, open the pack slightly two or three cards below the marked card. Then with your thumb release the cards one at a time until the marked card (**2**) (**a**) drops.

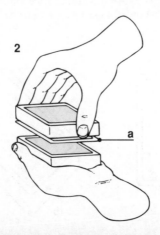

● Now place the two piles face down, side by side, in front of the spectator. Appear to change your mind and say: "No, I think you should cut the cards." Put one pile on top of the other so that the marked card is on top of the pack. Hand the pack over for the spectator to cut into two piles.

● From now on you will be directing the spectator, but apparently giving her free choice at key stages. In reality, you are deciding which cards to keep and which to discard.

● After the spectator cuts the cards ask her to place a finger on the pile of her choice. If it is the pile containing the marked card, say: "Good. We'll discard the others." If it is the other pile she points to, say: "Good. We'll discard these." Either way, you discard the unwanted cards.

● Next, ask her to deal the cards, the first card to you, the next to her, and so on, to form two piles. The marked card will now be at the bottom of your pile.

● Stop the spectator when she has dealt you seven cards. Ask her to discard the cards remaining in her hand, and discard the pile of cards she dealt to herself.

● Point to the pile she dealt you and say: "Now deal these again, the same way." You should get four cards, and she should get three. The marked card is now at the top of your pile.

● Ask the spectator to discard her pile once more, and then to deal two piles as she did before. You should both have two cards each. The bottom of your two cards will be the marked card.

● Have her discard her pile. Place your two cards face down side by side.

● Ask her to choose a card. Again, she appears to have
free choice but in reality she does not. If she points to
the marked card say: "OK, we'll keep that." If she
points to the unmarked card, say: "We'll discard that."
Either way you are left with the marked card – the Q of
hearts. Turn this card over to reveal it.

● At this point, ask the other spectator to open the
sealed envelope and read out the message enclosed. It
will identify the one remaining card – the one that was
"chosen" by the other spectator!

THE VANISHING CARD
Effect
The spectator places a chosen card on top of the pack. She then arranges her hands as instructed and says the magic word. When she goes to turn over the top card, it has changed. The performer then plucks the card from behind her ear.

Equipment
An ordinary pack of playing cards and a glass of water are needed.

Preparation
You will need to practice the palm (see p. 29).

Performing
● Hand the pack to a spectator and ask her to shuffle it.
● Take the pack back and fan the cards face down towards the audience.
● Ask the spectator to take a card, look at it and remember it.
● Place the pack face down on the table and ask the spectator to place her card on top of the pile.
● Explain that you are going to need some help with this trick. As you begin to talk, start to cough as though you have got "a frog in your throat." In reality, you can use this as an opportunity to moisten the back of one hand.
● Reach for a glass and as you are drinking, surreptitiously dip two fingers in the water. Out of view of the audience, secretly wipe these fingers on the back of your other hand.
● Now demonstrate what you want the spectator to do. Put your hands one on top of the other, with backs face down and with the moist back of the hand at the

bottom. As you do this, touch the pack of cards and the chosen card will stick to the back of your hand.

● Once you have the card you can hide it on your lap or palm it by transferring it to your other hand (see p. 29).
● Turn to the spectator and ask her to place her hands as you did and to say a magic word (eg "abracadabra").
● When she has said the magic word, ask her to turn over the top card. She will see that it has changed.
● Whether you have hidden her chosen card in your lap or elsewhere, palm this card and pluck it from behind the spectator's ear, or wherever you choose.

LUCKY 18

This is a simple mathematical trick which allows you to force a particular card onto the spectator.

Effect

The performer makes a prediction as to which card from the pack a spectator will choose. The spectator thinks of three numbers and then, by performing a simple calculation, selects a particular card from the pack. It is the predicted card.

Equipment

You will need an ordinary pack of playing cards, an envelope, a pencil, a pad of paper, and, if available, a single card from another pack.

Preparation

Prearrange the pack so that you know which is the eighteenth card. If you have another pack available, put a duplicate of this card in an envelope. Alternatively, write the name of the eighteenth card and place this "prediction" in the envelope. Do this in view of the audience just before you perform the trick.

Performing

● Ask a spectator to take the pad and pencil. Instruct him as follows: "Write down three different numbers between 1 and 9, making sure the highest value is written first and the lowest value last" (**1**, see over) (**a**). "Now, reverse the order of these numbers and write them below the other numbers" (**b**). "Imagine the first row of numbers is a three-digit number, and the second row is as well. Subtract the lower number from the upper one" (**c**). "Take the three digits of your total and add them together" (**d**).

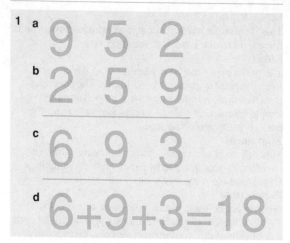

1 a 9 5 2
b 2 5 9
c 6 9 3
d 6+9+3=18

- Now ask for assistance from another spectator. Get her to note the final number and count down into the pack of cards until she gets to that number.
- Ask her to turn over that card. (If the sums are done correctly it will always be the eighteenth card!)
- Now get another spectator to open the envelope and reveal the written prediction or duplicate card.
- Your audience may be sceptical. Finish by turning over the pack and showing that all the cards are different!

Note: In the subtraction sum, the middle number of the total is always 9 and the outer two numbers always add up to 9, giving a total of 18.

RIP-OFF

This is an amusing trick with an unusual surprise.

Effect

A spectator cuts the pack, chooses a card, and then
returns the card to the pack and shuffles the cards. The
performer claims to have a matching card in a top
pocket. When this card is partly removed from the
pocket the audience see it is different from the chosen
one. When the card is completely removed from the
pocket, it matches the chosen one.

Equipment

You will need an ordinary pack of playing cards plus a
9 of hearts from an old pack, and a top pocket.

Preparation

Prearrange the pack so that the bottom card is the 5 of
hearts.

Take the 9 of hearts and tear it almost in half so that
only five of the hearts are shown on the face. Place the
card in a top pocket, with the card facing the audience
and the torn edge at the bottom (1).

You will need to practice the technique used in The Cut
Force (see p. 128).

1

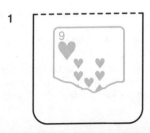

Performing

● Ask a spectator to cut the cards and put the lower pile crossways on the upper pile.

● Say: "This really is one of my best tricks." Ask the spectator to pick up the top pile, look at the bottom card and show it to the audience, and then place the pile on top of the other cards and shuffle the pack thoroughly.

● As he is doing this explain: "You have chosen a card. Meanwhile, I have its matching card in my pocket."

● Ask him to stop shuffling.

● Slowly pull the card out of your pocket so that only the number and the first row of hearts is visible (**2**), saying: "And here it is."

2

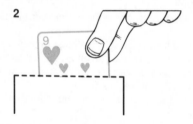

● At this point the spectator and the audience will disagree with you.

● Continue by saying: "Are you saying I've got it wrong?" They will reply: "Yes."

● Add: "Aren't I right in thinking that you chose the 5 of hearts? Well, count the hearts." At this point, remove the card from your pocket and throw it face up on the table.

SOMETHING UP YOUR SLEEVE

This magical trick will amaze a young audience.

Effect

A spectator picks up the top card of a shuffled pack and
writes the name of the card on a piece of paper. She
then returns the card to any part of the pack. The paper
is burnt to ashes, and the cold ashes are rubbed into the
performer's forearm. Marks on the forearm spell out
the chosen card.

Equipment

You will need an ordinary pack of playing cards, a bar
of soap, paper, a pencil, an ashtray and a box of
matches or a lighter.

Preparation

You will need to practice the false overhand shuffle
(see p. 12). Before performing the trick, make an
excuse to leave the room and go to a bathroom or
lavatory where you can find a bar of soap. Dampen a
corner of the soap and with this write the name of a
card on your left forearm (1). Allow the soap marks to
dry, roll down your sleeve and return to the room.
Arrange the pack so that the named card is on the top of
the pack.

1

4 OF CLUB

Performing

● Spread the cards face up to show the audience that the pack is well mixed, but do not show the audience the top card.

● Shuffle the pack using a false overhand shuffle which keeps the top card in place.

● Place the pack face down, and ask a spectator to take the top card, look at it, and put it anywhere in the pack.

● Ask the spectator to write the name of the card on the piece of paper provided. Turn your back while she does this.

● Ask her to fold the paper and place it in an ashtray.

● Ask another spectator to light the paper so that it burns completely to ash.

● Say: "This trick was taught to me by a Transylvanian magician – it is very magical."

● When the ashes have cooled, crumble them into a powder. With the fingers of your right hand pick up the ashes and wipe them on your left forearm (2).

● Where the soap marks remain, the ash collects and spells out the name of the card. Show your forearm to the spectator and exclaim: "This is your card!"

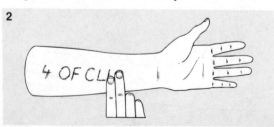

2

A STAB IN THE DARK

This trick is particularly effective because it combines the free choices of two spectators.

Effect

A spectator picks a card and returns it to the pack. The pack is shuffled and then wrapped in a newspaper. The spectator stabs a paperknife into the pack to cut the pack at a particular location. Amazingly, where the cards are cut is the location of the chosen card!

Equipment

You will need an ordinary pack of playing cards, a newspaper and a paperknife.

Preparation

You will need to practice the false overhand shuffle (see p. 12).

Performing

● Ask a spectator to shuffle the pack.

● Take back the pack, fan the cards face down and ask another spectator to take a card and remember it.

● Close up the pack and ask the spectator to return the card to any location within the pack. As he does so, hold the pack tightly so that it is difficult to insert the card all the way.

● Surreptitiously bend one corner of the chosen card to mark it temporarily. You can now freely shuffle the pack. The bent card will form a slight break in the pack and is easily located (**1**).

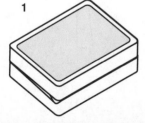

- Cut the cards at the break so that the selected card is now at the bottom of the pack.
- Use a false overhand shuffle to bring the selected card to the top of the pack.
- Hold the pack in your left hand and pick up a double page of a newspaper with your right. Hold the paper over the pack to start wrapping the paper around the cards.
- As soon as the paper hides the cards from view, turn the pack face up (**2**). At the same time unbend the corner of the chosen card.

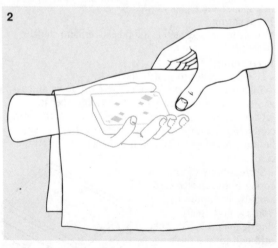

2

● Wrap the pack completely with paper.
● Hand the spectator a paperknife and ask him to thrust the knife through the newspaper and into the side of the pack. Leave the knife in position.

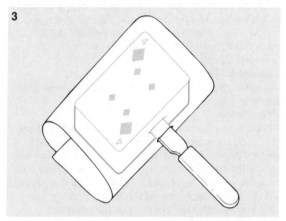

● Loosen the paper and reach underneath to take the cards from below the knife. Turn the cards over (face down) before you bring the cards into view. The top card – the one the spectator believes he has cut to – will be his chosen card.
● Ask another spectator to take this top card and reveal its identity as the selected card!
● To complete the trick, casually reach beneath the paper and turn the remaining cards over before bringing them into view.

STAB A TWIN

This trick uses a deck arranged according to the Si Stebbins system.

Effect

A spectator cuts the pack, takes the top card and puts it in her pocket. The performer proceeds to cut the deck in half with a paperknife and at the point of the cut takes out a card – it is the "twin" of the card in the spectator's pocket.

Equipment

An ordinary pack of playing cards and a paperknife are needed.

Preparation

Arrange the pack according to the Si Stebbins system (see p. 92). Practice cutting the pack exactly in two using a paperknife. With a good eye and a steady hand you will find it is quite easy to do. You will know how accurate you are, because the "twin" of the bottom card (**1**) (**a**) will be the twenty-seventh card from the bottom (**b**). You will also need to practice the glimpse technique (see p. 24).

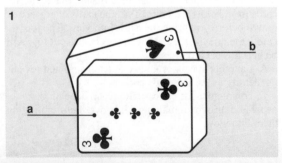

Performing

● Ask a spectator to cut the top half of the pack and place it underneath the bottom half.

● Instruct him to take the top card and, without looking at it, to place it into his jacket pocket or other safe place.

● As he is doing this, take back the pack and glimpse the bottom card.

● Pick up the knife and, with a grand gesture, insert the point into the side of the pack of the cards, as near to the center as you can get (**2**).

2

● Cut the pack at this point and glimpse the bottom card of the top pile.

● Knowing the bottom card of the pack, you can calculate the top card (the one the spectator has in his pocket).

● The "twin" of the spectator's chosen card (the card of the same color and value) will be 26 cards down in the pack.

● If the bottom card of the top pile is not the "twin" of the chosen card, then the card below it, the top card of the bottom pile, must be – providing, of course, that you correctly cut the pack.

● Explain, at this point, that each card in the pack has a twin – a card of the same value and color.

● Proceed to turn face up the card you have cut which you know to be the "twin" of the spectator's card.

● Continue by saying: "For example, here is the [name the card] and in this person's pocket is the twin." Ask the person to take out the card. It will match your card in color and value.

Note: If you wish to use the stacked deck again you must return the two cards to their correct places. Alternatively, finish by thoroughly mixing the cards using one or two riffle shuffles.

CARD THROUGH THE TABLE

This dramatic trick is particularly effective with a young audience.

Effect

A spectator chooses and remembers a card. The performer places the pack on a plate on the table and bangs a fist down on it. The chosen card leaves the pack and passes down through the plate and the table, and is retrieved from below.

Equipment

You will need an ordinary pack of playing cards and a plate placed on a table, and a chair on which to sit.

Preparation

You will need to practice the new moves described in this trick plus the false overhand shuffle (see p. 12).

Performing

● Hold the pack in your left hand and grasp it from above with the right hand, thumb at the inner end, fingers at the outer end (**1**).

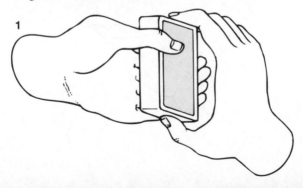

● Turn your back and riffle through the pack with your left thumb. Ask a spectator to tell you when to stop.
● Stop at the command, lift off the cards held by the right hand and turn this top pile over so that the bottom card can be seen by the audience. Ask them to remember the card.
● As you turn to face the audience and show them the bottom card, tilt your left hand slightly to hide the top of the bottom pile it holds. Squeeze this pile with your fingers so that the cards are bent slightly inward (**2**).

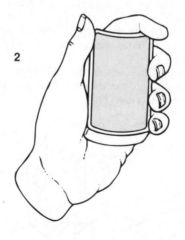

● Bring the pile in your right hand to land with a slap on top of the left-hand pile. Square the cards neatly. Because of the bend in the bottom pile, there will be a break between the two piles (**3**). Make sure the audience cannot see this.

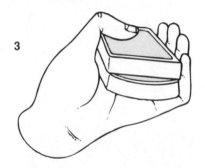

● Without looking, cut the pack at the break. Place the top pile under the bottom one. The chosen card is now at the bottom of the pack.
● Give the pack a false overhand shuffle which keeps the bottom card in place.
● Place the chair next to the table opposite the audience, so that the table is between the chair and the audience. Stand next to the chair.
● Place the plate upside down in the center of the table and put the pack face down onto it.
● Announce: "I am going to make the chosen card pass through the pack, through the plate, and stop on top of the table."

● Say: "Just to be sure that I haven't concealed a card
under the plate, will someone please look?" Lift up the
pack to allow a spectator to do this. Hold the cards from
above in your right hand between finger joints and
thumb (**4**).

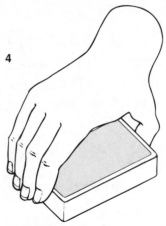

4

● While the audience is distracted looking under the
plate, bring your hand slowly back to the edge of the
table and allow your fingers to swing the bottom card to
the right (**5**). As you do so, casually pull out the chair
and sit down.
● Straighten your fingers slightly and release the
bottom card so that it falls in your lap. This must be
done quickly so that the audience doesn't see.

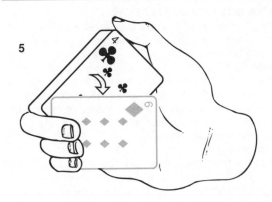

● Square the pack neatly with both hands and put the pack face down onto the plate.

● Close your right hand into a fist and count "One, two, three," then bring your fist down hard – but not too hard – on top of the pack. Say: "That should do it."

● Ask a spectator to remove the pack and look under the plate. There is nothing there.

● Act puzzled and say: "That's strange. It's always worked before. Perhaps I hit the pack too hard?"

● Say: "Hold on a moment," and with that reach down under the table, picking up the card from your lap as you do so. "Ah, that's what's happened." Pretend to be tugging at the card from underneath the table until suddenly it comes free. Bring out the card and throw it face up on the table.

THE GREAT EGG MYSTERY

This is a simple trick with a very novel means of disclosure – an egg! It is particularly effective with a young audience.

Effect

A spectator cuts the pack, remembers a chosen card, and then shuffles the card back into the pack. The spectator then shells a previously inspected hard-boiled egg and discovers the name of the chosen card is written on the egg white!

Equipment

You will need an ordinary pack of playing cards, a fresh egg, half an ounce (15g) of alum (potassium alum), half a pint (300ml) of vinegar, a wooden cocktail stick, a spoon, a saucepan of water and a stove ring. You will need adult supervision when boiling the egg.

Preparation

Dissolve the alum (potassium alum) in the vinegar. Write the name of a card (the one you will force) on the eggshell using the cocktail stick dipped in the alum solution. Place this card at the bottom of the pack. When the writing is dry and invisible, boil the egg for 12–15 minutes. Remove the egg from the saucepan with a spoon and allow the egg to cool. It is now ready to use. Throw away the unused solution and thoroughly clean and rinse your hands and the equipment you used. The trick uses the technique in The Cut Force (see p. 128) and the false overhand shuffle (see p. 12).

Performing

● Begin by explaining: "This is one of my most unusual tricks. Have a good look at this hard-boiled egg." Pass the egg to a spectator to examine carefully.

● Take back the egg and put it safely to one side. Continue: "Now throughout the trick I want you to keep one eye on the egg."

● Shuffle the pack using the false overhand shuffle that keeps the bottom card in place.

● Get a spectator to cut the cards and put the lower pile crossways on the upper pile. As he does this, say: "Don't forget to keep an eye on the egg."

● Ask the spectator to pick up the top pile, look at and remember the bottom card, and then place the pile on top of the other cards and shuffle the pack thoroughly.

● Get the spectator to put the pack to one side and then concentrate hard on a mental image of the card he has chosen. As he is doing this, take the egg and pass your hand back and forth over the egg, concentrating hard with your eyes shut.

● Finish with: "Yes, I think I've done it." Pass the egg to the spectator and ask him to carefully remove the shell. On the egg white will be the name of his card (**1**)!

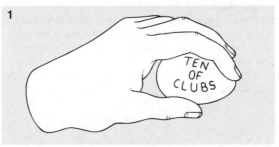

Note: At the end, throw the egg away. Don't allow anyone to eat it.

ON REFLECTION

Effect

A spectator chooses and remembers a card and writes
the name of the card on a piece of paper. The performer
then removes a card from the pack which the spectator
agrees is not her card. The card is placed in a tumbler
with its face towards the audience, and then covered
with a handkerchief. A second spectator reads out the
name of the card written on the slip of paper. The
tumbler is uncovered and the spectator's chosen card is
there for all to see.

Equipment

You will need a pack of ordinary playing cards that
includes an extra double-faced card of the same design
(a card with a face on both sides – say, a 3 of hearts on
one side and a 5 of spades on the other) – you can get
this at a novelty or magic shop. You will also need a
pencil, paper and a smooth glass tumbler of sufficient
size to accommodate a card.

Preparation

Shuffle the pack and then place the double-faced card
(**1**) (**a**) at the bottom of the pack. At the top of the pack
place the card (**b**) that is the duplicate of (**a**)'s upper
side – for example, the 5 of spades. Discard from the
pack the duplicate of (**a**)'s lower side – for example, the
3 of hearts.

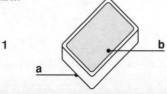

The trick uses the false overhand shuffle (see p. 12) and slip force (see p. 27) techniques.

Performing

● Begin by using a false overhand shuffle which keeps the cards in the same order.

● Riffle through the cards and stop when directed by a spectator. Cut the pack into two piles at the place where you stopped.

● Use the slip force technique to slip the top card of the top pile onto the top of the lower pile.

● Offer the lower pile to the spectator and ask her to look at and memorize the top card. At this stage, get her to write the name of the chosen card on a piece of paper, and fold the paper.

● Ask her to return the card to the top of the pile. Place your pile on top, and then cut the cards a small distance above her returned card. Show the audience the card you have cut to – to reassure them you haven't simply cut to the chosen card.

● Putting the lower pile on top of the upper (**2**) will now bring the chosen card (**b**) near the top of the pack, and the double-faced card (**a**) will now be somewhere in the middle.

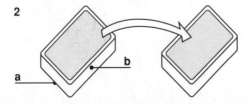

2

a

b

● Fan the cards with the faces towards the audience, but do not show them the chosen card (**3**) (**b**).

3

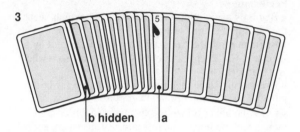

|b hidden |a

● Continue, saying: "I will take out a card – this is not your card is it?" At this point take out the double-faced card (**a**).
● "I will now put this card in the glass." As you do so, make sure the non-chosen card face is towards the audience (**4**).

4 (performer's view)

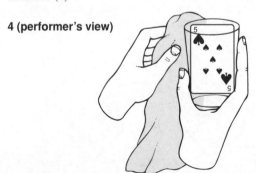

● Cover the tumbler with the handkerchief, and as you do so, turn your wrist so that the tumbler makes half a turn, bringing the chosen card face towards the audience (**5**).

5 (performer's view)

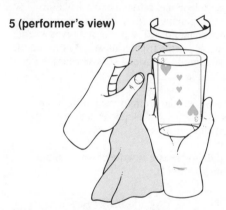

● Now ask a second member of the audience to read out the name of the card on the piece of paper. As he does this, gradually lift up the handkerchief to reveal the chosen card sitting in the glass.

THE LONG-DISTANCE TRICK

This trick works without you even having to be in the
same room or the same town as your "audience."

Effect

The performer telephones a friend and asks her to
shuffle a pack of playing cards and to cut them into two
approximately equal piles. The performer gives a series
of instructions which the friend follows. By the end the
performer can identify the friend's chosen card, without
ever having seen it.

Equipment

Your friend will need an ordinary pack of playing
cards, you will each need a telephone, and you will
need a pencil and paper.

Preparation

All you need do to prepare is write down a column of
numbers from 1 to 26 (**1**).

1

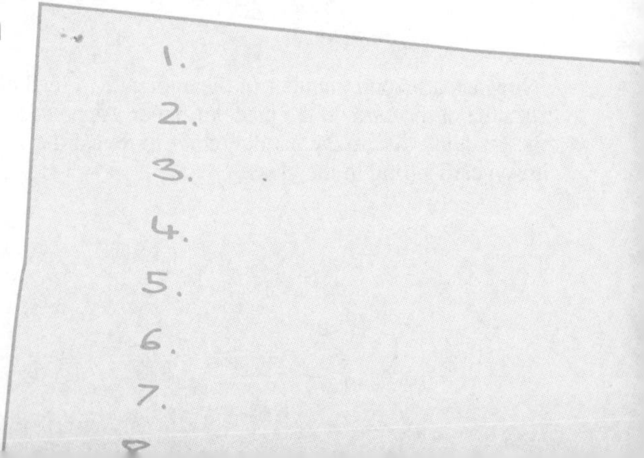

1.
2.
3.
4.
5.
6.
7.
8.

Performing

● Telephone your friend and tell her that you want to try out a new card trick.

● Ask her to fetch an ordinary pack of 52 playing cards and then instruct her as follows:

● "Shuffle the pack and then cut the cards into two approximately equal piles. Choose one pile and put the other to one side."

● "Silently count the number of cards in your chosen pile. Don't tell me what the total is. Then add together the two digits of the total. For example, if you have 23 cards, the digits 2 and 3 will add up to 5."

● "Remove from your pile the number of cards which equals this total. Discard these cards – you can put them with the discarded pile."

● "Now, think of a number between 1 and 10 and take that number of cards from your pile. Put these cards in your pocket or in another safe place."

● "With the cards you have left in your chosen pile, count down into the pile to the same number (the number of cards you have pocketed). Memorize the card at that position in the pile and then close the pile up again."

● Now summarize what has happened so far: "You have a number (the number of cards in your pocket) and you have the name of a card. At the moment I know nothing of these things."

● "All I want you to do now is deal each card remaining in your chosen pile, singly, face up on the table, and read out the name of the card as you deal it."

● As she names each card, on your piece of paper write
the name of the card against its number position in the
pile. For example, here the first card is the Q of
diamonds, the second is the 2 of spades, and so on (**2**).

2

1. Q D
2. 2 S
3. K H　←
4. 4 C
5. 6 H
6. A D
7. J D
8. 9 S
9. 2 H
10. 6 C
11. A S
12. 3 C
13. J H
14. 5 H
15. 2 D　←
16.
17.

● When she has finished naming her cards, look at the number against the last card called – this is the number of cards in her pile. If the number is less than 9, subtract the number from 9. If the number is between 9 and 17, subtract the number from 18. If the number is 18 or more, subtract the number from 27.

● For example, if she has 15 cards, subtract 15 from 18 to give you 3. You now know that her chosen card is the K of hearts – the card that is third in the pack – and that she has three cards in her pocket.

● Your friend will be baffled when you are able to make two correct predictions – and at a distance, too.

Note: The trick works on a similar principle to that of The Ninth Card (see p. 78).

8. Card novelties

This chapter contains a potpourri of tricks, puzzles and oddities. Some are card tricks; others are strange properties that the cards themselves possess. Sprinkle these novelties among the more traditional card tricks elsewhere in this book to keep the audience entertained throughout your performance.

SPELLING THE PACK

This is an alternative way of checking that there are the correct number of cards in the pack.

Effect

Count the cards by "spelling" them from A through to K. The number of letters gives you the number 52.

Equipment

You will need an ordinary pack of 52 playing cards.

Preparation

No preparation is required.

Performing

● Simply deal the cards face down, spelling out the names of all the cards in a suit (A to K) and dealing one card for each letter. Start by spelling out A (three cards: "a-c-e"), and dealing out three cards; then spell out 2 (three cards: "t-w-o"), 3 (five cards: "t-h-r-e-e") and so on, through to the K (4 cards: "k-i-n-g").

● Done correctly, the fifty-second card dealt will fall on the "g" of "king."

Note: This also works if you "spell" the pack in French.

English			French	
ace	3		as	2
two	3		deux	4
three	5		trois	5
four	4		quatre	6
five	4		cinq	4
six	3		six	3
seven	5		sept	4
eight	5		huit	4
nine	4		neuf	4
ten	3		dix	3
jack	4		valet	5
queen	5		reine	5
king	4		roi	3
Total	52		Total	52

THE CARD CALENDAR

This is a good opener for other tricks.

Effect

The performer tells a simple story showing how the standard card pack is designed around the calendar year – days and nights, the four seasons, 13 lunar months, 52 weeks and 365 days.

Equipment

You will need an ordinary pack of playing cards with jokers.

Preparation

Keep the two jokers to one side. Arrange the rest of the pack into four piles, each containing a suit in order from A through to K. Re-form the pack by putting the four piles in order, starting with a red suit on top and alternating with a black suit (**1**).

Performing

● Start with the pack face down in your hand.

● Begin the story by saying: "Did you know that the first pack of cards was designed by a wizard, living at a time when people were much more in touch with nature?"

● Continue: "One of the things he tried to do was show how his cards reflected nature."

● "The red cards represented the sun and daytime, the black cards darkness and night-time." Show the top card (red) and the bottom card (black). Then replace the cards in their original positions.

● "The four suits represented the four seasons of the year." Cut the pack into four piles of 13 cards and place the piles face up.

● "The number of cards in each suit is 13, the number of lunar months in a year. A lunar month is about 28 days." Spread one of the suits to show the 13 cards.

● "The number of cards in the pack is 52, the number of weeks in the year."

● "And last but not least, if you count the total number of spots on the cards (taking J as 11, Q as 12 and K as 13) you get 364. Add a single joker, and you get 365, the number of days in the year. Add both jokers, and you get 366, the number of days in a leap year. This wizard knew what he was doing."

● Scoop up the cards and give the pack two or three riffle shuffles. You are now ready to do your first trick.

BOMB AIMING

Effect

When a spectator tries to drop a card into a hat she can't. The performer can do it every time.

Equipment

You will need an ordinary pack of 52 playing cards and an empty hat or wastepaper bin.

Preparation

Practice "bomb aiming" so that you can do it accurately each and every time.

● To "bomb aim" a card, gently hold the card lengthwise between thumb and middle finger (**1**).

1

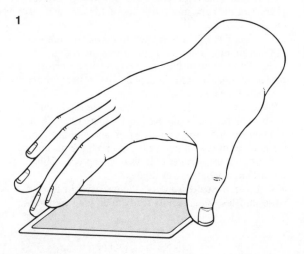

● Hold the card so that it is absolutely horizontal and move it into position over the target.

● Carefully sight the card so that you release it directly over the center of the target.

Performing

● Place the wastepaper bin or hat open end up on the floor (**2**).

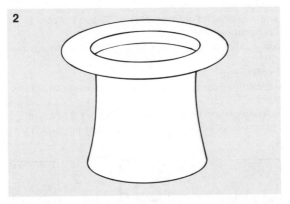

● Challenge a spectator to drop a card from chest height and get it in the hat or bin five times out of five.

● The spectator is very unlikely to succeed because she doesn't know the technique.

● Then take the same card and "bomb aim" it into the hat or bin five times. You should be able to drop the card into the hat or bin each time.

● When you have finished, you can choose to show the spectator the technique, or leave her to stew and try it again another day.

A CARD PUZZLE

This is a quick and simple puzzle to use any time in a performance.

Effect

The challenge for the spectators is to find a quick solution to a puzzle involving three cards. It's not as easy as it looks.

Equipment

You will need an ordinary pack of 52 playing cards.

Preparation

Make sure you know the answer before performing this one.

Performing

● Deal three cards face down in a row on the table in front of several spectators.

● Ask each spectator to turn the center card of his or her row of three face up. This is the start position (**1**).

1

● The rules of the puzzle are as follows: Each move involves turning over two cards. The challenge is – in exactly three moves, no more and no less – to finish with all three cards face up.

● Give the spectators a couple of minutes to try. After each attempt they can reset the cards to the start position and try again.

● If one of the spectators thinks he has found the answer, take him to one side to demonstrate it to you.
● When the two minutes is up, you (or the successful spectator) can demonstrate to the others how the trick is done.
● The solution is shown here (**2**) (the mirror image of this solution will work too):

2

Move 1: turn over the second and third card.
Move 2: turn over the first and third card.
Move 3: turn over the second and third card.

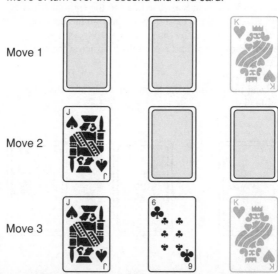

ANOTHER CARD PUZZLE

This is another simple puzzle using three cards.

Effect

The spectators must decipher written clues to arrive at the correct solution.

Equipment

You will need an ordinary pack of playing cards, a pencil and paper.

Preparation

Write out the following on the piece of paper: "There is at least one 3 to the right of a 2. There is at least one 3 to the left of a 3. There is at least one heart to the left of a club. There is at least one heart to the right of a heart. What are the three cards?" Sort through the pack of cards and arrange the three cards as follows: 2 of hearts, 3 of hearts and 3 of clubs in order at the top of the pack.

Performing

● Deal the three top cards face down in a row on the table (**1**).

1

● Explain: "The cards are numbered 1–3 from left to right. To find the solution you have to unravel this information." Place the paper in front of the spectators and read out the clues.

● Leave the paper there so that the spectators can refer to it.

● Give the spectators two minutes, and offer a prize to see who can come up with the solution first.

● When someone has the answer, or time has run out, turn over the cards (**2**) and show the correct solution.

2

THE MAGICIAN ALWAYS WINS

This provides quick entertainment at any time in a performance and enhances your reputation as a magician.

Effect

A spectator is apparently given a free choice of three cards. The performer will always correctly predict which is the chosen card.

Equipment

You will need an ordinary pack of 52 playing cards.

Preparation

Practice the patter so that you can perform the trick quickly and without having to think about what to say.

Performing

● Fan the cards with the faces towards you.

● Remove an A and place it face down on the table to one side (**1**), adding: "This card predicts what will happen."

1

● Continue looking through the cards and pull out any two cards and one other A. Remember where this A is located among the three cards and place the three cards face down on the table (**2**).

2

● Say: "Here are three cards. Pick up any two of them." What happens next depends on which cards the spectator chooses.

● If she leaves behind the A (whose location you will have memorized), the trick is over. In that case say: "I predicted you would leave the ace," and simply turn over the other A that you had set aside earlier.

● If she picks up the A as one of her two chosen cards, ask her to hand you one of her cards. If she gives you the A, respond with: "There was a one-in-three chance that you would give me the ace. And you have." Then turn over your set-aside A to prove your prediction was right.

● If, after handing you one of her two cards, the spectator is left with the A in her hands, simply say: "You have kept the ace. I predicted you would," and turn over your set-aside A.

● Whatever happens, the magician always wins.

FOUR-CARD INDEX

Effect

The spectator thinks of a card. The performer asks what the card is, then delves into a pocket and, without looking, takes out, in the right order, up to four cards which depict the card's value and suit.

Equipment

You will need an ordinary pack of 52 playing cards and a jacket with deep side pockets.

Preparation

Arrange the following four cards in number sequence, with the A on top: A of clubs, 2 of hearts, 4 of spades and the 8 of diamonds (**1**). Remember their order. This is easily done, because each card is double the value of the one before. The order of suits is remembered using the word CHaSeD (see p. 92). Place the cards horizontally in your pocket, with the backs facing out (**2**).

1

2

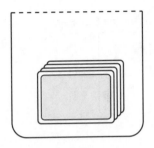

Set the remainder of the pack aside.

Performing

● Ask a spectator to shuffle the pack and then think of any card.

● Take back the pack and place the cards vertically in your pocket behind the four horizontal cards already there.

● Continue: "I haven't yet reached the stage where I can take out your card without looking for it. But at the very least I can take out some cards which are equivalent to it. Let me show you."

● Say to the spectator: "Name your card." No matter what card is named, you can make up the combination using the four cards from your pocket. Whichever suit is chosen, you can show as the first or last card you lay down. The values of the cards can be made to add up to any number between 1 and 13.

● Two examples are shown (**3**, see over).

3

Spectator chooses the 5 of hearts:

gives you the 5

gives you the suit

Spectator chooses the J of clubs (value 11):

adds up to 11;
the first card
gives the suit

● Think before dipping your hand into your pocket. Try
to come up with the best combination to illustrate the
chosen card. By placing a finger between each of the
four horizontal cards, you should be able to pick up
cleanly the precise cards you need, each and every time.
● In rare cases, someone's chosen card will be one of
your four. Then you have a real miracle!

YOU BET

Effect

The performer places a coin on a card and balances the card on a finger. The performer then challenges a spectator to remove the card without touching the coin, and to leave the coin balanced on the finger. The spectator tries and fails. The performer shows how it is done.

Equipment

You will need a single card from a new or nearly new deck and a 25¢ coin.

Preparation

Practice the technique, so you can do it right every time.
● The coin needs to be exactly in place over the ball of your finger.
● Flick the index finger of your right hand against the edge at one end of the card.
● The card should fly through the air, leaving the coin balanced on your finger.

Performing

● Balance a playing card on the ball of your index finger (**1**).

1

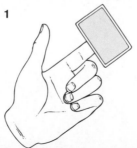

● Carefully position the coin on the card directly over the ball of the finger.

● Challenge the spectators by saying: "I'm willing to bet that I can remove the card and leave the coin balanced on my finger."

● Allow a spectator to try it a few times. Without knowing the technique, the spectator is likely to fail each time.

● With a flourish, show how it is done (**2**).

2

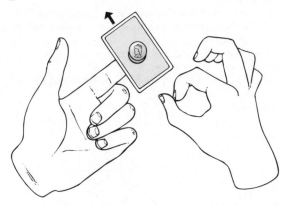

STEPPING THROUGH A CARD

Effect
The performer challenges the onlookers by claiming to be able to step through a card, then proceeding to do so.

Equipment
You will need an ordinary pack of playing cards and an additional card that you are willing to damage, such as a joker or an instruction card. You will also need a pair of scissors.

Preparation
Prepare the card (**1**) by first cutting a slit in it lengthwise along its center (**a**), leaving about ⅛ in thickness of card intact at both ends (**b**).

1

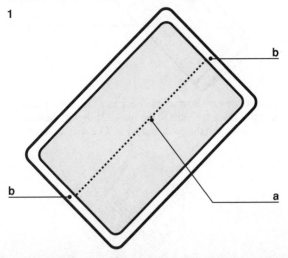

Fold the card along the cut and, with sharp scissors,
make several straight cuts into the doubled card (**2**)
alternately from the center slit nearly to the edges (**a**)
and from the edges nearly to the slit (**b**).

2

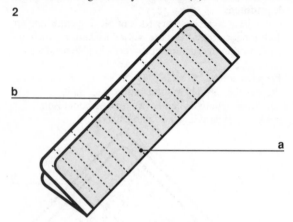

Flatten the card so that it is back to its original shape,
and then hide the card in the pack (**3**). It will make an
obvious gap in the pack and so will be easy to locate.

3

Performance

● Begin by saying: "Have you ever seen a performer step through a playing card? Impossible? Oh, no it's not. Here's one I prepared earlier."

● Riffle through the pack and take out your prepared card. Slowly and carefully, and with maximum suspense, open up the card into a large zigzag loop (**4**).

● Step through the loop, and then take a deep bow.

4

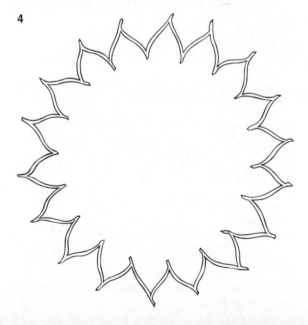

SIX-CARD LIFT

Effect

The performer challenges the spectators to arrange six cards in such a way that lifting one card lifts all the others, while the faces of all the cards remain visible. When the spectators fail to do this, the performer shows how it's done.

Equipment

You will need six cards from an ordinary pack of playing cards.

Preparation

Practice the technique so that you can quickly and easily show how it is done. The arranging technique is as follows:

● Place the first card (**1**) – the master card – face down vertically on the table in front of you.

● Place the next card (**2**) horizontally on top.

● The remaining four cards (**3–6**) are tucked in around the first two. This is done by placing two cards (**3** and **4**) tucked horizontally behind the master card.

● The last two (**5** and **6**) are placed vertically, tucked over card **2** and behind cards **3** and **4**.

● The arrangement can be lifted up by card **2** and turned over to show the faces of the cards.

Performing

● Spread six cards on the table face down.

● Challenge the spectators to come up with a way of arranging the cards so that they can lift all six cards by holding only one card by its edges. There is a further snag – all the faces of the cards must be visible when the cards are lifted.

● When the spectators have tried and, most likely, failed, show how it is done.

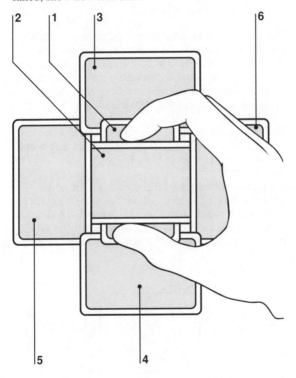

CARD THROUGH THE HOLE

This is a very adaptable trick that is particularly
suitable for a young audience.

Effect

The performer asks a member of the audience to push a
card through a small hole without bending the card.
When the spectator fails to do this, the performer shows
how. If the spectator discovers the technique and is able
to perform the trick, the performer can nevertheless
complete the trick in style, with a humorous flourish.

Equipment

You will need a standard-size playing card, a 4-in
square of thin card, a modeling knife and cutting board,
a drawing compass and a pencil.

Preparation

Using the compass, draw a circle 1½ in wide in the
center of the card square. Cut out the circle using the
knife on the board, so that you are left with a hole in the
center of the card (**1**). Have the card square, the playing
card and the pencil to hand when you start the trick.

1
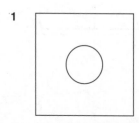

Performing

● Challenge a spectator to push the playing card through the hole in the square without bending the playing card or tearing the card square.

● When he fails, as is likely, show him how the trick is done.

● Fold the card square in half (**2**) and then gently bend down the edges at the fold, so that the hole opens wider. Done carefully, the hole widens until it is big enough for the playing card to be pushed through (**3**).

● To finish with a light touch (or as a backup should the spectator succeed), finish with: "Of course, there is another way to do the trick."

● Pick up the pencil and push it through hole in the the card so that it touches the playing card (**4**). Add: "See, I am pushing the card through the hole!"

2

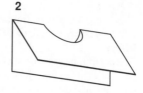

3

4

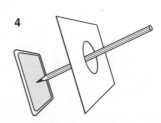

FINALE

This is a good way of finishing your routine – but you
will be destroying a deck of cards in the process!

Effect

The performer asks the strongest spectator to tear the
pack of cards in half. Providing the pack is kept tightly
together, and the cards are not separated, the spectator
is likely to fail. The performer then takes back the pack
and tears it in half.

Equipment

You will need two well-used packs of linen-backed
playing cards of the same design (one of which you are
willing to destroy), an elastic band and a jacket with
deep side pockets. You also will need a sharp modeling
knife and cutting board or a hot oven, heatproof plates
and oven gloves. Note: Adult supervision is needed if
oven is used.

Preparation

Prepare one of the packs of cards for tearing. There are
two ways of doing this.

● Spread the cards out on clean plates (**1**) and place
them in an oven at 275°F for about 90 minutes. Use
oven gloves to lift out the plates and allow the cards to
cool to room temperature. They will now be dry and
brittle, and easily torn, so handle them carefully.

● Alternatively, with great care, make a ¾in-deep cut in
one side of 50 cards in the pack (**a**). Hide the cut by
placing the two uncut cards (**b**) at top and bottom of the
pack (**2**).

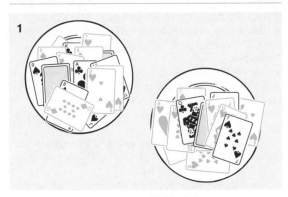

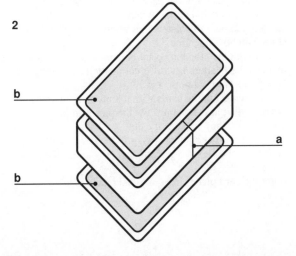

Prepare the packs for switching (see p. 31), with the prepared pack in your pocket held together by an elastic band. The normal pack is in your hand.

Performing

● Pick out the strongest-looking member of your audience and ask him or her to tear the pack in half, but keeping the pack tightly together, not separating the cards. Give the spectator about a minute to perform the task.

● It is likely that some of the cards will be slightly mangled or dog-eared, but the spectator won't actually be able to tear the pack in half.

● Take the pack back, shuffle it and say: "We'll leave it for another day." Put the pack in your pocket and as you do so, switch over the two packs of cards. Then suddenly appear to change your mind and say: "OK. I'll show you how it's done."

● Bring out the "treated" pack of cards and proceed to tear it in half. There is a different method depending on how you have treated the cards.

● If you have cut the cards with a knife, tear them by twisting the pack. Do not show the pieces to the spectators – they will see the cut.

● If you have baked the cards, grip the pack tightly at both ends and flex the pack up and down until the pack splits in half (**3**).

● Put the card pieces in your pocket, take a bow and leave.

3

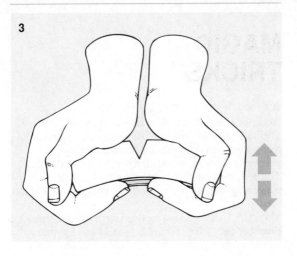

Section 2
MAGIC
TRICKS

A SHORT HISTORY OF MAGIC

According to Arthur Conan Doyle's famous detective Sherlock Holmes, "We see but we do not observe." In many ways this describes the reaction a magic performer is trying to instill in his (or her) audience. The performer wants the spectator to see what is happening, but not observe what is going on behind the scenes.

Magic tricks have been practiced since ancient times. Probably the earliest record is found in an Egyptian papyrus dating from 1700 BC. It shows an illusionist, Dedi of Dedsnefu, performing a trick in front of the Pharaoh.

The ancient Greeks and Romans had a fondness for tricks, particularly those using hidden mechanical

2

devices which produced miraculous effects. Using such devices, priests could make temple doors open automatically and wine flow from the mouths and arms of statues. The Cups and Balls trick (see p. 483) was described by a Roman named Seneca in the 1st century BC. It is still commonly performed today.

In medieval Europe, the practice of magic became associated with witchcraft, a practice which was punishable by death. Nevertheless, some performers used their abilities to exert power and influence over God-fearing people.

In 1584, the Englishman Reginald Scot, in his book *The Discoverie of Witchcraft*, tried to show how magic tricks were performed – by sleights of hand, not the work of the devil. His text explained the secrets of

many magic tricks, including those using coins, cards and ropes. He wrote the book to expose the work of magicians, but instead it became the first manual for practicing magicians.

Even by the late 16th century, performing magic tricks was not considered respectable. Nevertheless, novelty acts such as fire- and sword-swallowing, and performances using "intelligent" animals, were popular in fairs and markets.

In 18th-century Britain, performers of magic tricks had gained some respectability, and perhaps the most famous was Isaac Fawkes. He amassed a fortune from performing close-up tricks at fairs and at private parties in the homes of wealthier citizens.

The late 18th and early 19th centuries saw the appearance of several hundred professional magicians. By the early 19th century "scientific" tricks were in vogue and performers calling themselves Doctor or Professor wove inventive stories to explain their tricks in terms of "science." For example, the French magician Jean Eugène Robert-Houdin explained his famous levitation trick (raising a person in the air without any apparent support) in terms of the newly discovered gas, ether. His explanation was false, but it was a convincing part of his performance. Robert-Houdin was to become a legendary figure among magicians and was later dubbed "The Father of Modern Magic." Originally a watchmaker and inventor, he did not become a full-time magician until over 50 years old. He made many improvements to the techniques and equipment then fashionable. He developed his magic craft to a very high standard and was instrumental in bringing greater respect to the profession.

The late 19th century and early 20th century was the great age of traveling shows. Spectacular magic shows travelled from theater to theater, in Europe and the United States. Such was the popularity of magic shows that one magician and entrepreneur, John Nevil Maskelyne, was able to run a permanent magic theater in London for over 40 years from 1873.

As magic shows became more popular, and there was greater competition between performers, specialty acts arose and performers developed special personas (theatrical characters). One of the most famous was William Ellsworth Robinson, a white American, who wore makeup and performed as the Chinese magician Chung Ling Soo, even inventing a "mock-Chinese" language. He took the performance far beyond the stage, and kept up his Chinese persona at all times in public. He died on stage in 1918, attempting his famous trick in which he caught a bullet in his mouth. The gun was faulty and fired a real bullet that killed him.

Perhaps the most famous magic performer of all time was Harry Houdini, who was born in 1874 in Budapest, Hungary, as Ehrich Weiss. During his career as an escapologist he challenged several police forces to lock and bind him in chains and sacking. On each occasion he was able to free himself, sometimes in very unusual circumstances (on one occasion he was lowered into New York Harbor in a safe, and escaped). He died in performance on October 31, 1926, Hallowe'en. Several

Chung Ling Soo

days beforehand he had challenged some students to punch him in the stomach, saying that he could withstand any blow. One student punched him before he had time to tense his stomach muscles. This blow ruptured his appendix and was the cause of his death several days later.

One of the more interesting 20th-century performers was Cardini, who learnt his card-handling skills in the long days spent as a soldier in the trenches during World War I. He wore gloves to keep out the cold. Later, as a performing conjuror, white gloves and a monocle were his trademark, and on stage he would produce dozens of fans of cards from nowhere. His performance also included pretending to be drunk while producing a succession of bizarre articles while handing his clothes to a valet.

The demise of variety and vaudeville shows in the 1950s reduced the opportunities for performing magic on stage. However, the best magicians who specialized in close-up magic or stage magic for cabaret or television continued to make a living, and many traveled internationally. There are still many opportunities for performing magic in small venues such as social clubs, and in larger venues such as theaters and nightclubs, and, through the medium of television, performers can reach a worldwide audience.

TYPES OF MAGIC PERFORMANCE

Children's magic

Many magicians make a full- or part-time living by presenting magic shows to children. The performance usually lasts the best part of an hour. The conjuror dresses in bright clothes, uses colorful equipment, and gets the children to join in with performing the tricks.

Close-up magic

Close-up magic is done before a small audience, at home or in a venue such as a restaurant, although a performance can be shown on television to a large audience. The performer uses small items such as cards, coins and rope. In a restaurant, the conjuror may move from table to table, performing an act which lasts just 5–10 minutes.

Stand-up magic

A general term for the larger-scale forms of magic which are performed on stage or for television. Large props are used and the visual spectacle forms an important part of the act. Often an assistant is involved. Performances of the types of magic described below often fall into this category. The well-known British magician, Paul Daniels, performs both close-up and stand-up magic on television.

Escapology

This form of magic involves performers escaping from devices into which they are locked or bound. The performer needs to be strong and supple. Escape usually involves the performer untying knots and picking locks while in a very constrained position. Harry Houdini was the most famous exponent of this form of magic.

Illusions

Illusions are seemingly impossible feats performed with large objects, often people; for example, making a person disappear or sawing a person in half. Performing illusions usually requires large and expensive equipment plus the help of one or more assistants. The American David Copperfield and the double-act Siegfried and Roy are famous illusionists.

Mentalism (mind-reading)

These tricks give the appearance of being performed by superhuman feats of the mind. They vary from predicting the future and mind-reading (clairvoyance) to bending metal forks and stopping watches. Al Koran, Kreskin and Uri Geller are famous exponents of mentalism.

Silent magic

A performance without any speech. The performer's gestures and expressions are used to convey meaning. This is a very challenging form of magic, since the visual aspect is so important and speech cannot be used to misdirect attention. Success depends on costume, visual props and the effective use of mime.

Harry Houdini

WHAT YOU WILL NEED

Before you start on the road to becoming a magician, you need a few things – a surprisingly few things: some everyday items (coins and a handkerchief will do for starters), this book, and patience and enthusiasm. The rest will follow. If you want to plunge straight in and learn a trick, turn to p. 277. If you want some background – and you will need this later anyway – read on.

Props

Props – the theatrical term short for "properties" – refers to the equipment and other items used by the performer. Props vary from everyday items, such as handkerchiefs and elastic bands, to specially bought or made equipment. You may use a prop simply to demonstrate your conjuring prowess; by making the object disappear, for example. Or the prop itself may make the magic work, such as a wand which can extend and retract or which is hollow. Props are also useful for distracting the audience's attention from secret moves, such as using a magic wand to direct the audience's gaze. Some props, though seeming to be everyday objects, are specially made for the job. For example, wands, silk scarfs and soft rope are best bought from a magic shop, but you can start by using ordinary handkerchiefs and ropes.

The clothes you wear can be props in themselves: a silk scarf tied about the head, concealed pockets in a jacket, or a belt or sash around the waist concealing items. A top hat or pointed hat and wand are traditional props which are strongly associated with magic. Seeing them instantly tells people you are a magician.

Here are some dos and don'ts when using props.

Dos

- Mix special magic props with everyday objects. People are often more amazed by magic done with everyday items than with made-for-the-purpose props.
- Be imaginative and use objects different from the norm. Use an apple or orange, for example, instead of a ball.
- Match the props to your audience. Brightly colored props work well with a young audience. A mind-reading act with an adult audience will require more subdued colors.
- Think about how your props will appear to the audience. Are they attractively set out? Will they be visible? (Red props will not show up against red clothing.) Will the colors clash?
- Keep your props clean and in good order. They are all part of your image and they need to look good and work well.
- If you can, choose a theme – say, an Oriental or Egyptian one – and make sure your props follow this theme.
- Think carefully about your clothes. If necessary, make sure they have suitably placed pockets (secret or otherwise) for holding your props.
- Make a suitably colored magic box – decorated with magic signs – to keep your smaller props in.

Don'ts
- Don't use too many props. If you can use the same prop in several tricks, do so.
- Don't leave your props lying around so a spectator can inspect them.

Examples of magician's props

rope

magician's silks

dice

fake boxes

cups and balls

wand

A persona

Your persona is the character or image you project as a performer. As a conjuror, you want to be liked and you want to be remembered. How can you achieve that? What you say and do, and how you appear to the audience, all build up to give the audience a picture of who you are. Think carefully about this. What impression do you want to create? How do you want your audiences to remember you? What kind of audiences do you want to play to anyway?

When you have decided what your character (your persona) will be, this will make your choice of costume, props and the tricks themselves much clearer. You will be on your way to developing your own style. Do you want to be funny or simply friendly and casual? Do you want to concentrate on close-up tricks? Or do you want to perform on a stage doing tricks with larger props? Do you want to do both? Do you want to incorporate mind-reading (mentalism) in your act? In this book we have concentrated on those tricks which need the minimum of equipment and do not require large props. This is, in any case, your most likely starting point as a performer. Later, you may wish to perform as an illusionist using larger props on a big stage.

Consider what to wear. Some performers like to assume a different character altogether. Do you want to be an Oriental magician or an Indian swami? Perhaps dressing as a clown, or taking on the persona of Merlin or even a mad professor appeals to you? Whatever you decide, your clothes, your props and your entire presentation – what you say and do – need to be convincing. They all need to work together to create an overall impression. So, if you have chosen to be Merlin, make sure that your props reflect this, and are painted with suitable symbols and in appropriate colors. Whatever you decide, make sure you are comfortable as this character. If not, be yourself.

Patter

Your patter is what you say and how you say it – during your performance. This will depend, among other things, on the persona you have adopted, the nature of your audience, and how confident you feel. Most of us are somewhere between being shy and being very confident. Performing itself increases self-confidence, and some people who are otherwise quite shy find they blossom on stage and have no trouble in commanding the attention of an audience. In many cases, a casual and friendly style of presentation works well. Use humor if you are comfortable doing so and it fits in well with your persona, and is geared to your audience.

Here are some dos and don'ts regarding patter.

Dos
- Plan carefully what you are going to say, from start to finish. It helps to write this down in note form, indicating each point you want to make.
- Practice your presentation in a room on your own with a tape recorder. Stand up and deliver your performance as though an audience is there. Play

continued

back the tape and you will probably discover that there are many mistakes, pauses, repetitions and so on. Don't worry. Keep practicing, and taping, and you will discover that your performance will soon improve.

- Once you have developed some confidence, practice your patter in front of those you know and trust. Ask them for their comments.
- Do respond to the audience. As your confidence develops you will find that you talk with greater and greater ease.
- Invent stories to explain and enhance your tricks.
- Use patter to misdirect the audience from what you are doing.
- Speak clearly and slowly.
- Make sure you speak loudly enough so that the person at the back can hear.
- If you are going to use a microphone, practice using it before a performance. On the day, check that the microphone is properly set up and then leave it alone. Wherever possible, use a clip-on microphone rather than a microphone on a stand, so that you are not restricted from moving around.

Don'ts

- Don't talk too much. Avoid a running commentary.
- Don't state the obvious, such as "Here is a yellow box."
- Don't insult anyone.
- Don't drop your voice at the end of a sentence. If anything, raise it.

Working with an assistant

Working with an assistant does have several advantages.

- Instead of having to work with all the props in place beforehand, each trick can be brought in as it is needed.
- The assistant can distract the audience's attention while you, the performer, complete a move.
- The assistant may even perform the trick move him- or herself.
- Having an assistant increases the range of tricks you can do and the banter between you and your assistant creates greater interest for the audience and helps fill out the act.
- Your assistant can also help you develop and improve your tricks.

But having an assistant means that there is, so to speak, an extra mouth to feed. If you are performing for money, the money will need to be split. Many conjurors and magicians cannot, or choose not to, have an assistant.

Working with an assistant is very different from working with a confederate (or stooge). This is a person who pretends to be an ordinary member of the audience but who secretly helps the performer accomplish the trick. Using a stooge is frowned upon by most magicians – they consider it a form of cheating.

PREPARATION

Simply knowing how a trick is done and how to carry it out will not make you a successful performer. You are still only halfway there. You need to entertain the audience and convince them – by all your actions – that something exciting is happening. This takes practice – and lots of it.

Here are the dos and don'ts of preparation for mastering a trick.

Dos
- Learn one trick at a time.
- Learn the trick thoroughly so that you are absolutely confident how to present it.
- Learn a few tricks well, rather than many tricks sloppily.
- Imagine what the trick will be like from the audience's point of view. Will it be interesting? Will they spot something they aren't meant to see? How can you distract them so they won't notice what you're doing with the props? How can you finish the trick in a dramatic way?
- Continue working on a trick, and making adjustments, until you are completely happy with it. This may mean the trick is slightly different from the way it is described here – but you will have made the trick your own.
- Adjust your finger positions if you find a particular move difficult or awkward – not everyone's hands are the same.

continued

- Track down the weak spots in a trick and work out ways to get around them, using misdirections if necessary.
- Practice frequently but in small doses. You are more likely to overcome a problem when you come to it afresh.
- Practice in front of a mirror. It helps "fine-tune" your performance and allows you to see how it looks from the audience's point of view. It also encourages you to look away from your hands and at the audience.
- Try a new trick on friends and family, and listen to their comments.
- Make the props yourself or buy them from a reputable dealer in magic equipment. You can then be sure you are using reliable equipment which looks good, does the job and will last.
- Remember, first and foremost, you are an entertainer – you must make your performance lively, interesting and enjoyable.

Don'ts

- Don't show any trick until you have practiced it thoroughly.
- Don't perform a trick until you can do it so well that you don't have to worry about "what comes next."
- Don't tense up at the crucial point in a trick. Practice until you make the difficult move look casual and easy.
- Don't tell anyone how the trick is done.

There is a saying among magic-trick performers:
"Practice. Practice again. Practice until you can do it
perfectly. Then practice some more."

PERFORMING

A performance of magic – whether a single trick or a
whole routine – is not merely a collection of bits
cobbled together. You need to prepare your
performance as a whole piece, with a start and a finish.
Think through your act carefully so that it is smooth
and polished. One trick or part of the act should follow
on naturally from another.

The structure of a performance

When you plan your performance you need to take into
account the kind of audience and the venue. Is it a small
venue where you can perform close-up magic, or is it a
larger one, where you will be performing on stage? A
performance of close-up magic for an adult audience
would typically last 10–15 minutes and use six to eight
tricks. A performance on stage would normally last
slightly longer. If you were performing at a children's
party, you would probably use fewer tricks, but make
each trick last much longer and involve the children
more. You might weave a story around each trick.
Here are some suggestions as to what you might
include, whatever the type of performance:

● At the beginning do quick and easy tricks which
allow you to relax and let the audience get to know you.
Simple production or vanishing tricks are suitable here.

● In the middle of the performance, when you and the
audience are more relaxed, use longer, more
complicated tricks which involve the spectators more.

Tricks with long story lines or those involving mentalism (mind-reading) are suitable here.

● Build up to the end of your performance with a couple of straightforward tricks, and then try to finish on a spectacular visual trick. The production of a large number of items – the more silks, or whatever, the better – or the reappearance of an object you made vanish earlier in your performance – are good tricks with which to finish your act.

Here are the dos and don'ts in preparing for and during the performance.

Dos – Preparing the performance

● Choose tricks which are suitable for the kind of audience you are expecting.

● Read about magic and magicians, and use every opportunity you can to look at magicians as they perform. Analyze what they do and learn from it.

● Plan your performance in detail.

● Think about having music playing in the background when you first enter the room to perform. This music should fit in with your persona, the type of performance and your audience.

● Decide in which order you are going to do the tricks, and how one trick will lead on to the next.

● Inject variety into your act. To the performer, the tricks work in different ways. To the spectator, the tricks may appear similar. Make sure you emphasize the differences between tricks and include a variety of tricks that involve more than one person, where

continued

objects are revealed in different ways, and where various props are used.

- Work out what to say from start to finish.
- Vary the pace of your performance; for example, intersperse slow tricks with fast ones.
- Be aware of your own strengths and weaknesses and tailor your performance to make the most of your strengths.
- Make sure your hands and fingernails are clean and that you are neat and well groomed. Even if you are wearing casual clothes, make sure you look clean and tidy.
- Make sure you have all your props in the right places at the start of the performance. Decide carefully what you wish the audience to see.
- Expect to get excited and anxious before a performance. Professionals do.
- Practice regularly and pay attention to detail. This increases confidence in your performance and reduces the chances of getting stage fright – an attack of nerves on stage.
- Run through everything in your routine and check that everything is where it should be – and works.
- Make sure that you have an alternative plan – a trick held in reserve – should something unexpectedly go wrong or because, for whatever reason, you have to abandon a trick.
- Take a dozen deep breaths before walking on stage. It calms your nerves and allows you to concentrate on entertaining your audience.

Dos – During the performance

- Walk confidently to the spot where you are going to perform.
- Beam a smile at your audience and move your eyes around the room to try and make everyone feel as though you have noticed them – as individuals.
- Choose a trick you can do well as your first number.
- Speak clearly and slowly.
- Tell a story, make a joke – above all, entertain – but do it naturally. Be yourself. Find your own style.
- Be prepared to make changes during your performance if things go wrong.
- Use your hands and eyes to direct the audience where you want them to look.
- Use explanations and patter to misdirect the audience from what you are actually doing.
- Ask a spectator to show a chosen item to someone else. This prevents the possible embarrassment of the spectator later forgetting the item, or even purposely naming another item to spoil the trick.
- Act relaxed and smile. Look as though you are enjoying yourself.
- React to your own tricks. Scratch your head, shrug your shoulders, and so on to help convey your feelings.
- Use the rhythm of your speech to create drama. Talk slowly to show concentration and build suspense. Talk louder and faster at the climax of a trick.
- At appropriate points in your performance when you can expect some applause, take a small bow or open

continued

- your palms towards the audience and pause, looking at them. Such actions usually trigger applause.
- Think about your performance and constantly strive to improve your presentation.
- Aim to make the audience believe – by your words, movements and appearance – that you are truly a successful magician.
- Leave the audience wanting more.
- At the end of the performance, thank your audience and take a bow. Leave before the applause finishes.

Don'ts – During a performance

- Don't do two similar tricks in the same performance.
- Don't repeat a trick (unless the trick is specifically designed to be repeated).
- Don't try to do a trick if you are not confident about it – you are likely to give a poor performance.
- Don't speak too fast. This is easy to do if you are nervous. Slow down.
- Don't spoil a surprise by stating what will happen before it does.
- Don't turn your back on the audience if you can avoid it. To move backwards, step back or move diagonally across.
- Don't insult anyone – whether they are present or not.
- Don't take everything so seriously that if things go wrong your act falls apart. Laugh with everyone else and then get on with the next trick.

1. Coin magic

Magic tricks using coins are popular not only because of people's inherent interest in money, but because coins are small props, immediately to hand, and can be supplied by spectators. In tricks where the performer makes a spectator's coins disappear, the audience feels more involved because someone's money is at stake. Most tricks require medium- to large-sized coins; coins with milled or angled edges are particularly useful as they are easier to handle. Some tricks, such as The Traveling Coin (see opposite), Two Heads Are Better Than One (see p. 279) and Behind The Ear (see p. 290) require no props other than the coins themselves and so can be done anytime and anywhere. Other tricks such as The Dissolving Coin (see p. 300) and Coin In The Wool (see p. 308) are more sophisticated and use several props. Such tricks can provide a dramatic finale to a magic routine.

THE TRAVELING COIN

A quick and easy trick which is very convincing if you get the timing right.

Effect

The performer makes a coin magically move from one hand to join a coin in the other hand.

Equipment

Two similar medium- to large-sized coins.

Preparation

The trick depends on the precise positioning of the coins in the hand, and the speed and smoothness with which the hands are turned over. Practice talking as you turn over your hands to help misdirect the audience's attention.

Performing

• Ask members of the audience for two coins of the same type (make sure that you have practiced the trick using coins of this type).

• Now show the coins to the audience, one on the palm of each hand. The coins need to be positioned carefully (**1**). The coin in the left hand should be placed between

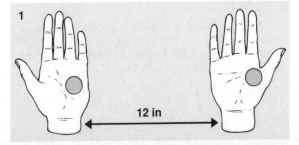

12 in

the third and fourth fingers. The one on the right should be near the base of the thumb.

● Hold the hands, palms up, about 12 in (30 cm) apart on a table top.

● Explain to the audience that you can make any coin travel through the air at the speed of light.

● At precisely the same moment, turn both hands over so that the thumbs come close together and then draw the hands immediately apart. Your audience will believe that there is one coin beneath each hand. In fact, because of the original positioning of the coins, the coin from the right hand has been thrown under the left (**2**).

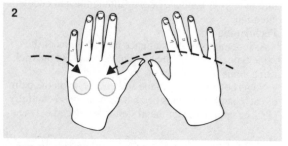

● Lift the right hand to show that the coin from that hand has gone.

● Now lift your left hand and show – to your surprised audience – that both coins are there.

TWO HEADS ARE BETTER THAN ONE

This trick is particularly suitable for a young audience.

Effect

In this trick, of moderate difficulty, a spectator's coin appears to have a head on both sides.

Equipment

A medium-sized coin.

Preparation

The trick calls for the precise timing of rapid hand movements which must be practised.

Performing

● Borrow an ordinary coin from a member of the audience.

● Place the coin on the palm of your right hand, with the head side up. Raise the right hand so that it is slightly above and to the right of your left hand (**1**). Show the coin to your audience.

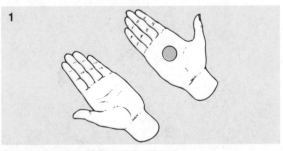

1

● Now do the following move to give the appearance that you are turning over the coin. It is described here one step at a time. In reality, you will do the move swiftly and smoothly in a fraction of a second.

● Move your right hand sharply to the right, and move your left hand slightly to the right, so that the coin slides off and drops on to your left hand, still head side up (**2**).

● As the coin falls onto your left hand, turn your right hand over and slap it down on your left hand (**3**). Doing this quickly gives the appearance that the right hand has turned the coin over.

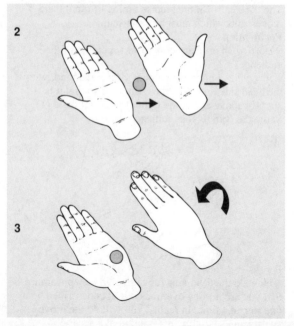

4

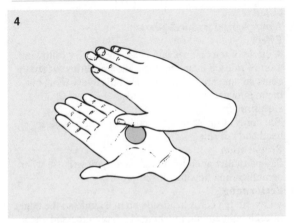

● Now remove your right hand and show the audience
that the "other" side of the coin is also a head (**4**).
● You can repeat the move using both hands. For
example, with the coin in your left hand slightly higher
than the right, you can pass the coin to your right and
appear to make the coin turn over when in reality it
hasn't. By passing from right hand to left, and then
from left hand to right, it will appear that the coin
genuinely has two heads.
● At the end, pick up the coin between the finger and
thumb of your right hand and show the audience that it
is a genuine two-sided coin. Then return it to the person
you borrowed it from.

NINE TAILS

A simple mathematical puzzle.

Effect

A circle of ten coins is laid head side up. By following a set of rules, a member of the audience tries to turn the coins so nine are tail side up. He fails every time, but the magician can do it in seconds.

Equipment

Ten coins of the same type, and which have a clear head and tail side.

Preparation

Pay particular attention to the patter you will use when demonstrating how the puzzle works.

Performing

● Lay out ten coins head side up in a circle so the edges of each coin are not touching (**1**). Say to the audience that the object of the exercise is to turn nine coins tail side up.

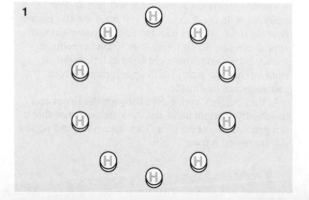

● Explain that there are rules. For each move the player must start on a head, finish on a head and count four places. Each move thus involves starting on a head, counting four coins in a clockwise or anticlockwise direction, and then turning over the fourth coin (which initially is a head but is then turned over tail side up).
● For each move, the player can start anywhere in the circle, providing it is a head.
● Now demonstrate what you have just said (in doing so you will actually demonstrate how the problem is solved, but you will discover that onlookers will not be able to repeat what you have done).
● Reinforce the rules as you go along, but don't explain why you have chosen to start each move from a specific coin.
● Starting anywhere, count one, two, three and turn the fourth coin tail up (**2**). Stop and have a few words with your spectators.

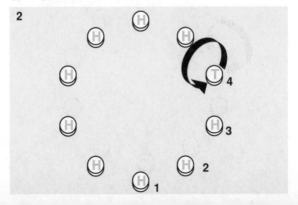

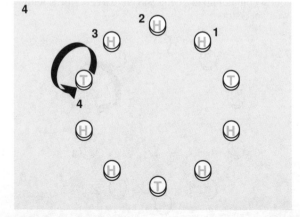

● For the second move, start your count so that it will
finish on the coin that you started your first count on
(**3**). Stop and chat before the next move.

● For the third move, start so that you finish on the coin
you started your second count on (**4**).

● Continue in this way, and you will finish with nine
coins tail side up, and one face up.

● Now turn over all the coins so they are face up and
ask a member of the audience to follow the rules and
finish with nine coins tail side up. He is very unlikely
to succeed!

Note: If the audience ask you to show them again how
it is done, start in a different place on the circle, and
move in a different direction from that of your original
demonstration. Don't repeat the demonstration more
than once.

EXTRA MONEY

This straightforward trick is particularly suitable for a
young audience.

Effect

In this trick, three coins are joined magically by four others.

Equipment

Seven medium-sized coins of the same type. Three
sheets of thick card, each measuring 8 x 5 in (20 x 12
cm). A strong adhesive. A modeling knife and cutting
board.

Preparation

Take one sheet of card and with the knife cut a diagonal
slot in it (**1**) of length and width just sufficient to hold
four coins of the type you intend to use.

1

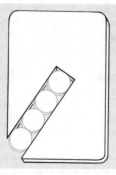

Glue the two other pieces of card, one to each side of the first card so that the cards form a flat tray with a hidden cavity (**2**). Put four coins in this cavity and you are ready to perform the trick.

2

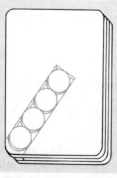

Performing

● Holding the tray by the corner to conceal the cavity, take three coins and count them out one by one onto the top of the card tray.

● Now show the audience that first your right hand and then your left hand are both empty. As you do this you will need to transfer the tray from left to right hand and then back again. When you do this, make sure that you do not let the audience see the opening to the concealed cavity.

● Now tip the tray so that the coins (including the four in the concealed cavity) slide into the palm of your left hand (**3**).

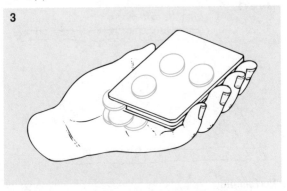

● At this point the audience expects you to have only three coins in your left hand. Put the tray to one side and open your hand to reveal that it actually holds seven coins. Then take a bow.

THE HANKIE VANISH

A fairly easy coin vanish involving a member of the
audience.

Effect

The performer makes a coin disappear from a
handkerchief while a spectator is holding it.

Equipment

A small coin and a large silk handkerchief with a
similar second coin sewn into the hem.

Preparation

Prepare a large silk handkerchief by opening the hem at
one corner, inserting a small coin, and then sewing the
hem up again, making sure the coin is held securely in
place (**1**).

1

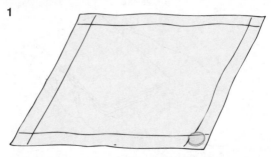

Performing

● Take the coin in your right hand and hold it up to the
audience between finger and thumb.

● With your left hand holding the coin corner of the
handkerchief, drape the handkerchief over the coin. In

one smooth movement take the coin corner up
underneath into the center of the hankie and thumbpalm
the real coin in your right hand (**2**).

2

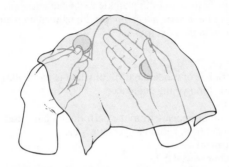

● Keeping the palmed coin carefully concealed, remove
your right hand from under the handkerchief.
● Now get a member of the audience to hold the sewn-
in coin through the hankie (**3**).

3

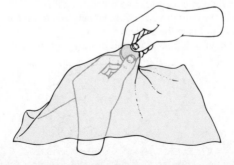

● Now grab hold of a corner of the hankie in your left hand and whisk the hankie away. The coin has vanished!

● Show both sides of the hankie to the audience and then put the hankie away, pocket the palmed coin and get on with the next trick.

BEHIND THE EAR

This trick is of moderate difficulty and is particularly suitable for a young audience.

Effect

The coin disappears from the performer's hand and reappears from behind a spectator's ear.

Equipment

A medium-sized coin.

Preparation

The trick depends on the timing and smoothness of hand movements and needs plenty of practice.

Performing

● Ask a member of the audience for a coin (make sure it is a type of coin you have practiced with).

● Hold the coin in your left hand between thumb and fingers and face the audience (**1**).

● Bring your left hand up and bring your right hand

1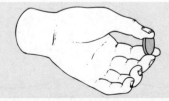

across as if to take the coin. Put your right thumb
behind the coin and your fingers in front (**2**) so
shielding the move from the audience.

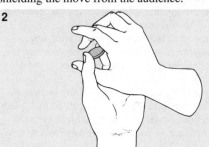

● With barely any movement, open the thumb and
fingers of your left hand slightly, letting the coin fall
into the palm of your left hand (**3**). This move is called
the French Drop.

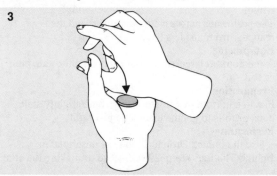

● A split second later, press your right thumb and
fingers together as if holding the coin and move them to
your right, looking at your right hand as you do so.
Your eyes should misdirect the audience into believing
that the coin is now in your right hand.

● Casually drop your left hand down by your side,
gently gripping the coin with the joints of your fingers.

● Blow on your right hand and open it slowly, showing
that the coin has disappeared.

● Now with your left hand reach up behind the ear of
the person who gave you the coin. As you do this, push
the coin up to your fingertips and let it make contact
with the person's ear as you pull your hand away from
his head.

● Show the coin in your left hand as you did at the
beginning of the trick. Hey presto!

COIN IN THE BUN

A rather unusual vanishing coin trick.

Effect

The performer makes a coin disappear and then
reappear from inside a bun.

Equipment

A medium- to large-sized coin and a slightly stale bun
or roll.

Preparation

Practice in front of a mirror using some slightly stale
buns or rolls to get the technique just right.

Performing

● Use the French Drop technique as described in
Behind The Ear (see p. 290). Instead of making the coin

appear from behind the ear of a spectator, make it
appear from inside a bun.

● After showing the audience your empty right hand,
pick up the bun with your left hand (this hand contains
the palmed coin).

● Explain that you have a hunch that the missing coin is
in the bun.

● Start to break open the bun by first bending the sides
up so that the underside of the bun breaks open (**1**).

1

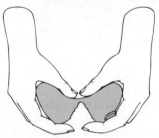

● With the fingers of your left hand, surreptitiously slip
the coin into the break in the bun (**2**).

2

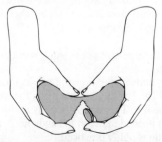

● Now bend the sides of the bun down keeping the lower broken halves together, and the coin will pop up from the middle of the bun (**3**).

3

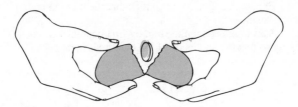

THE MAGIC WAND

A straightforward vanishing coin trick suitable for performing near the beginning of a magic routine. Make up your own patter and gags to make this trick truly your own.

Effect

The performer transfers a coin from the right hand to the left apparently to make way for another object. In doing so the coin disappears.

Equipment

A medium- to large-sized coin and a wand or pencil.

Preparation

The trick depends on the French Drop sleight of hand (see Behind The Ear, p. 290) but using the right hand instead of the left. This sleight, together with the misdirection needed to divert the audience's interest, needs to be thoroughly practiced.

Performing

● Place the coin and wand (or pencil) on a table.

● Pick up the coin with your right hand and show it to the audience, holding the coin by its edges between thumb and first finger (**1**).

● Look at the wand (or pencil) as if you want to pick it up but cannot because the coin is in your right hand. This creates a reason for doing the next step.

● Keep looking at the wand (or pencil) and put your left hand over your right as if to transfer the coin to your left hand. In reality, drop the coin into the fingers of your right hand (**2**, see over). Your left hand hides what is really happening while your eyes direct the audience's attention to the wand.

2

● Now pick up the wand with your right hand, still keeping the coin concealed by holding it in your palm or in the crease of your fingers.

● Turn to look at your left fist, where the coin is meant to be. Tap the left fist with the wand, as if working magic.

● Uncurl your left hand slowly, watching with interest. React with surprise or delight that the coin has gone. Turn and face the audience with your left hand open. This should elicit appreciative applause.

● Now place the magic wand in a pocket and, as you do so, drop the coin surreptitiously into the pocket.

COIN FOLD

A quick and easy trick, particularly suitable for a young audience.

Effect

The performer makes a coin disappear from a folded paper.

Equipment

A 6 x 6 in (15 x 15 cm) sheet of colored paper and a medium- to large-sized coin.

Preparation

The trick works well when making a grand show of folding the paper and sprinkling the "magic dust." Practise to get the paper folding just right.

Performing

● Fold the bottom edge of the paper up to about ½ in (1 cm) short of the top edge and make sure the shorter side is towards you and not the audience (**1**).

● Drop the coin into the folded paper (**2**).

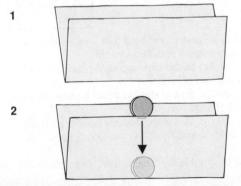

1

2

- Fold the sides of the paper towards the audience (**3**).
- Fold the top half inch towards the audience (**4**) and the paper will have the appearance of a secure packet, with the coin trapped inside. In reality, the top edge of the packet is open.

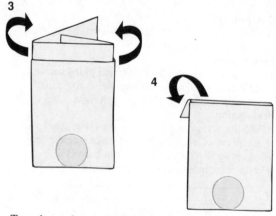

- Turn the packet over and hold it in your left hand so that the open edge is at the bottom (**5**).
- Tap the packet on the table top so the audience can hear that the coin is inside.
- Now allow the coin to slip out of the packet and palm it in your left hand (**6**).
- Reach into a pocket with your left hand to pick up some pretend "magic dust." As you do so, pocket the coin.
- Pretend to sprinkle the "magic dust" over the packet.

● Now tear up the packet. The coin has disappeared!
● Make sure you pick up the torn bits of paper
afterwards. You don't want the audience to find out
how the trick is done.

5

6

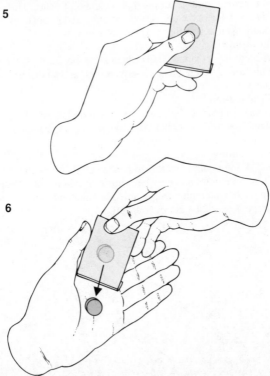

THE DISSOLVING COIN

An impressive trick using several props and with
spectator participation.

Effect

A borrowed coin is dropped into a glass of water. The
audience hears the coin enter the glass and a spectator
confirms that it is there. The coin then vanishes.

Equipment

A medium- to large-sized coin, a clear glass tumbler
half full of water, a large handkerchief, and an elastic
band.

Preparation

Prepare a tumbler half full of water and place an elastic
band in your left pocket. You can use a coin provided
by a spectator.

Performing

● Ask for a coin from the audience and then hold the
coin in the left hand between finger and thumb (**1**). Pick
up the handkerchief with your right hand and then
drape it over the coin in your left.

1

● Now hold the coin inside the handkerchief between your right thumb and first finger (**2**), so freeing your left hand.

● Ask a member of the audience to place the beaker in the palm of your left hand (this also provides an opportunity for them to check that it is an ordinary tumbler of water).
● Hold the coin over the water with the handkerchief draped around the glass (**3**).

● Now allow the coin to drop but before doing so secretly tilt the glass backwards so that when the coin drops it hits the side of the glass and falls into the left hand (**4**).

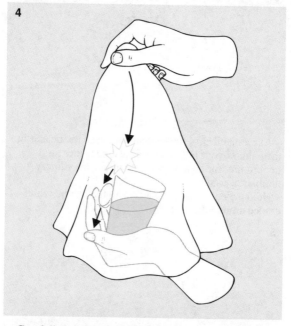

4

● Carefully move the glass so that it rests on top of the coin. You can now lift the handkerchief and allow someone to look straight down into the water. It appears that the coin is in the glass (**5**).

5

● Cover the glass again and lift it with the right hand
(**6**). The audience will now think that the coin
(supposedly inside the glass) is in your right hand. In
reality, the coin is palmed in your left hand.

6

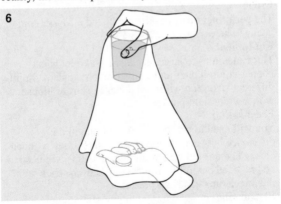

● Put your left hand into your pocket to take out the
elastic band. As you do so, pocket the coin.
● Place the band around the mouth of the tumbler and
put it down on a table.

● Get a spectator – perhaps the one who provided the coin – to remove the band and handkerchief. The coin has disappeared!

● While the audience's attention is concentrated on the spectator with the glass, palm the coin. You can now make the coin appear from some other place – perhaps from behind the spectator's ear.

SILVER AND COPPER

A slick trick, using more advanced moves, and suitable for doing near the middle of a magic routine. Make up your own patter and gags to make this trick truly your own.

Effect

The performer makes a silver coin and a copper coin change places.

Equipment

Three medium- to large-sized coins: two identical copper-colored ones and a silver-colored one of slightly different size. You will need a jacket, shirt or blouse with a wide, right pocket.

Preparation

You will need to practice until you can tell the difference between a copper and a silver coin by touch alone. The normal finger- and thumbpalms will need to be practiced carefully. You need to start the trick with the three coins in a right pocket.

Performing

● Put your right hand into your pocket and as you do so, fingerpalm one of the copper coins. Do this by bending the second and third fingers around the coin in a natural manner (**1**).

1

● Now take the two remaining coins between your thumb and first finger and show them to the audience (**2**).

2

● Place the silver coin to your left and the copper one to your right on a table in front of you (**3**).

3

● Pick up the silver coin with your right fingers, saying you will hold it in your left hand.

● As you move to pass the silver coin from right hand to left, switch the silver coin for the copper one so that the copper coin is surreptitiously passed across. This switch is done by dropping the silver coin into your palm at the same moment as you tip the palmed copper coin into your left hand (**4**).

4

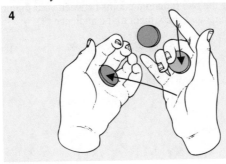

● Hold the silver coin in the palm of your right hand (**5**).

5

● Pick up the copper coin on the table with your right
fingertips and as you do so, thumbpalm the coin (**6**).

● Now tell the spectators to watch carefully.

● With hands well apart, form two fists and tap these on
the table as though in a magic gesture. The audience
now expects to see a silver coin in your left hand and a
copper coin in your right hand.

● Uncurl the fingers of your left hand to leave behind a
copper coin on the table top.

● Release the silver coin from the palm of your right
hand and leave the coin on the table. The silver and
copper coins have miraculously changed places!

● Scoop up the two coins and return them (together
with the thumbpalmed copper coin) to your pocket.

6

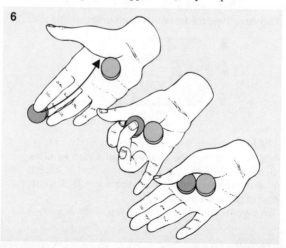

COIN IN THE WOOL

A nice twist on the disappearing coin trick and one
which involves a member of the audience.

Effect

The performer makes a coin disappear and then
reappear from the center of a ball of wool.

Equipment

A medium-sized coin, a colored or patterned medium-
sized beaker, adhesive tape, at least 40 ft (10 m) of
fluffy colored wool and a 3 x 1½ in (8 x 3.5 cm) sheet
of thin card matching the color of the wool.

Preparation

Prepare the ball of wool in the following manner. Take
the sheet of card and roll it into a tube that is 1½ in
(3.5 cm) long and has an internal diameter of 1 in
(2.5 cm). Tape the end of the card to secure the tube (**1**).

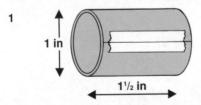

1

1 in

1½ in

Hold the tube on your thumb and carefully wind the
wool around the tube to form a ball. Don't wind too
tightly. Make sure that you leave one end of the tube
protruding very slightly from the wool (**2**). Tuck the
end of the wool into the ball.

Arrange the ball of wool in the top of the beaker with

2

the tube end pointing downwards so that the tube is not visible to the audience (**3**).

3

Performing

● Bring out the beaker and wool and place them on a table in front of the audience.

● Ask a member of the audience for a coin (make sure that you get a coin which will be small enough to fit inside the tube you have constructed).

● Get the person to mark the coin in some way, or note its date, so that he can make sure that it is his coin that he gets back again.

● Hold the coin up to the audience and then use a
thumbpalm (see Silver and Copper, p. 304) to make the
coin disappear.
● Now say that you will look for the missing coin. Pick
up the wool with your left hand and place the wool in
your right hand, putting the open end of the tube
directly over the palmed coin (**4**). This frees your left
hand to lift the beaker.

4

● Take the beaker in your left hand and turn it upside
down to demonstrate that it is empty. At the same time,
turn your right hand over so that the coin drops into the
tube.
● Put the beaker down on the table right way up and
take the wool in your left hand. As you do so, stick
your right thumb into the tube and pull it out of the
wool and palm it in your right hand (**5**).
● Direct the audience's attention to the ball of wool in
your left hand. Squeeze the ball of wool to close up the
opening, so keeping the coin inside.
● Place the ball of wool back on the beaker and start to

5

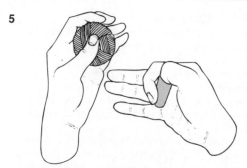

unravel the end of the wool from the ball.
● Invite the person who gave you the coin to pull gently
on the end of the wool and so unravel the ball. Stand
back and casually put your hands in your pockets and
so pocket the paper tube. As the spectator unwinds the
wool, the coin drops into the glass (**6**). He picks up the
coin. It is his own. How did it get there?

6

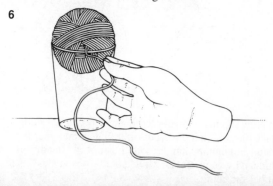

TOP POCKET VANISH

A good trick to confuse people who think a vanished
coin must be hidden in one or other hand.

Effect

The performer makes a coin disappear.

Equipment

A medium- to large-sized coin and a jacket, shirt or
blouse with a top pocket containing a handkerchief.

Preparation

You will need to practice the thumbpalm (see Silver
and Copper, p. 304). A handkerchief placed in the top
pocket will hold the pocket open ready to receive the
coin.

Performing

● Hold the coin in your right hand between first and
second fingers (**1**).

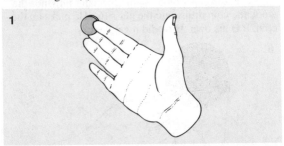

● Now slightly cup your left hand as if you are going to
take the coin in it. Put your right fingers into your left
hand and thumbpalm the coin in your right hand while
hidden by your left (**2**). Move your left hand away as if
it has the coin.

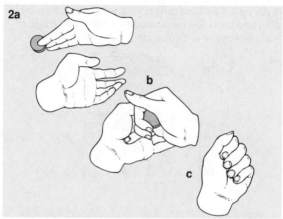

• Now with your right hand point and show how you will make the coin go up your left arm, across your chest, and down your right arm to your right hand (**3**).

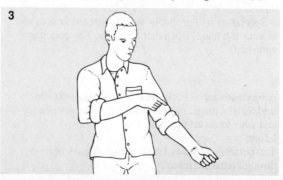

● As your right hand passes your top pocket, drop the
coin into it (**4**). Do this smoothly without any pause in
your movement or explanation.

4

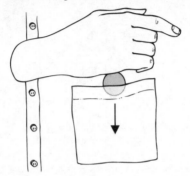

● Now pretend to make the coin move as you described
earlier. Follow its supposed path with your eyes.
● Open your right hand. Look puzzled. The coin is not
there.
● Spectators will probably assume that the coin is still
in your left hand. Open that hand too. The coin has
vanished!

COIN THROUGH THE HANDKERCHIEF

A more advanced trick suitable for doing near the
middle of a magic routine. Make up your own patter
and gags to divert the audience.

Effect

The performer makes a coin appear to pass right
through a handkerchief.

Equipment

A medium- to large-sized coin and a thick linen handkerchief.

Preparation

The trick depends on the use of a sleight of hand called the fingerpalm which, together with the patter needed to divert the audience's interest, needs to be practiced thoroughly. Practice the sleight of hand on its own first, together with the transfer of the coin from right to left hand, and back again.

Performing

● Pick up the handkerchief and show it to the audience to indicate that there is no hole in the fabric.

● Hold the handkerchief in your left hand and then pick up the coin with your right. Hold it up between the thumb and first two fingers of your right hand.

● With your left hand, drape the handkerchief over the coin. There is a bump where the coin is (**1**).

1

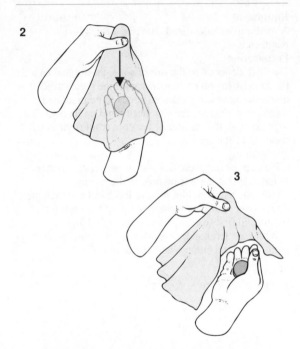

● Take the bump with your left hand. As you do so, drop the coin into the fingers of your right hand (**2**). Grasp the bump as though the coin is still there.
● Lift the handkerchief off your right hand, still gripping the bump, but actually leaving the coin in your right hand (**3**).

● Lay the handkerchief on your right palm, on top of the coin that is hidden there. The audience should still be thinking that the bump in the handkerchief contains the coin.

● Pass your left hand back towards you close under your right hand, taking the coin from your right hand (**4**).

● Grip the handkerchief with your left hand. Pretend to squeeze the coin out through the end of the handkerchief with your right hand (**5**).

4

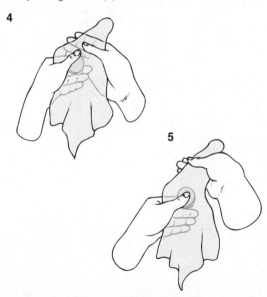

5

● Under the handkerchief, transfer the coin from your
left hand to your right. Let the coin gradually emerge
from below the bump as though it has passed through
the material (**6**).

6

2. Silk and handkerchief magic

Magic tricks using handkerchiefs or silk scarfs provide a strong visual element to a performance. These props can be easily secreted away in a small space and provide a dramatic flourish when they are produced. Silk handkerchiefs and scarfs can be compressed to a tiny size. Linen handkerchiefs, being thicker and less supple, can be used to create shapes and hide small objects. Whether silk or linen, scarfs and handkerchiefs provide a very effective means of masking a magician's moves as he or she manipulates objects "under cover." Some tricks, such as The Invisible Thread (see p. 324), Handkerchief Cleaver (see p. 330) and Blow That Knot Away (see p. 341) require no other props and so can be done almost anytime and anywhere. Other tricks, such as Handkerchief in a Glass (see p. 332) and The Inner Tube (see p. 344), require several props and can provide a dramatic climax to a magic routine.

PRODUCING A HANDKERCHIEF

Tricks involving the use of a handkerchief (or scarf)
can be enhanced if the handkerchief is produced
magically at the beginning of the trick.

Effect

A handkerchief is produced from the performer's
apparently empty hands.

Equipment

A large silk handkerchief or silk scarf.

Preparation

● Lay out a handkerchief flat on a table and fold the
four corners into its middle (**1**) to form a smaller
square.

● Holding the corners in place, fold the new corners
into the middle of the handkerchief (**2**) to form an even
smaller square.

● Continue folding in this way until the handkerchief
becomes very small.

1   **2**

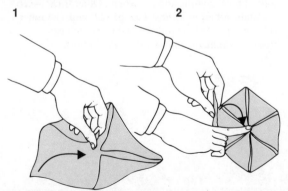

● Place the folded handkerchief on your left sleeve, at the inside of the elbow joint, and hide it by pulling a fold of your sleeve over it (**3**).

● Bend your arm slightly to hold the handkerchief in position.

Performing

● Approach your audience and show them that your hands are empty.

● Put your right hand on your left sleeve and the left hand on the right as if to pull up the sleeves.

● As you do so, take hold of the hidden handkerchief in your right hand, being careful to keep it concealed.

● Put both your hands together and, using your thumbs to unfold the handkerchief, cause it to appear slowly (**4**).

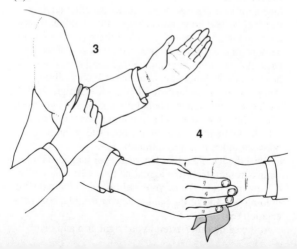

THE BOW AND ARROW HANKIE

More of a novelty than a trick. You can teach this one to a young audience.

Effect

The performer's hankie shoots from the hand, like an arrow from a bow.

Equipment

A large linen handkerchief. Use a plain-colored one which is clean and ironed.

Preparation

This feat depends on the precise timing of the release of the left hand and the flicking action of the right. You may find the moves easier to perform using the opposite hand.

Performing

One approach is to ask the audience whether anyone has ever played bows and arrows with a hankie. If they have, get them to show how. Give them your hankie to demonstrate. If they then proceed to show you their trick, that is fine. Congratulate them and show them how *you* do it. You could even make it into a little competition. At the very least you will have grabbed the audience's attention and hopefully got them on your side. This is how you make a hankie into a bow and arrow.

- Hold the handkerchief by the opposite corners between index finger and thumb (**1**).
- Twirl the handkerchief between your hands so that it wraps around itself like a gnarled twig (**2**).
- Now turn the wrist of your right hand so that you are holding one end of the hankie as you would a bow or catapult (**3**).
- At the same time, extend your right arm and bend

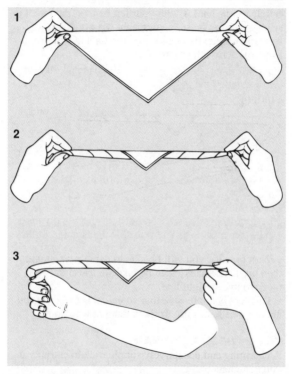

back your left so that you are in a similar position to an archer drawing a bow, but with the right arm bent rather than straight.

● Increase the tension on the taut hankie as you move both hands back slightly.

● Release the hankie with your left hand a fraction of a second before you snap your right wrist and arm forwards and let the hankie go. The hankie will shoot forwards across the room (**4**).

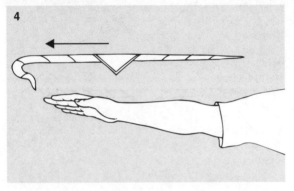

● With practice you will be able to name a target and then hit it. The hankie can be made to travel 12–15 ft (4–5 m) in a straight line.
● This feat is impressive to a young audience. You can choose whether or not to show them how to do it.

THE INVISIBLE THREAD

A charming and deceptively simple trick to entrance a young audience.

Effect

The performer attaches an invisible thread to the center of the handkerchief. By pulling on the thread, the performer makes the hankie bend back and forth. The performer bites the magic thread in two, and the hankie no longer moves when the thread is pulled. The hankie is then shaken open and given to the audience for examination.

Equipment

A large linen handkerchief. Use a plain-colored one which is clean and ironed.

Preparation

Practice in front of the mirror to make sure that your thumb movements will not be detected. Presentation is all in this trick. It can be done in mime, with no speech.

Performing

● Hold the hankie in your left hand and pull it through the open fist of your right hand so that it stands upright (**1**).

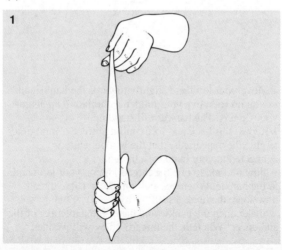

● Pluck an "invisible" thread from midair and then pretend to pass it through the tip of the hankie and tie it.
● Now pretend to pull on the thread and, as you do so, bend the hankie towards you (**2**) by moving your right thumb down slightly against your fingers. This move will be shielded by the hankie.

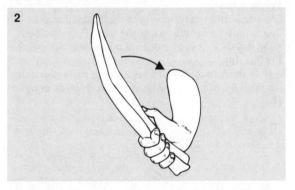

● Move your left hand slightly towards the hankie, and as you do so, move your hidden right thumb up against your fingers. The hankie will stand up.
● Repeat this back and forth pulling effect several times to give the appearance that the hankie really is connected to your hand by a thread.
● Now pretend to bite the thread joining your left hand to the hankie. When you pull on the invisible thread now, keep the hankie still.
● Shake open the hankie and hand it to a member of the audience. "Where is the thread?" they will wonder.

THE BROKEN MATCH

An easy trick involving a member of the audience.

Effect

A member of the audience places a match on a
handkerchief. The hankie is folded and the person is
invited to break the match in half inside the
handkerchief. This done, the performer makes a magic
gesture or incantation and lifts up the hankie. The
match falls out – it is unbroken.

Equipment

A large white linen handkerchief, clean and ironed,
with a match placed in its hem. A box of matches in
case no members of the audience have a match.

Preparation

Open up the hem at one corner of the handkerchief and
insert a match (**1**). Fold the handkerchief and place it in
a top or side pocket ready for use.

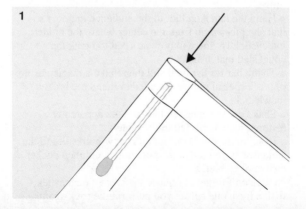

Performing

● Take out the handkerchief from your pocket. Hold it up and show both sides to the audience.

● Spread the handkerchief on the table with the hidden match at the top left corner, towards the audience.

● Invite someone to throw a match into the center of the handkerchief (provide a match if none of the audience has one).

● Fold the handkerchief (**2**) in half over the match (**a**), then quarters (**b**), then eighths (**c**) and finally sixteenths (**d**). The spectator's match will now lie along one edge of the folded handkerchief.

● Invite a member of the audience to come up and break the match in two. As you say this, move your fingers to locate the matchstick in the hem of the handkerchief. Fold this corner up to the center of the handkerchief, making sure the audience cannot see this move.

● Hand the handkerchief to the audience member so that she picks it up from the center where the hidden matchstick is. She will now proceed to break the concealed matchstick.

● Thank her for her help and then make a magic gesture or use a special phrase intended to mend the broken matchstick.

● Shake out the handkerchief and the apparently restored match will fall to the table.

● Hold up the handkerchief and show both sides to the audience as you did at the beginning, and then pocket the handkerchief.

Note: Don't forget to replace the broken matchstick with a fresh one before you perform the trick again.

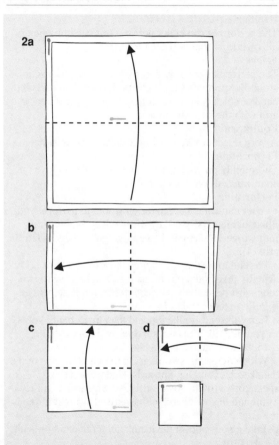

HANDKERCHIEF CLEAVER

The performer can either perform this trick on one of
his own legs or on a spectator's arm.

Effect

The performer securely knots a handkerchief or scarf
around a spectator's arm. The performer then pulls the
handkerchief or scarf straight through the spectator's
arm with the knot still intact.

Equipment

A very large handkerchief or a square silk scarf.

Preparation

Thoroughly practice making the loop folds to give the
appearance of tying a knot.

Performing

● After choosing a spectator on whom to perform your
illusion, diagonally roll up the handkerchief or scarf
into a rope-like length. Place it on top of the spectator's
arm (1).

● Pretend to tie the ends below the arm in a knot (2) but
actually take both ends of the handkerchief, form two
loops just beneath the arm and fold them together (3).

● Pull the loops tight (4).

● Carry the ends to the top and then tie as many knots
as you like (5). The handkerchief will appear to be
firmly tied around the spectator's arm.

● With a magic password, grasp the knotted ends of the
handkerchief and tug upwards. Underneath the
spectator's arm the loops will give way and it will look
as though the handkerchief has passed straight through
the arm.

● Take a bow, pocket the handkerchief and get on with
the next trick.

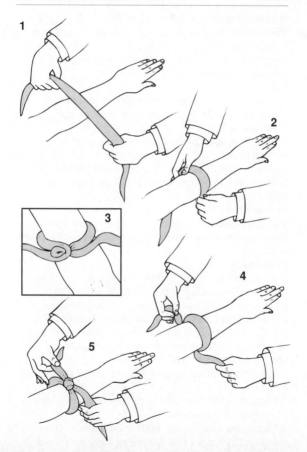

HANDKERCHIEF IN A GLASS

This simple trick can be performed with music in the background or you can tell an amusing story while performing it. A little flair and showmanship will enhance the overall effect.

Effect

A handkerchief "escapes" through the bottom of a sealed glass as the performer talks about escapology.

Equipment

A glass or plastic tumbler, a square silk scarf large enough to completely cover the tumbler, two silk handkerchiefs of different colors, cotton thread 8–10 in (20–25 cm) in length, and a medium-sized rubber band.

Preparation

Take the handkerchief that is going to escape and tie the cotton to one of its corners. Knot the thread at the other end.

Performing

● Explain to the audience that you are setting out to become an escapologist but you have decided to practice on scarfs before trying it out on yourself.

● Put the first handkerchief (**a**) into the tumbler. Ensure that the cotton is hanging outside the glass (**1**) on the side facing you (and ensure that this is the side facing you throughout the trick).

● Put the second handkerchief (**b**) on top of the first in the glass.

● Place the scarf over the top of the glass so that it and its contents are concealed.

● Secure the scarf with a rubber band near the rim of the glass (**2**). Ensure that the rubber band isn't too tight.

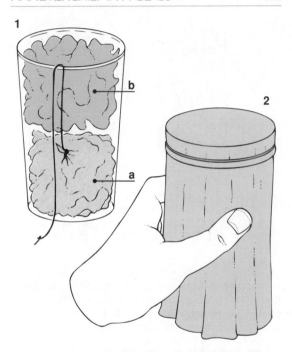

• Turn the glass upside down to show that everything is held in place by the band. Tell the audience that it is impossible for the first handkerchief (**a**) to "escape" from the glass.

• Utter a magic password, pull the knotted end of the cotton and handkerchief (**a**) will be pulled out of the glass (**3**).

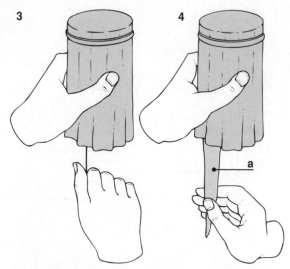

● Take hold of the corner of handkerchief (**a**) and pull it into view. It will look as though you are pulling it through the bottom of the glass (**4**), leaving handkerchief (**b**) and the scarf in place.

IT TIES ITSELF IN A KNOT

A simple but visually effective trick to show the power the performer has over inanimate objects.

Effect

Holding one corner of a handkerchief and letting the rest dangle, the performer lifts up the opposite corner with her other hand and gives the handkerchief a downward shake. She tries this two or three more times until, magically, a knot appears in the dangling corner of the handkerchief.

Equipment

A large handkerchief.

Preparation

Tie a knot in a corner of the handkerchief.

Performing

● Tell the audience that you will make a handkerchief tie itself in a knot just by using a sharp flick of your wrist.

● Take the knotted corner of the handkerchief, hiding the knot in your cupped right hand (**1**).

● With your left hand, bring the dangling opposite corner up and grasp it with the thumb and first finger of your right hand.

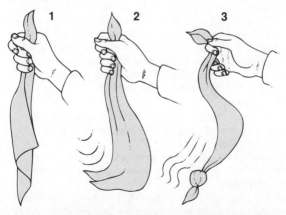

● Give the handkerchief a sharp downward shake, releasing the untied end as you do so. It will appear to the audience that you have failed in your intention to make the handkerchief tie itself (**2**). Seem puzzled by the handkerchief's failure to obey your will.

● Repeat these actions twice more, the left hand always bringing the untied corner up to the right one.

● On the final shake, retain the untied corner between your thumb and first finger but open your other fingers to release the knotted end (**3**). It will look as though, after two attempts, the handkerchief has obliged you by tying itself in a knot.

IT WAS A KNOT BUT NOW IT'S NOT

A truly illusive trick requiring rudimentary sleight of hand.

Effect

After allowing two colored silk handkerchiefs to be closely examined by a spectator, the performer throws them into the air: the handkerchiefs come down tied together. The knotted handkerchiefs are thrown upwards a second time and, when they return to earth, they are no longer tied to one another.

Equipment

Two large, colored handkerchiefs (preferably of silk) and a very small, thin flesh-colored rubber band.

Preparation

There is none apart from some practice, so that the performer's actions might be as smooth as possible.

Performing

● Place the rubber band over the first finger and thumb of the same hand, keeping them very close together (**1**).

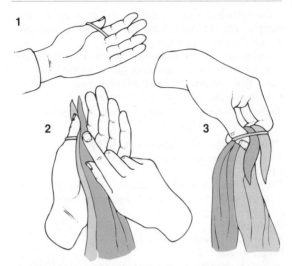

● With your other hand, pick up the two handkerchiefs and ask the spectator to examine them closely.

● When the spectator hands back the handkerchiefs, ensure that you take each by a corner and put them between the first finger and thumb, above the rubber band (**2**).

● Stand so that your handkerchief-holding hand is furthest away from the audience.

● Drop your hand slightly and allow the rubber band to slip from your hand onto the ends of the handkerchiefs (**3**).

● Throw the handkerchiefs into the air. They will seem to be tied together as they land.

- Carefully pick up one handkerchief by its corner, so that the audience can see that the other is hanging from it, as if they were tied together.
- Throw the tied handkerchiefs into the air and give the one you are holding a sharp tug just as it leaves your hand. This will pull the handkerchiefs apart.
- As they float downwards, the audience will see that the handkerchiefs are no longer "knotted" together.

PEN THROUGH HANDKERCHIEF

This is a simple and visually effective trick.

Effect

The performer borrows a spectator's handkerchief and seems to make a pen pass right through it without damaging the handkerchief.

Equipment

A borrowed handkerchief and a pen or pencil.

Preparation

It is the presentation and patter that bring this trick to life.

Performing

- Ask a spectator for a large handkerchief.
- Hold your left hand out, keeping your left elbow against your body. Draw attention to this hand as you close it to make a fist (**1**).
- Place the borrowed handkerchief over your fist.
- Now that your fist is hidden, open it as though holding a beaker (**2**).
- With your right thumb facing downward, bring your right hand against the handkerchief, moving the thumb

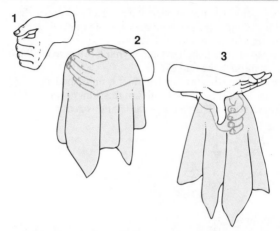

into your left hand, thereby creating a vertical fold (**3**).

● Enclose your right thumb with your left hand, at the same time moving your hands towards your body, so that both thumbs face your body.

● Once you've finished this action, move your right thumb up and down a couple of times and then remove it, leaving your left hand where it is. You have created a vertical fold, although it will appear to the audience that you have created a dead-end depression by pushing the middle of the handkerchief into your fist.

● Take the pen, push it into the depression (really the fold) and move it up and down a couple of times, pretending that you are having some difficulty in making it penetrate the handkerchief.

● On the last attempt, push the pen halfway down, then hit the top of the pen with the palm of your right hand to force it down into the fold (**4**).

● Move your right hand under your left fist and pull the pen through the fold (**5**).

● To show that the handkerchief is unharmed, open up your left fist beneath it and turn the palm upwards. The secret fold will drop out because of this action.

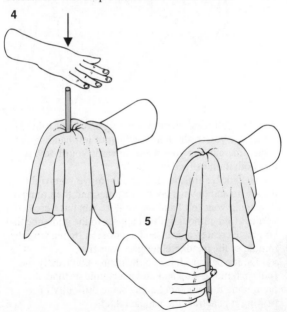

BLOW THAT KNOT AWAY

A rather elegant trick that involves some nimble finger play.

Effect

A knot is tied in the middle of a large handkerchief. The performer blows on the knot and it vanishes.

Equipment

A large linen or silk handkerchief.

Preparation

The twist of the wrist as the knot is tied needs to be practiced as a smooth movement that conceals the trickery.

Performing

● Diagonally roll up the handkerchief and present it to your audience, holding it at the ends.

● Hold end (**a**) between the first and second fingers of your left hand, with the third and fourth fingers curled around the handkerchief (**1**).

● Hold end (**b**) between the first and second fingers of your right hand.

● Your palms should face upwards and both ends of the handkerchief should extend about 3 in (8 cm) beyond the hands.

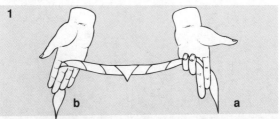

● Place end (**b**) in your left hand, so that it is held
between the base of your left first finger and thumb (**2**).
● Reach through the loop from above and, using your
right thumb and first finger, take hold of end (**a**) (**3**).
● Bring end (**a**) through the loop, turning your left hand
so that your fingertips point downwards as you do so,
allowing your left second finger to catch in the knot and
form a smaller loop in the handkerchief (**4**). Don't let
the audience know that you've sabotaged your knot in
this way.

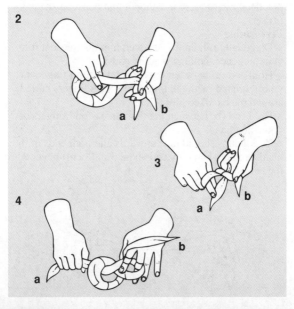

● Tighten the knot and slip your finger out of it as you do so.

● Hold the handkerchief in your left hand, showing the knot to the audience, and then press down on the knot with your right hand, so loosening it (**5**).

● Keep holding the knot in your right hand and place the topmost corner of the handkerchief over your right first finger.

● Release your right hand's pressure on the knot as you blow on it (**6**). It will look as though you have blown that knot away!

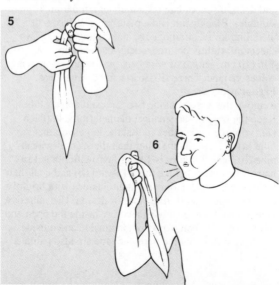

THE INNER TUBE

An impressive trick that can provide a stunning climax
to a performance.

Effect

The performer shows the audience two hollow tubes –
one inside the other. From these apparently empty
tubes, the performer produces several silk scarfs, and
then, as a finale, a wine glass.

Equipment

Three large cardboard or plastic tubes of similar height
and slightly differing diameters (dried skimmed milk
and drinking chocolate containers or similar are
suitable). Black paint and a paintbrush. Scissors or a
modeling knife, straight edge and cutting board. Two
sheets of brightly colored, sticky-backed paper. A
4 in (10 cm) length of wire bent into a narrow U-shape.
Adhesive tape. Three silk scarfs and a wine glass.

Preparation

Remove the ends from the two largest diameter tubes.
Keep the base of the smallest diameter tube in place
(**1**). Trim the three tubes so that the largest diameter
tube (**a**) is 1¼ in (3 cm) taller than the second-widest
tube (**b**), which in turn is 1¼ in (3 cm) taller than the
narrowest tube (**c**). Take tubes (**a**) and (**b**) and coat their
insides with black paint and their outsides with brightly
colored paper of differing color or design. Use adhesive
tape to attach the bent wire securely inside the open end
of tube (**c**) and then paint both the inside and outside
black, ensuring that the wire and tape are also painted.

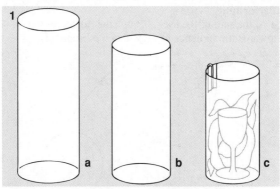

In preparation for the trick, place the wine glass and three scarfs inside tube (**c**). Then hook the tube inside tube (**b**) and place the two inside tube (**a**) (**2**). Ideally, place the tubes on the table where you intend to perform.

Performing

● At the start of the trick, lift up tube (**a**) and turn it towards the audience to show that it is empty (**3**).

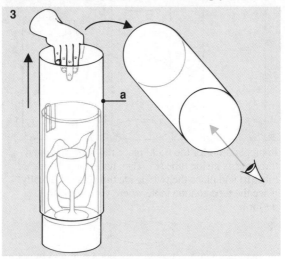

● Explain that one tube fits snugly inside the other and that tube too is empty. As you say this, put tube (**a**) down and then pick up tube (**b**) (with tube (**c**) hidden inside) and put it inside tube (**a**) (**4A**).

● As you do this, make sure that the hook on tube (**c**) catches the lip of tube (**a**).

● Lift up tube (**a**) and tube (**c**) will come with it (**4B**). With the other hand you can lift up tube (**b**) and show the audience that it too is empty.

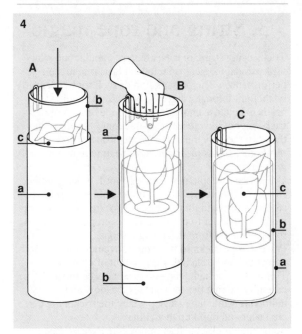

- Now place the middle tube (**b**) on the table and set the largest one (**a**) over it so that the smallest, hidden tube (**c**) is nesting in the middle (**4C**).
- Make a magic incantation or gesture and then produce the items you have previously loaded, starting with the scarfs and finishing with the wine glass.
- Take a bow and expect applause. You deserve it.

3. String and rope magic

Tricks using string or rope are very popular and many professional magicians include at least one in their performances. The presentation of such tricks needs to be thought through carefully, because the audience needs to be close enough to see the cleverness of the trick, but not too close (or in the wrong place) so that they can see how the trick is done. Rope tricks, like most other forms of magic, have been with us for a very long time.

Use soft and supple white rope or cord, or large white shoelaces. These are much more pliable than ordinary rope or string and their light color means they show up well. Even easier to perform with is proper magician's rope, available from most magic shops.

Practise rope tricks so that your movements are smooth, and your hands relaxed, with no hint of clumsiness. Timing is important, and you need to pace the trick carefully, so that the early stages are slow and deliberate while later stages, where the trickery occurs, are faster and build up to a climax.

Some rope tricks, such as Impossible Release (see p. 358) and A Mug's Game (see p. 370), can be done on quite a grand scale and involve several people. Others, such as Instant Knot (opposite) or Vanishing Knots (see p. 353), can be performed almost anywhere and require no equipment other than a length of rope or string.

INSTANT KNOT

Less of a trick and more of a novelty. You tie a knot in record time!

Effect

The performer shows the unknotted string to the audience. She brings her hands together and a knot appears instantaneously.

Equipment

A 4 ft (1.3 m) length of string.

Preparation

A quick and easy trick requiring no special preparation.

Performing

● Hand the string to a member of the audience so that he can check there are no knots in it. Take back the string.

● Hold the string with the left hand, palm up, about 6 in (15 cm) from end (**a**) and with the right hand, palm down, about 6 in (15 cm) from end (**b**) (**1**). Hand position is crucial.

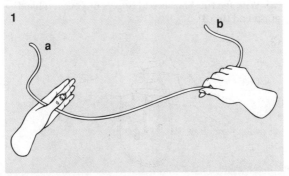

● Now, turn the right-hand palm towards you, with the fingers going under the string (**2**).

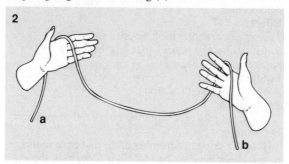

● Explain, "I will now try to break the world record for tying an overhand knot. Ready! Steady! Go!" Bring your hands together quickly.
● Bring your right hand behind the left and with the first and second fingers of your right hand grasp end (**a**). With the first and second fingers of your left hand grasp end (**b**) (**3**).

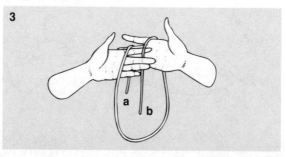

● Move your hands apart and when you pull the string taut, a knot appears instantly in its center (**4**).

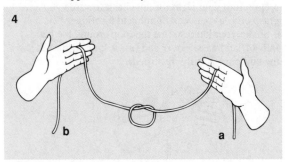

4

b   a

ONE-HANDED INSTANT KNOT

One better than the previous trick. You tie the knot with one hand!

Effect

The performer shows the unknotted string to the audience. He holds the string in one hand, shakes the rope slightly, and a knot appears.

Equipment

A 4 ft (1.3 m) length of string.

Preparation

A quick and easy trick requiring little preparation. Practice until you can do the moves quickly and smoothly.

Performing

● Hand the string to a member of the audience so that she can check there are no knots in it.

● Hold the rope in your right hand (or left) so that it passes between the second and third fingers and over the thumb (**1**). End (**a**) should hang down about 10 in (25 cm).

● Now turn your right (or left) hand towards you and grasp end (**a**) between thumb and forefinger (**2**).

● Shake your hand so that the loop around the hand falls off and passes over end (**a**). A knot forms (**3**) and the audience is truly mystified.

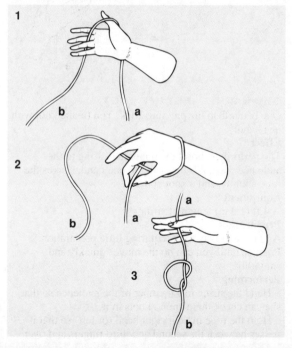

VANISHING KNOTS

A good effect to follow the Instant Knot or the One-Handed Instant Knot.

Effect

The performer shows a knotted string to the audience and then adds one knot and then another. When a volunteer pulls on the ends of the string, the knots fall apart.

Equipment

A 4 ft (1.3 m) length of string.

Preparation

Practise this trick so as to aim for as much audience participation as possible. The string should have a half-hitch knot in it (**1**), as formed using the Instant Knot (see p. 349) or the One-Handed Instant Knot (see p. 351).

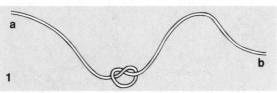

Performing

● Hand the knotted string to a member of the audience to check.

● Explain, "The easiest way to undo a knot is to tie a couple more."

● Holding the string up so the audience can see, tie another half-hitch in the string to form a reef knot (**2**) (see overleaf). Do not pull the ends too tight, but leave the loops of the knot open slightly.

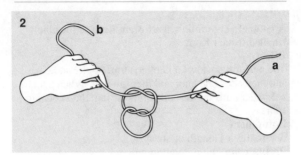

● Continue, "Now we join the two parts of this knot with a third knot." As you say this, push end (**a**) through the lower loop from the far side (**3**).
● Now push end (**a**) through the top loop, again from the far side (**4**).

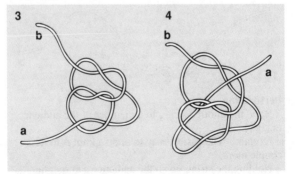

● Ask a member of the audience to gently pull on the two ends of the string. When he does this the knots get smaller and smaller and then fall apart.

MAGIC SCISSORS

Performed slowly, the trick is clever; performed quickly
it is magical.

Effect

The performer threads a string through the handle of a
pair of scissors. She then invites a member of the
audience to release the scissors without breaking the
string and with another member of the audience holding
the string by its ends. The volunteer does not succeed.
The performer then shows him how.

Equipment

A 6 ft (2 m) length of string. A pair of large scissors
with fully looped handles.

Preparation

A straightforward trick. No special preparation is
required, although if you plan to do the quick version of
the trick, you need to practice it rigorously.

Performing

● Fold the piece of string at its center and push this
loop through one handle of the pair of scissors (**1**).

1

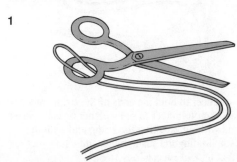

● Put both ends of the string through the central loop and then through the other handle (**2**).

2

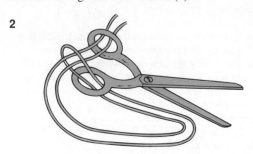

● Pull the ends of the string to form a neat arrangement and show the scissors and string to the audience (**3**).

3

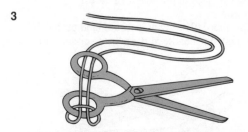

● Ask a volunteer to hold the ends of the string and then get another volunteer to see whether he can release the scissors without breaking the string and with the other person holding the string by its ends. It is very unlikely that he will succeed.

● Take back the scissors and string and then proceed to show them how it is done. Note: If the neat arrangement has been altered, you may need to rearrange or even rethread the string. If so, show the arrangement to the audience to show that you are not cheating.

● Get the first volunteer to hold the ends of the string.

● The next part you can do slowly, explaining as you go, or quickly, without explanation, for a more dramatic effect.

● Pull the central loop out and pass it through the other handle of the scissors (**4**).

4

● Next, being careful not to twist the loop, open it out further, and then pass the loop right over the scissors (**5**).

5

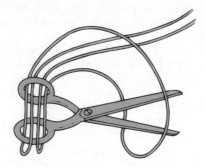

● Now ask the volunteer to pull gradually on the ends of the string. The string will unthread itself from the scissors and come free!

IMPOSSIBLE RELEASE

An impressive feat of escapology with plenty of audience involvement. It is particularly suitable for a young audience.

Effect

A scarf is tied around the performer's wrists and a rope then threaded around the scarf. Another scarf is draped over her wrists and in less than a minute she releases herself from the rope.

Equipment

A 12 ft (4 m) length of soft rope and two large silk scarfs.

Preparation

Make sure the props you need are placed on a table
ready for use. The trick works particularly well if you
grab the audience's attention by telling them an
escapology story while freeing yourself from the rope.

Performing

● Get a spectator to check that the rope you are using is
strong and that there is nothing unusual about it.

● Meanwhile, get a second spectator to tie your wrists
together with one of the scarfs. Keep your fists closed
while this is being done.

● Ask the first spectator to pass the rope between your
wrists (**1**) and then get him to keep hold of both ends of
the rope.

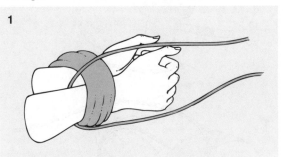

● Now get the second spectator to drape the other scarf
over your wrists.

● Open your hands and pull backwards slightly. As you
do so, explain that the rope is secure around your tied
wrists. Pulling backwards will have brought the rope
hard against the tied scarf.

● Begin telling the story of Harry Houdini, the great
escapologist, his feats and how he died (see p. 257).
While doing this, open your hands and rub the heel of
one hand against the other to trap and then move the
rope towards your palms (**2**).

● As you continue talking, make a step towards the
spectator holding the rope. As the rope slackens, work
your hands backward and forward until you can bend
your fingers and slip the loop over one hand (**3**).

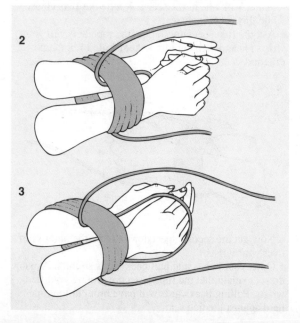

● Now ask the spectator to pull the rope taut. As he does so, the rope will be drawn beneath the scarf and come free.

● Ask the volunteer to remove the scarf draped over your wrists. This exposes the other scarf which is still securely tied in place.

● Get the volunteer to undo the silk around your wrists. Then take your bow.

RING RELEASE

A neat trick that will perplex your audience.

Effect

The performer threads a small ring onto a length of string. Two spectators each hold one end of the string, with the ring hanging at the center. A handkerchief is then thrown over the ring and the performer places his hands beneath the handkerchief. Seconds later the handkerchief is removed to reveal the ring secured in place by a matchstick. A spectator removes the matchstick and the ring falls to the ground free of the string.

Equipment

A 5 ft (1.5 m) length of string. Two identical metal or plastic rings of about 1 in (2.5 cm) diameter. A matchstick, a silk handkerchief and a wristwatch.

Preparation

Use a thumbpalm as described in Top Pocket Vanish (see p. 312) to hide one of the rings in your left hand. Hide the matchstick beneath your wristwatch (**1**) (see overleaf).

1

Performing

● Ask one of the spectators to check the string, the ring (not the hidden one!) and the handkerchief.

● Thread the visible ring onto the string and then get two spectators to hold either end of the string.

● Move the ring to the center of the string and then place the handkerchief over it (**2**).

2

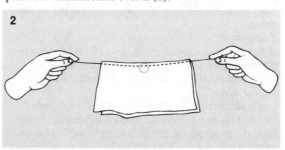

● Explain that you are just going to check everything is OK. As you say this, put both hands under the

handkerchief and, under cover, take out the matchstick
from under your wristwatch.

● Quickly secure the palmed ring to the string using the
matchstick (**3**). Put your left hand over the previously
threaded ring and then remove the handkerchief.

3

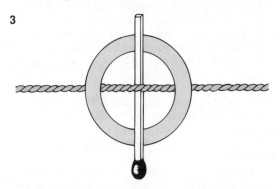

● Exclaim in surprise as you notice the match threaded
through the ring.

● Run your left hand (with the threaded ring concealed)
along the string to the person on your left, as you ask
him to remove the match. To do this he has to let go of
the string and this gives you the opportunity to take
your left hand (still holding the concealed ring) off the
left end of the string.

● While the spectator is removing the match from the
central ring, palm or pocket the other ring.

● When the match is removed the ring is released from
the string. No one will be any wiser as to how the
trick is done.

CHINESE ROBBERY

An easy trick using a volunteer and suitable for a young
audience.

Effect

Six traditional Chinese coins (or metal washers) are
threaded onto a string. The string is knotted and the
ends tied around a person's waist. The coins (or
washers) are then covered with a handkerchief. The
magician, playing the part of a Chinese pickpocket,
steals the money by removing it magically from the
string.

Equipment

A 6 ft (2 m) length of string. Six traditional Chinese
coins or metal washers. A large handkerchief.

Preparation

No special preparation is required.

Performing

● Explain, "Until only recently, the Chinese preferred
clothes without pockets. They had an unusual way of
carrying loose change. They made coins with holes in
the middle and carried the coins on a piece of string
hanging from around the waist. Chinese pickpockets
used a very cunning method to steal the coins."

● Show the audience the coins or washers and the piece
of string.

● Fold the string in half and push its center through one
of the coins (or washers). Then pass both ends of the
string through the loop to secure the coin to the center
of the string (**1**).

● Continue, "Other coins are put on top," and saying
this, thread both ends of the string through several more
coins (**2**).

● Now tie a single half-hitch about 4 in (10 cm) above the coins and then tie the string loosely around the waist of one of the spectators so that the coins are hanging from his or her side (**3**).

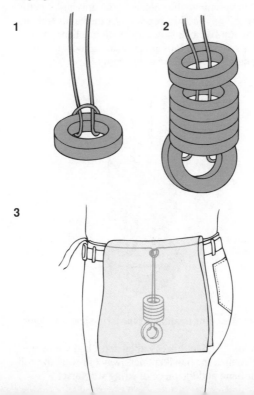

● Place the handkerchief over the coins, explaining, "This is how the coins might be carried, hidden by the handkerchief."

● Continue, "The amazing thing is how the pickpocket was able to remove the coins without untying or cutting the string." Saying this, reach under the handkerchief, slide the top five coins upwards with one hand, and with the other hand loosen the securing loop and then pull it down over the remaining coin (**4**).

4

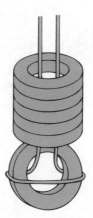

● Allow the coins to slide off the string and into your hand.

● Adding, "And to this day, they don't know how it's done." Whisk the handkerchief away to reveal the coins in your hand and the piece of string still intact.

CUT AND RESTORED ROPE

A classic trick which has been popular for hundreds of years.

Effect

A length of string is cut in half by a spectator. The performer restores it into one piece.

Equipment

A 5 ft (1.5 m) length of soft rope, ideally magician's rope. A large pair of scissors.

Preparation

Plenty of practice is needed to make sure the crucial move is done smoothly and discreetly.

Performing

● Give the rope to a member of the audience to check.

● Take the rope back and then hold it between the thumb and first finger of the left hand about 1 in (3 cm) from the ends of the rope (**1**). The back of your hand should be towards the audience.

1

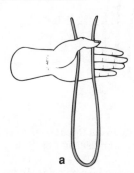

a

● With your right hand grasp the middle of the rope at point (**a**) and bring it up to your left hand (**2**).

● When (**a**) has reached your hand, without stopping pick up the rope at point (**b**) and bring the resulting loop up beside the two ends of the rope (**3**). This needs to be practiced carefully, and done as one smooth movement. To the audience it will seem that you have simply picked up the center of the rope and placed it as a loop beside the two ends.

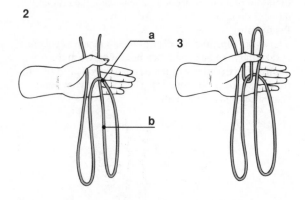

● Ask a spectator to cut through the top of the loop (**4**) making sure the arrangement of rope in your hand is well hidden.

● Next drop the two long ends (**5**). To the audience you now appear to have two roughly equal lengths of rope.

● Tie the two short ends of rope into a knot around the
the long length (**6**). Make sure you keep the knot well
shielded from the audience until it is complete.

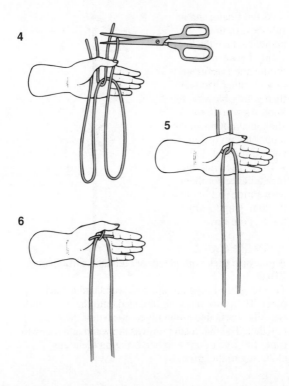

● Now hold the rope at one end, showing that it
(apparently) consists of two pieces of roughly equal
length joined by a knot in the middle (**7**).

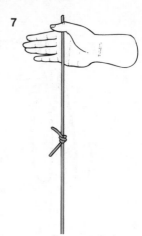

7

● As the finale, and in
full view of the
audience, take the knot
gently between the
thumb and forefinger
of your other hand and
then gently blow on the
knot. As you do so,
slide the knot down the
longer length of rope
and off the end.
● Throw the knot into
the audience for them
to examine and hold up
the long length, while
taking your bow.

A MUG'S GAME

A platform trick with plenty of audience participation.
Effect
Two lengths of rope are tied to a wand and to each
other. Then two mugs are threaded onto the ropes
and two silk scarfs tied around them to anchor the ropes
together. The magician removes the wand and the two
ropes fall free of one another, bringing the mugs
clattering to the ground.

Equipment
Two identical 12 ft (4 m) lengths of soft rope. A magic
wand, two enamel coffee mugs and two silk scarfs.

Preparation
Practice a very smooth performance with plenty of
patter to direct attention away from the crucial knot tied
around the wand.

Performing
● Get two spectators to assist you. Place one assistant
either side of you about 10 ft (3 m) apart and facing
each other. Give them the two ropes to hold so that the
ropes are parallel. Place the magic wand under the
center of the ropes (**1**).

1

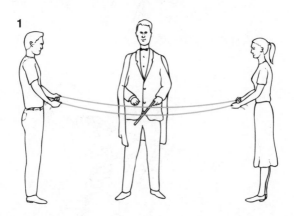

● Ask the assistants to release the ropes and then get them each to hold one end of the wand (**2**). The ropes are now supported in the middle by the wand.

● Gather the two ropes together (**3**) and then explain that you will tie them both to the wand. Unknown to the audience and assistants, you tie them in such a way that they are held together by the wand (**4**).

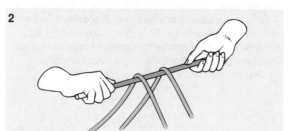

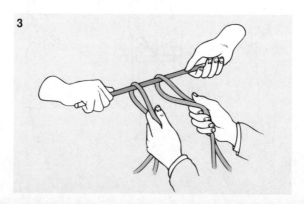

4

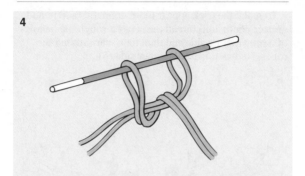

● Now give two ends back to each spectator. What the assistants do not know is that the two ends they now hold each belong to the same rope (**5**). When they walk backwards to their original positions, the ropes will hang across with the wand tied in the middle.

5

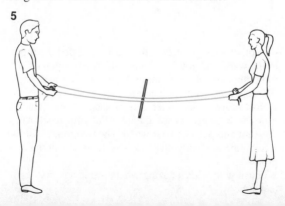

● To make the trick appear more dramatic (and to add greater confusion) thread the ropes through the handles of a mug on one side and then tie a scarf around the ropes. Repeat this for the other side (**6**).

6

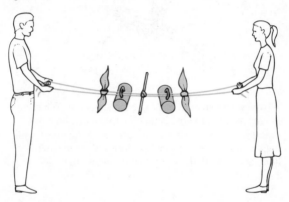

● Explain what you have done. You have tied the ropes to the wand and you have joined the ropes together in more than one place (point to the mugs and the scarfs). The ropes are securely held together.

● Now move to the center of the ropes, saying, "But now I want to get my wand back." Put your hand over the knot and pull out your wand. The two ropes will fall free of one another with a crash as the mugs hit the ground.

● Finish with, "It's amazing what a wand can do," and take a bow.

ROPES CHANGE LENGTH

This is one of the most impressive rope tricks to show children. It sounds complicated when you first read the instructions but it is quite easy to work out if you have the ropes in your hand and you follow the steps one at a time.

Effect

In the hands of a performer, a short, medium and long length of rope all become the same length and then revert back to their original lengths.

Equipment

Three lengths of soft rope – one 24 in (60 cm) long, a second 12 in (30 cm) long and a third 8 in (20 cm) long.

Preparation

Plenty of practice is needed to make sure you get the looping moves and the counting just right.

Performing

● Show the pieces of rope to the audience and then put them in your left hand and place them under your thumb with the back of your hand towards the audience. The longest rope (**a**)(**b**) is to the left, the medium rope (**c**)(**d**) is in the middle, and the shortest rope (**e**)(**f**) is to the right (**1**).

● Grab the bottom end (**b**)

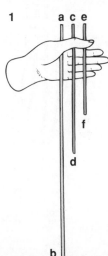

of the long rope with your right hand and put it under
your left thumb between the top ends (**c**) and (**e**) of the
medium and short pieces (**2**).

● Take the bottom end (**d**) of the medium piece with
your right hand and put this in a position to the right of
the top end (**e**) of the short piece (**3**).

● Next, put your right hand through the loop formed by
the long piece and take the bottom end (**f**) of the short
piece and place it to the right of its other end (**e**), so that
the short rope (**e**)(**f**) loops around (**a**)(**b**) but is above
(**c**)(**d**), as shown in (**4**).

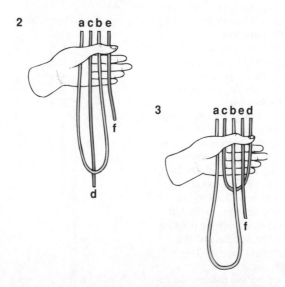

4

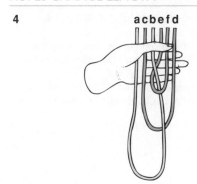

a c b e f d

● Now, with you right hand, pick up ends (**e**) (**f**) and (**d**) and draw these to your right, hiding the loop (**e**)(**f**) behind the fingers of your right hand. Done smoothly, the move gives the appearance that the three ropes are now all the same length (**5**).

5

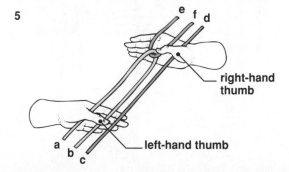

e f d

right-hand thumb

a b c

left-hand thumb

● Hold the ropes in your right hand with the ends
dangling down (**6**).
● To convince the audience that the three ropes really
are of the same length, you count the ropes singly from
hand to hand.
● Bring the right hand over to the left and transfer the
medium length rope to the left hand (**7**), counting "one"
as you do so.

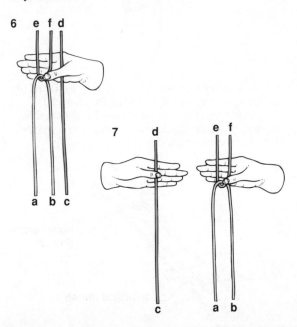

● Now bring your right hand back to the left again, and transfer the medium rope back to the finger and thumb of the right hand and, at the same time, pick up the looped short and long ropes between the first and second finger of the left hand, counting "two" as you do so (**8**).

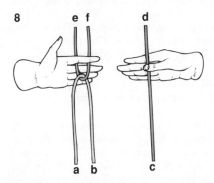

● Finally, bring your right hand back to the left once more and transfer the medium rope to the left hand, counting "three" as you do so. You have now "counted" the three ropes from right to left.

● Now scrunch the three ropes together in your left hand, and then slowly pull them out, one at a time, starting with the shortest and ending with the longest. Hold the ropes up as you did at the start of the trick and take a bow for your richly deserved applause.

4. Paper magic

Paper napkins, newspapers and sheets or loops of paper are light and flimsy props which lend themselves very well to a variety of tricks. The five tricks described here require some other props, and four of them require special preparation but are well worth the effort. Torn and Restored Newspaper (see p. 389) works well as a stage performance. Linking Clips (below) can be done on the spot with little or no preparation.

LINKING CLIPS

A trick that works of its own accord.

Effect

The performer folds a piece of paper and attaches two paperclips to it. He pulls on the ends of the paper and the clips become linked together. The trick is repeated but this time using two chains of paperclips and with a volunteer holding the ends of the two chains. When the performer pulls on the ends of the paper, the two chains become magically linked in the hands of the volunteer.

Equipment

A strip of paper 6 x 3 in (15 x 7.5 cm) or a novelty banknote. Two individual paperclips and two chains of five paperclips each.

Preparation

No special preparation is needed. Make sure you have all the materials readily to hand. The two chains of paperclips are simply made by linking clips together as shown (**1**).

1

Performing
● Fold the strip of paper so that its top edge forms the letter S and carefully attach the two paperclips to hold the loops of the S together (**2**). The precise positioning of the clips is important.

2

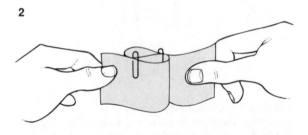

● Check that no one is standing too close (flying paperclips are dangerous), then begin, "Everything is automated these days. Even paperclip joining . . ." On saying this, pull the two ends of the paper apart smoothly and quickly. The clips will fly off and link themselves together.
● "Here are two chains I did earlier," and bring out the two paperclip chains.
● Ask for a volunteer from the audience and get him to

hold one end of each chain while you attach the other
ends to the paper as before (**3**).

● "It even works with chains," and pull on the ends of
the paper. The two chains of paperclips will link
together in the hands of the volunteer.

3

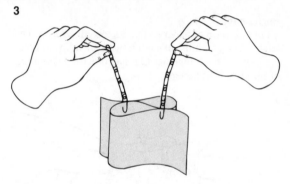

MYSTERIOUS LOOPS
This one is based on the classic trick called The Afghan
Bands. It works particularly well with older children.
There are many ways of presenting this trick. Here is
one.
Effect
The performer invites two members of the audience to
help her. She takes a loop of paper and carefully cuts
along its center line to produce two separate loops. One
of the spectators copies her actions but ends up with a
single long loop. The second spectator follows suit. He
finishes up with two loops – but they are linked
together, not separate.

Equipment
Three colored strips of paper, say red, blue and green,
each 6 ft (2 m) long and 3 in (7.5 cm) wide. Glue and a
pair of sharp-pointed scissors.

Preparation
Take one strip of paper, the red (**a**), and glue the ends
together without twisting the strip. Take the second
strip of paper, the blue (**b**), and twist it once before
joining the ends together with glue. Finally, take the
third strip of paper, the green (**c**), and twist it twice
before gluing the ends (**1**). Start the performance with
the three loops of paper and the scissors close at hand.

1

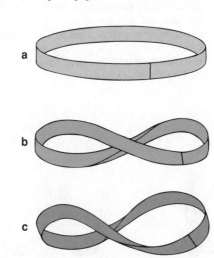

a

b

c

Performing

● Explain to the audience that you have three magic loops that seem to have a will of their own.

● Pick up the red loop of paper and hold it high to show the audience. As you do so, explain what you are going to do. "I am going to cut this loop of paper along its length. Let's see what happens . . ."

● Now start to cut the loop along its length but stop after a few seconds (**2**). Ask the audience, "What do you think I will be left with when I've finished?" Listen to the various answers and look where they come from. Then continue, "Well, let's see."

● Continue cutting along the length of the loop and when complete you will be left with two separate loops of paper. Hold them up and show them to the audience.

● Now, seek out a member of the audience who expected you to finish up with one large loop. Ask him to come up and repeat what you did and see what happens.

2

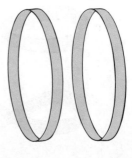

● Hand him the blue loop. When he carefully cuts along its length he will be left with one large loop (**3**) – what he predicted!

3

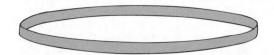

● Continue, "I got two separate loops. My friend here got one. Did anyone expect something different to happen?" Listen to their answers and then pick a second volunteer: "Well, let's see what happens when you try."
● Give him the green loop of paper. When he finishes cutting he will be left with two loops of paper – but linked together (**4**).

4

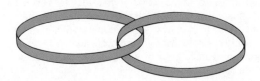

● Finish with, "I told you so. They're magic loops. They seem to have a mind of their own!" and take a bow.

A SWEET SURPRISE

A trick to be performed at the dinner table! Presented in a casual manner it will certainly take your dinner guests by surprise.

Effect

The performer takes a paper napkin from someone at the dinner table. With a pen he draws a circle and dot on a sugar cube and then drops the cube into a glass of water where it dissolves. He presses the folded napkin down on top of the glass and the circle and dot are magically transferred from the sugar cube to the napkin.

Equipment

Two identical paper napkins. A felt-tip pen, a sugar cube and a glass of water.

Preparation

Whether you perform this trick at the dinner table in your own home, or whether you perform it in a restaurant, you will need to prepare a napkin in advance (the same type of napkin that the other guests are using). Fold the napkin into four and then draw a faint circle and a dot in the center of one side (**1**). This is the same mark that you will later draw on the sugar cube. Conceal the napkin neatly folded in a pocket until you are ready to do the trick. There needs to be a bowl of sugar cubes and a glass of water on the dinner table before you start.

Performing

● While sitting at the dinner table, secretly take out the concealed napkin and place it on your lap.

● Ask someone to pass you a clean paper napkin. Fold it carefully into four to produce a neat square (this should be similar to the paper square you have on your lap).

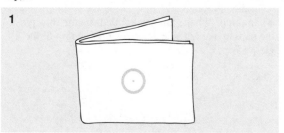

● Casually explain to the onlookers, "I learnt this from a friend recently. It doesn't always work, but let's try it and see."
● Take a sugar cube from the bowl and draw a circle and a dot on it (**2**).

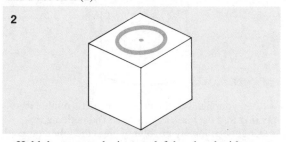

● Hold the sugar cube in your left hand and with your attention fixed firmly on the glass of water, drop the sugar cube into the water, saying, "Now let's see what happens." At the same time, casually pick up the fresh napkin with your right hand and place it in your lap.

● Still with your concentration on the glass, pick up the concealed napkin with your right hand, thus exchanging it for the new one.

● Continue, "I hope this works" and, saying this, press the napkin marked side down over the mouth of the glass (**3**).

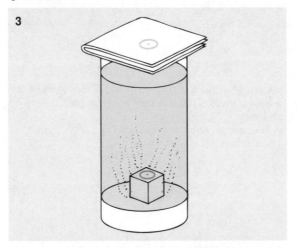

3

● Keep your hand on the napkin for half a minute or so, peering into the glass as you do so and noticing the sugar cube gradually dissolve. This is the time to use your left hand to pocket the napkin which is lying on your lap.

● Finish with "That should do it" and, saying this, lift up the napkin to show the circle and dot magically transferred to the paper.

TORN AND RESTORED NEWSPAPER

An impressive trick that works on a deceptively easy principle. It depends on careful preparation and slick presentation.

Effect

A newspaper is torn into shreds and is then magically restored to its original form.

Equipment

Two copies of the *same* newspaper, a glue stick, a warm (not hot) iron and an ironing board.

Preparation

Practice by using the identical inner pages of the two newspapers. Use the cover pages of the two newspapers to perform the trick in front of the audience. The labeling below applies to the performance itself, not the practice sessions.

Take the cover pages of the two newspapers (**a**) and (**b**). On the inside front cover (page 2) of paper (**a**) apply a small patch of glue (**g**) from a glue stick (**1**).

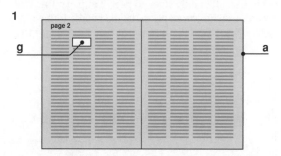

Place paper (**b**) back-to-back with paper (**a**) so that page 3 of paper (**b**) is stuck to page 2 of paper (**a**) (**2**).

2

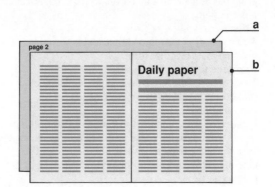

Now fold paper (**b**) in half, then in quarters (**3**), eighths, sixteenths, and so on (**4**), until you are left with paper (**b**) in a small bundle stuck to page 2 of paper (**a**). With a warm (not hot) iron, press flat the bundle formed by paper (**b**) so that it lies inconspicuously inside paper (**a**).

3

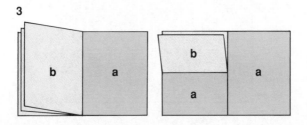

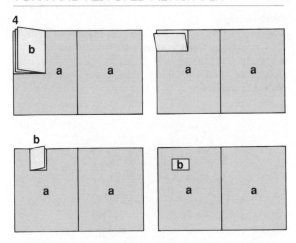

Now fold paper (**a**) so that the newspaper bundle (**b**) is inside (**5**). You are ready to perform.

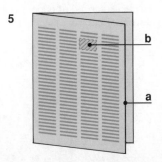

Performing

● Make a big show of rolling up your sleeves so as to convince the audience you have nothing to hide.

● Pick up paper (**a**), open it out, and casually show both sides to the audience, taking care to cover bundle (**b**) with your hand (**6**).

6

● Explain to the audience that you like this trick – it allows you to rip something to pieces and it's a good way of letting off steam.

● Now tear down the centerfold of paper (**a**) and place the back page in front of the front page (**7**).

7

● Fold paper (**a**) across the middle and then tear it across (**8**), putting the lower half in front of the upper half.

8

● Continue folding and tearing the paper in half, each time putting the torn pieces in front, so that bundle (**b**) always stays at the back.
● When the torn paper (**a**) is only slightly larger than the bundle (**b**), place the two between your hands and turn your hands so that paper (**a**) is below bundle (**b**). With the lower hand squeeze paper (**a**) into a ball (**9**).

9

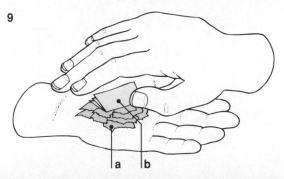

● Close your eyes and say your favorite magic word or phrase.

● Open your eyes and lift off your top hand to reveal bundle (**b**) neatly folded (**10**).

10

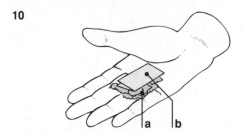

● Unfold bundle (**b**), a step at a time, until you reveal the double page quite restored and whole (**11**).

11

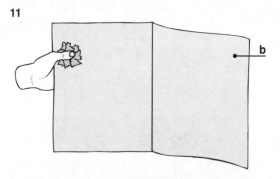

● You can even show the reverse side of the paper, with
the bundle of torn bits held under your thumb. They are
glued down on the bottom piece only, so make sure
none fall and give the game away.
● Squeeze the whole thing into a ball and put it in your
pocket or discard it safely.

MAKING MONEY

This trick will have the audience eating out of your
hand. It works on a similar principle to the previous
trick.

Effect

The performer takes a piece of paper and folds it in half
several times. When he unfolds it, the paper has
changed into a banknote.

Equipment

A $10 note or a novelty banknote. A piece of paper of
exactly the same size cut from a glossy magazine. A
medium-sized envelope and two small pellets of re-
usable adhesive. A wallet or purse in your pocket.

Preparation

Lay the banknote on a table with the face side face up.
Fold the note in half (**1**) and then in half again

1

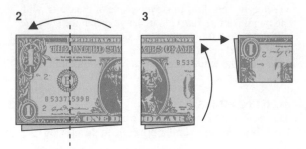

(**2**) and then fold the lower half upwards (**3**).
Now do exactly the same with the glossy paper. Stick
two small pieces of re-usable adhesive to the paper (**4**).
Now turn the banknote upside down with respect to the
glossy paper and stick the two folded pieces of paper
together (**5**).

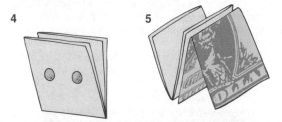

Now unfold the glossy paper (with the folded banknote
attached to its back) and place it in an envelope with
the banknote side face down (**6**). You are ready to
perform the trick.

6

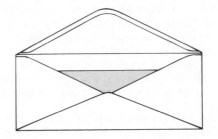

Performing

● Pick up the envelope and explain to the audience, "I got this in the post the other day from a magician. It's a magic piece of paper. He said I'd make a lot of money from it."

● Take out the paper, taking care to keep your left hand obscuring the folded banknote (**7**). Show the paper to the audience.

7

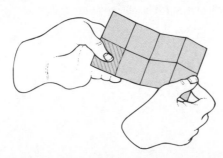

● Continue, "He told me how it works" and, on saying this, fold the paper in half, and in half again, in exactly the same way as you did during the preparation. The previous folds will guide you.

● When the paper is small, turn it over, and the $10 note will suddenly become visible. Unfold the banknote slowly, taking care not to show the now hidden paper to the audience.

● Finally, when the banknote is fully unfolded, pull it away from the paper so that it breaks free of the re-usable adhesive.

● Take the banknote in one hand, and keeping the paper concealed in the other, hold the banknote up to the light to check that it is real.

● While you are doing this, and with your eyes fixed on the banknote, reach into a pocket with your other hand to take out your purse or wallet. As you do so, pocket the piece of paper.

● Take out the purse or wallet and put the banknote inside it saying something like, "If I carry on making money like this, I'll be able to retire early."

5. Mind magic

Entertainers who perform mind magic, or mentalism, claim to use special mental powers to perform apparently superhuman feats. Such demonstrations include predicting the future, reading people's minds (telepathy) and matching an object to a person (psychometry). In a performance of mental magic much depends on the magician's ability to convey a sense of mystery and wonder. Although some magicians specialize in this kind of magic to the exclusion of all else – and they cultivate unusual looks or behavior to distinguish them from other performers – just one or two mentalist items in your performance can do much to enhance your reputation.

There are some specific points to consider when performing mind magic. Use the word "test" or "experiment" rather than "trick" to describe what you are doing. This reinforces the idea that you are using special powers, not a conjuring trick, to achieve a particular effect. Do not invent complicated explanations for your powers – it is better to simply leave it as a mysterious process. If a coincidence or unusual event happens, claim, with a knowing smile or wink, that you might have planned it all along. Be slightly wrong now and then. Making a guess which is nearly right, but not quite, adds authenticity and helps make the audience believe than you trying to "read people's minds." Use everyday items, rather than special props, to help maintain the idea that it is you, not the props, that are special. Most mentalist feats depend on knowledge about how the human mind works but also use simple conjuring principles to produce an effect. Try these tricks and see for yourself. Some are truly mind-boggling.

RIGHT EVERY TIME

A quick and easy first trick to perform with a young audience.

Effect

A "mind-reading" trick in which a volunteer chooses one of three picture cards. The performer correctly predicts which card is chosen.

Equipment

A medium-sized envelope, a smaller envelope, and a card to fit inside this envelope. Three sheets of white card, each 6 x 4 in (15 x 10 cm). A marker pen and an ordinary pen.

Preparation

Use the marker pen to draw a picture on each of the three cards. On one card draw a house, on the second draw a car, and on the third draw a bicycle (**1**).

1

Now carefully set up your prediction envelope. On the small card write with an ordinary pen, "I knew you would pick the house!" Put the card inside the smaller envelope, seal the envelope, and on its front write, "I knew you would pick the car!" Put this envelope inside the larger one and on the front of this write, "I knew you would pick the bicycle!" Check that you have set up the prediction envelope correctly (**2**).

2

I knew you would pick the house!

I knew you would pick the car!

I knew you would pick the bicycle!

Now, whichever card a spectator chooses you can
correctly predict the card by showing the appropriate
message which you have set up beforehand. You need
to be careful, of course, only to show the right message,
and not one of the others. Start the trick with the
envelope face down so that the message on the front is
not visible.

Performing

● At the start of the trick openly place your prediction
envelope down on one side, saying, "This is my
prediction as to what will happen."

● Hand the three picture cards to one of the audience.
Ask her to shuffle them and then get her to choose one.
Add, "Are you sure you want to choose that one?" so
allowing her the opportunity to change her mind if she
wants to.

● Continue, "Well, that is strange, because that is the
card I predicted." Reach for the prediction envelope
and display the message which matches her choice. For
example, if she chooses the bicycle, simply turn over
the envelope and show your message. Is she chooses
the car, open the large envelope and take out the
smaller one and turn it to face the audience. If she
chooses the house, open the smaller envelope without
showing its face to the audience, and then take out the
card inside and show this to the audience. Whatever the
choice, you can match it with the right message.

● Quickly move on to the next trick before your
audience has time to figure out how the trick is done.
Ask for your cards back and dispose of the envelopes
carefully, so the audience does not see them.

COLOR MYSTERY

A highly effective trick to use with a young audience.

Effect

The performer is able to determine correctly the color of a crayon placed in a tube behind her back.

Equipment

Six wax crayons of the same length and shape but of different colors. An opaque plastic tube with a stopper at one or both ends and which is big enough to hold a crayon (an old-fashioned cigar tube or similar is suitable) (**1**).

1

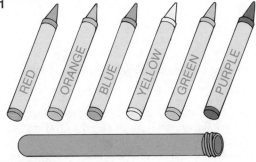

Preparation

Practice the trick thoroughly so that you can unseal the tube behind your back while carrying on a conversation with the audience. Also practice acting out your "second sight" as convincingly as possible.

Performing

● Hand the six crayons to a member of the audience and, turning your back to him, ask him to choose one crayon and put it in the plastic tube and seal the top.

● Still with your hands behind your back, get him to place the tube in your hands and ask him to put the rest of the crayons in his pocket or hide them somewhere else.
● Now turn to face the audience and tell them what has happened so far. Meanwhile, with your hands behind your back (away from the audience's view), unseal the tube and tip it gently to allow the crayon to emerge slightly from one end. Scrape a finger or thumb nail against the crayon (**2**) and then reseal the tube with the crayon inside. All this is happening while you are talking to the audience.

2

● Continue, "I will now try and use my second sight to see which color crayon is inside the tube." Saying this, bring the tube slowly up to your forehead. As you do so, glance at your finger or thumb nail and note the scraped off wax beneath it. You now know the color of the crayon inside the tube.
● Close your eyes and take your time using your "second sight" to "see" the color of the crayon inside the tube. The more effective your acting, the more dramatic the presentation of the trick.
● Finally, state the color, and finish by opening the tube and taking out the crayon to confirm that you are right.

NEWSPAPER PREDICTION

A trick best performed on an audience of older
children.

Effect

The performer predicts precisely where a spectator will
tell him to cut a newspaper column.

Equipment

A newspaper, a pair of scissors and glue or clear
adhesive tape. An envelope, paper and pencil.

Preparation

Carefully cut a column from the newspaper, choosing
one where the headline is large. Cut off the headline
(**1**), turn the column of text upside down, and then
neatly stick or tape the headline to the now upside
down column. Do this so that the join is not visible.

1

Now trim the bottom end of the column so that the cut end is close to the text (**2**).

2

Jail Breakout

yesterday five prisoners

On the slip of paper write out the line of type furthest from the headline. This is your "prediction." Put it in a sealed envelope.

Performing

● Give the sealed envelope to a member of the audience.

● Hold up the column so the audience can see the headline (but they should not be so close that they can see the column text is upside down).

● Read out some text from about one-third of the way down the column. If you cannot read upside down easily, memorize a line or two. Remember, you are trying to give the appearance that the newspaper column is the right way up.

● Now take the scissors in your other hand, saying to a member of the audience, "I will run the scissors up and down the column. Say 'Stop' and I will cut the column at that point. OK?"

● Go ahead and follow the spectator's instructions, making the cut at the chosen place (**3**). Cut carefully so

3

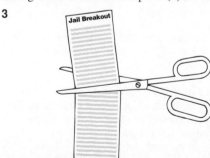

the break is exactly horizontal and between one line of text and the next. The cut-off end of the column will now flutter to the ground.

● Get a member of the audience to read out the top line of the cut-off column.

● Now ask the spectator holding the sealed envelope to open it and read out the message – it will match the line read out.

● Discard your headline and text in a safe place, away from prying eyes.

BOOK TEST
Another trick best performed on an audience of older children.

Effect
The performer hands a book to a member of the audience and then enlists the help of three people in choosing a random number between 1 and 99. This number determines which page is chosen from the book. The performer then "mind-reads" the first word on that page.

Equipment
A book containing at least 100 pages, 78 rectangles of card, each 5 x 3 in (12.5 x 7.5 cm), a marker pen, a pencil and a rubber band.

Preparation
Prepare a pack of alphabet (lexicon) cards as follows. For each letter of the alphabet prepare three cards. For each card use the marker pen and simply write the appropriate capital letter in the center of the card (**1**). Now take one of the cards for letter Q (this letter rarely comes up more than once in a word). With a pencil

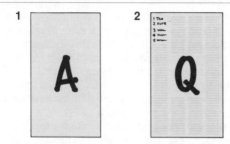

write on this all the page numbers from 1–99. Next to each number write the first word found on that page of the book you are using (2). Assemble the cards in alphabetical order. The Q card with the information you want will therefore be in the center of the pack. Enclose the cards in a rubber band and place them in your pocket. You are ready to perform the demonstration of your powers.

Performing

● Give the book to a member of the audience and ask her to flick through it to check that it is just a normal book – each page is different.

● Now explain that you are going to ask for help in choosing a random number between 1 and 99.

● Ask one person to call out a number from 1 to 9, ask another to call out another number from 1 to 9, and then ask a third to decide which of these two numbers (if they are different) should go first. The resulting two-digit number determines which page is to be selected.

● Ask the person with the book to turn to that page number and look at the first word on the page. Ask him to concentrate hard on that word.

● Explain that you are going to try and find that word
by using telepathy – thought transference. Take out the
cards from your pocket and explain that you are going
to use these cards to spell out the word. Turn the cards
to face the audience and riffle through the cards to
show that they are simply cards with letters on (the
pencil marks on the special Q card will not show up if
you riffle through the pack quickly).

● Ask everyone to be quiet and still and say that you
are going to try and "read" the sender's mind.

● Start sorting through the cards, and take out the
vowels – A,E,I,O,U – and lay them on the table (3). As
you do this, secretly hunt for the special Q card and
when you have located it, find the word which appears
at the beginning of the chosen page.

3

● Ask the "sender" to concentrate hard. Meanwhile,
close your eyes as if deep in thought. Slowly, open
them and then take the cards for the vowels in the
chosen word. For example, if the word is BEAR take an
E and an A and place them in front of you (4).

● Still concentrating, hunt for the remaining letters, but
seem to make a mistake or two along the way, which
you later correct. This misleads the audience into
thinking that you really are "mind-reading." In our

4

example, you might hunt for the letter B and then, to confuse the audience, search for the letter T, to make the word BEAT. Concentrate hard, change your mind, and correct the word to BEAR.

5

● Pretend that this demonstration has been a real effort of will. Thank the "sender" for his help, pocket the cards, and then take a bow.

MYSTERIOUS MAGAZINES

A more subtle variation on the Book Test (see p. 408).
Effect
The performer asks a volunteer to choose one of six magazines. He then enlists the help of four other people in choosing a particular word on a particular line of a particular page of the magazine. The volunteer finds this word and concentrates on it. The performer then proceeds to "read her mind" and correctly writes down the chosen word on a piece of paper.

Equipment

Six different magazines (Sunday newspaper color
supplements are best), plus a further three magazines
which are exact duplicates of three of them. Staple
extractor and a stapler. Paper and pencil.

Preparation

With the aid of a staple extractor carefully remove the
covers from the three duplicate magazines (**1b**, **2b**, **3b**).
In the same way, remove the covers of magazines
(**4**, **5**, **6**) and use these covers to form the outside of the
duplicates. Replace the removed staples with new ones
carefully positioned in the same holes. Done properly,
the three doctored duplicates should appear not to have
been tampered with. You now have six magazines, the
covers being all different, but the interiors of three of
them are identical with the other three. Pair them off in
your mind so that you know which covers contain
matching interiors.

Performing

● Show the magazines to the audience and, without
actually saying so, indicate that they are all different.
● Get a volunteer to pick one of the magazines. Stress
that her choice is not influenced by you in any way. She
can, in fact, change her mind at this point, if she
wishes.
● Once she has made the choice, put the remaining five
magazines to one side.
● Now ask the volunteer to turn to the back of her
magazine and say how many pages it contains, say 50.
● Get a second person to choose a number between 1
and 50, say 26. This will be the chosen page which the
volunteer should then turn to.

• Ask the volunteer to say how many columns of print are on this page. A third person then chooses one of the columns, say the second, and says this out loud.

• Get a fourth person to give a number which represents the line in this column. The volunteer finds this line, say line 21, and then says how many words are on it. A fifth person then chooses one of the words, say the fourth, and the volunteer finds it.

● At this point, casually pick up one of the discarded magazines, making sure it is the duplicate of the volunteer's magazine. Pretend to run through the process carried out so far, using your own magazine to show the steps (but do not show the contents of the magazine to the audience). For example, "You've chosen page 26, the 2nd column, the 21st line and the 4th word." As you do this, you turn and count to the right place, and you find, of course, the chosen word – but don't say anything. Check with the volunteer, "Is that right?"

● You now discard your magazine, pick up the pencil, pass it to the volunteer and ask her to circle the chosen word.

● Take back the pencil, and ask the volunteer to concentrate hard on the chosen word. Meanwhile, close your eyes and appear to be concentrating too.

● After a few seconds, take a paper and pencil and start to write out the chosen word. Make sure you make one or two errors, for example, writing LOFT, and then LIFT. Then ask the volunteer to concentrate harder and close your eyes once more before crossing out your earlier tries and writing LIGHT – the correct word (**2**).

2

IT'S ALL DONE WITH THE HANDS

A very convincing demonstration of "psychometric" powers – the ability to match an object to its owner.

Effect

Five members of the audience are asked to sign their names on a slip of paper. Each person puts their signed paper in an envelope which is then sealed. The envelopes are collected by one of the spectators. The performer takes the envelopes and then correctly "divines" which envelope belongs to which person.

Equipment

Five envelopes (enclosed by a paper band), five sheets of paper 3 x 2 in (7.5 x 5 cm) and five pencils. Also a blunt cutlery knife.

Preparation

The "trick" relies on an ingenious method for marking the envelopes. Lay an envelope on the table and then firmly press on a knife blade, running it along the edge next to the flap (**1**). This becomes envelope (**a**).

1

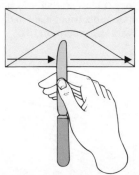

Repeat the procedure with the next envelope, but
running the blade along the left edge with the flap
uppermost. This envelope is (**b**). Envelopes (**c**) and (**d**)
are treated in a similar fashion, but pressing the right-
hand and bottom edges of the envelope respectively (**2**).
The fifth envelope (**e**) is untreated.

2

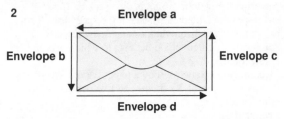

All the envelopes are now distinguishable by touch.
Envelopes (**a**), (**b**), (**c**) and (**d**) have one edge which is
flattened. It is then simply a case of remembering, and
then detecting, which envelope has which side
flattened. Envelope (**e**) has no flattened sides.
Pack the envelopes into a paper band in the right order
from (**a**) to (**e**), with (**a**) uppermost (**3**).

3

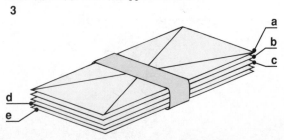

Performing

● Show the five slips of paper to the audience. Hand them to a volunteer and ask him to check them. While he is doing this, hand a pencil to five other members of audience.

● Ask the volunteer to give a slip of paper to each person who has a pencil.

● Now get the five people to sign their slip of paper. While they are doing this, remove the paper band from around the envelopes and then go round and hand an envelope to each of the five (mentally noting the order in which you have given out the envelopes).

● Get each person to put their slip of paper inside the envelope and then seal it.

● Ask the volunteer to collect the envelopes, and shuffle them.

● Take the envelopes, place them on the table in front of you, and then take one and carefully hold it between your fingers so that you are holding all four sides of the envelope with the flap uppermost (**4**).

4

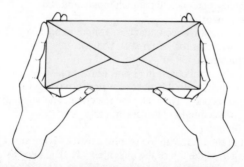

● With your eyes closed, concentrate as though you are trying to sense which person's signature is inside. You should be able to tell which envelope it is by noting which side, if any, has a sharp edge.

● Open your eyes and then give the envelope to the appropriate person, but ask him or her not to open it.

● Continue in this way, taking your time, and apparently "divining" which envelope (and enclosed signature) belongs to which person.

● When you have handed out all the envelopes, ask the five people to open them. Inside, each will find the piece of paper with their signature.

TIPPING THE BALANCE

This demonstration of mind over matter is aimed at an adult audience. It works best in a warm, dry room.

Effect

The performer balances two matches on the edge of a matchbox. He then gets a spectator to choose one of two matches. By exercising the power of the mind, the magician can make the match topple and fall.

Equipment

Two unused wooden matches, a small matchbox and a glass of water (or, better still, vodka).

Preparation

Secretly dip about $1/2$ in (1 cm) of the non-striking end of the match into the glass of water (or vodka) for 30–40 seconds. Then take the match out and wipe off the surface liquid with your fingers.

Performing

● Start the trick with the two matchsticks lying side by side across the top of the matchbox (**1**). You need to

1

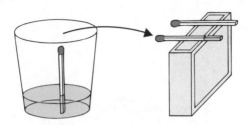

know which is the "dipped" matchstick.

● Now ask a spectator to pick one match for her and one match for you. In reality you make the choice. If she points to the non-dipped match say, "Alright, you have that one and I'll have the other." If she points to the dipped match say, "OK, so that's the one I'll use. Now while I concentrate on it I want you to concentrate on the other one."

● Now move the matches over slightly, one at a time, so that they are delicately balanced on one edge of the matchbox. This is best done by gently nudging the tail end of the match with one hand while using the other hand to stop the match overbalancing (**2**) (see over). If the match overbalances, gently nudge it the other way. When you have finished, both matches should be parallel and with their heads tilted down by the same degree (**3**).

● Continue, "Right. Concentrate on your match and I'll concentrate on mine." Alternatively, you can both concentrate on the same match (the dipped one) and get the rest of the audience to concentrate on the other one.

2

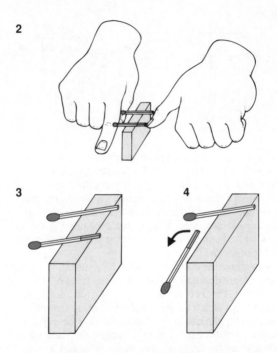

3

4

Whatever you decide, in time the liquid will evaporate from the dipped match and slowly but surely the match will tip further and then fall (**4**). If you set the trick up properly, you can convince the audience that it is your concentration that has made the match fall. A true case of "mind over matter."

THE PENDULUM WILL FIND YOU OUT

You will need to practice this one to convince yourself
that it really does work!

Effect

The performer is able to find out what a person is
thinking simply by getting that person to hold a
pendulum.

Equipment

A white cotton thread about 16 in (40 cm) long. A
finger ring. Three white cards 5 x 4 in (12.5 x 10 cm).
A pen.

Preparation

Tie the ring neatly to the end of the thread (**1**). Practice
the trick several times with friends or relatives to
convince yourself that it actually does work.

1

Performing

● Hand the three cards and the pen to a member of the
audience. Turn your back and ask him to sign his name
on one of the cards.

● Still with your back turned, get him to lay the three
cards in front of him in a row, with the signature on the
marked card face down. He decides where the marked
card is positioned.

● Now turn back and face the spectator. Explain that
you do not know which card he signed, nor where he

has placed the card. Continue by saying, "But you are
going to help me find the card, believe it or not."

● Continue, "I'm going to ask you three questions
shortly to which your answer will be yes or no. Don't
tell me the answer – the pendulum will speak for you. If
the truthful answer to my question is yes, the pendulum
will swing backward and forward in a straight line. If
the truthful answer is no, the pendulum will swing
around in a small circle. Have you got that? Just nod if
the answer is yes."

● Now show him how you want him to hold the
pendulum, absolutely still to start with, between his
thumb and first finger (**2**).

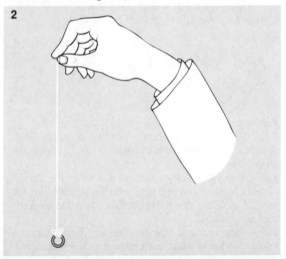

2

● Now run through everything once again: "If the truthful answer is yes the pendulum will swing to and fro; if no, it will swing in a circle. Right. Here are the three questions."

● Point to one of the cards and ask, "Is this the signed card? Concentrate. Think yes or no." Now watch what the pendulum does. If it swings back and forth you have found the card first time (**3**). If not, move on to another card, and repeat the question, while pointing at the next card. The pendulum needs to be stationary before each "reading" is taken.

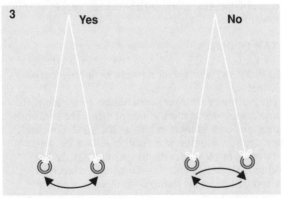

3   Yes   No

● As the performer, you can choose to stop as soon as you find the card for which the answer is yes. Or you can continue until you have checked all three cards and confirmed that one is yes and the other two are no. When you are ready, turn over the card which is the marked one.

Note: This trick really does seem to be mysterious!
According to psychologists, the pendulum signal works
by a combination of suggestion and response. You have
suggested to the spectator that the truthful answer yes
will produce a back and forth movement of the
pendulum, while a truthful no response will produce a
circular movement. His unconscious mind is triggered
by your questions to produce minute, imperceptible
movements in the pendulum-holding hand so
generating the required pendulum movement. Such a
reaction is called a psychomotor response, and, believe
it or not, the trick works well with most people most of
the time.

TAP IT OUT

A trick best done in your own home. You need a good
memory and your volunteer needs to be able to spell.

Effect

The performer arranges seven objects on the table. He
asks a spectator to think of one of them. The performer
then taps each of them in turn with a wand. For each
tap, the spectator has to mentally spell out one letter of
the name of the object she has in mind. On the last
letter spelt she should stop. Amazingly, the performer's
wand will be on the same object thought of by the
spectator.

Equipment

A cup, a bowl, a glass, a saucer, an ashtray, a matchbox,
a corkscrew. A pencil and paper. A wand (or a pencil).

Preparation

Commit the seven items and their corresponding
numbers to memory:

1. Cup   5. Ashtray
2. Bowl   6. Matchbox
3. Glass   7. Corkscrew
4. Saucer

Arrange the objects on the table before the trick starts.
Do not put them in sequence, but it helps if you arrange
them in a similar pattern each time you do the trick (**1**).
This helps you remember where they are and means
that you have one less thing to worry about.

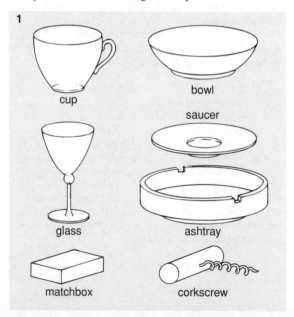

1

cup

bowl

saucer

glass

ashtray

matchbox

corkscrew

Performing

● Point out each object you have on the table and as
you do so, give its name. Do this in a random order.

● Now ask a spectator to think of one of the objects.

● Explain what you want her to do. "I will tap an
object, and as I do so I want you to mentally spell out
one letter of the name of the object. For example, if you
think of cup and I tap the glass first, think of C for cup,
on the second tap, the letter U, and so on. Simply spell
out the word in your mind, with one of my taps
representing each letter. Get me to stop as soon as I
have tapped out the last letter of your word."

● Now deliberately and slowly tap out the seven objects
in the following sequence:

First tap	-	Any object
Second tap	-	Any object
Third tap	-	1. Cup
Fourth tap	-	2. Bowl
Fifth tap	-	3. Glass
Sixth tap	-	4. Saucer
Seventh tap	-	5. Ashtray
Eighth tap	-	6. Matchbox
Ninth tap	-	7. Corkscrew

● Providing you do this correctly and your spectator
doesn't cheat (or can't spell) you will always arrive at
the chosen object on the last tap – to the amazement of
your spectator and the audience.

6. Mathematical magic

Mathematical discoveries provide a rich harvest for performers who choose to exploit the magical properties of numbers. Most of these tricks come under the category "self-working." Simply follow the instructions and the tricks work by themselves, without any sleight of hand or other deception. In many cases, you can use a mentalist approach to describe your magic feat. As with other performances of mental magic, much depends on your ability to convey a sense of mystery and wonder. Use the word "test," "demonstration" or "experiment" rather than "trick" to describe what you are doing. Again, this reinforces the idea that you are using mental powers, not a conjuring trick, to achieve the special effect.

I'VE GOT YOUR NUMBER

This quick and easy trick works every time, providing your volunteer can carry out your instructions and can do simple arithmetic. You, the performer, have little to do.

Effect

The performer writes a prediction on a slip of paper. He then asks a volunteer to think of a number, and then gets her to perform some simple arithmetic with the number. At no stage is the performer given any indication of what the original number is. The volunteer completes the arithmetic and the number with which she is left matches that predicted by the performer.

Equipment

Two pieces of paper and a pencil.

Preparation

No special preparation is required. You will, of course, need to memorize all the instructions.

Performing

● At the start of the trick write this prediction on a piece of paper, taking care not to show the writing to any member of the audience: "You will finish with the number 1089."

● Ask a volunteer to call out any three-digit number in which all the digits are different; for example, 257.

● Give the volunteer a pencil and paper and ask her to write this number in reverse; in this example, she would write 752.

● Now get her to subtract the first three-digit number from the second, or vice versa, subtracting the smaller number from the larger. In this case, the calculation would be:

$$\begin{array}{r} 752 \\ -\ 257 \\ \hline 495 \end{array}$$

● Now ask the volunteer to reverse this total, and add the two three-digit numbers together:

$$\begin{array}{r} 495 \\ +\ 594 \\ \hline 1089 \end{array}$$

● Sometimes she will end up with 99, a two-digit number:

$$\begin{array}{r} 483 \\ -\ 384 \\ \hline 99 \end{array}$$

- In this case, ask the volunteer to add 99 to 99 to get a three-digit number:

$$99$$
$$+\ 99$$
$$198$$

- Now ask the volunteer to reverse the total, and add the two three-digit numbers together:

$$198$$
$$+\ 891$$
$$1089$$

- Get someone else to open your piece of paper, which has been in full view throughout, and read out what is written upon it. Your prediction proves to be correct! Note: Try this trick several times. Whatever three-digit number you choose, when you follow the instructions correctly, you always finish up with 1089.

THINK OF A NUMBER

A variation on the previous trick. It requires the performer to do a small amount of mental arithmetic.

Effect

The performer asks a volunteer to choose a two-digit number and gets him to tell her and the audience what this is. The performer then asks the volunteer to perform a series of simple calculations which involve the volunteer's own personal details (and which the performer cannot be expected to know) plus other information provided by the audience. At an early stage, the performer writes a prediction on a slip of paper. Later, when this prediction is compared with the volunteer's answer, they are found to match.

Equipment
Two pieces of paper and two pencils.

Preparation
No special preparation is required other than memorizing the instructions and practicing some simple mental arithmetic.

Performing

● Ask a volunteer to think of a two-digit number and get him to tell you and the audience what this number is; for example, 65.

● Get the volunteer to write this number on a piece of paper, explaining that you want him to do some simple arithmetic. Say you will do the same (in fact, you write down another number – a prediction – that is easily calculated in your head once you have the volunteer's chosen number).

● Now ask the volunteer to write his year of birth underneath the number but keep this to himself. For example:

65 (*volunteer's chosen number*)
1979 (*year of birth*)

● Ask someone else to call out a famous event and the year that it happened; say, 1776 and the Declaration of Independence. The volunteer should add this to his list.

● Finally, ask a volunteer to write down how old he will be at the end of the year and how many years it has been since the event called out by the spectator. He may need to do a separate calculation to work this out.

● Now run through again what you've asked him to do, emphasizing those items you did not know when you wrote on your paper, and those items which even now you do not know.

● Now get the volunteer to add up his list of numbers and tell you what the final total is. His calculations, taking the current year as 1996, should look like this:

> 65 (*volunteer's chosen number*)
> 1979 (*year of birth*)
> 1776 (*year of Declaration of Independence*)
> 17 (*volunteer's age at end of year*)
> <u>220</u> (*years since Declaration of Independence*)

Total = 4057

● Ask someone else to unfold the piece of paper on which you've written a number. Your prediction – and the volunteer's answer – are the same!

● What is the secret? All you have to do is carry in your head twice the number of the year in which you are performing. In 1996, for example, this number is 3992 i.e. 2 x 1996. When the volunteer's two-digit number is mentioned, you add his number to 3992 and write this answer on a piece of paper which is disclosed at the end. Thus, if the volunteer's number was 65, the final answer (in 1996) will be 3992 + 65 = 4057 (the same answer as that calculated by the volunteer).

MAGIC SQUARE

The effect of this trick on your audience has to be seen to be believed. You will go up in their estimation!

Effect

The performer asks a member of the audience for a number between 50 and 100. The performer then draws a square on a piece of paper and divides this into 16 smaller squares. He rapidly fills the squares with numbers in an apparently random manner. The large

square, now filled with numbers, is passed to the
spectator. The spectator discovers her chosen number is
the sum of each vertical line of numbers, each
horizontal line, the two diagonals, and the central block
and corner blocks of four squares.

Equipment
Paper, pencil and a ruler.

Preparation
You will need to memorize the method for constructing
the square of numbers and the positions of numbers
1–12. Once this is achieved, practice using different
guessed numbers to develop your ability to enter
numbers quickly. About 10 minutes' practice a day
over a fortnight will make you an expert!

Performing
● In full view of your audience use pencil and ruler to
draw a square on the piece of paper. Then divide the
square into 16 smaller squares (**1**).
● Ask a spectator for any number between 50 and 100.
● Now write the numbers 1–9 in the squares as shown

1

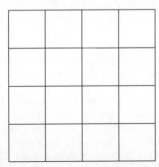

(2). (It is probably best for you to devise your own strategy for remembering where these numbers go. One way of checking is to ensure that each vertical group of numbers adds up to nine, with the number 9 on its own in the bottom right-hand corner. The number 6 – an upside-down 9 – is next to the 9.)

● Now add the numbers 10, 11 and 12 in the positions shown (3).

2

	1		7
	8		2
5		3	
4		6	9

3

	1	12	7
11	8		2
5	10	3	
4		6	9

● You are now left with four spaces to fill. Subtract 20 from the spectator's chosen number – for example, if the number is 66, subtract 20, giving 46. Call this number **N** and enter this number in the first square of the first line (**4**).

4

Enter N	1	12	7
11	8	Enter N-1	2
5	10	3	Enter N+2
4	Enter N+1	6	9

● Move to the second line and enter the number **N - 1**, in other words 46 – 1 = 45, in the empty square.
● Move to the third line and enter the number **N + 2**, in other words 46 + 2 = 48, in the empty square.
● Finally, in the fourth line, enter **N + 1** as the missing number.
● The magic square is now complete (**5**). Hand it to your spectator. She – and the audience – will be amazed at how the different combinations of four numbers –

verticals, horizontals, diagonals and blocks – will add up to her chosen number, 66.

5

46	1	12	7
11	8	45	2
5	10	3	48
4	47	6	9

THE NINES HAVE IT

Superficially similar to the Book Test (see p. 408) and Mysterious Magazines (see p. 411), this trick works on a very different principle and is foolproof.

Effect

The performer hands a magazine to a spectator. She then asks another person to think of a four-figure number made up of four different digits. The performer does not know this number, but simply asks the spectator to perform a series of calculations on it until he is left with a single-figure number. The performer knows what this is, and directs the other spectator to turn to that page of the magazine – the performer has predicted that page and a message is waiting there!

Equipment

A magazine, a marker pen, a paper and pencil.

Preparation

On page 9 of the magazine write in bold letters with the marker pen GOT THERE BEFORE YOU! and sign it.

Performing

- Hand the magazine to a spectator, asking him not to open it.
- Hand the paper and pencil to a volunteer and get him to think of a four-figure number made up of four different digits; for example, 7923. Tell him not to disclose his number to you, but to write it down on a piece of paper (**1**).

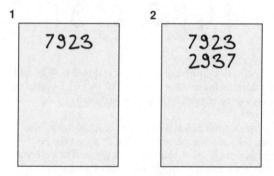

- Now get the volunteer to jumble up the four digits of the number and write these down below the first number (**2**).
- Get him to subtract the smaller number from the larger one (**3**).

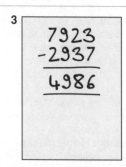

3

7923
−2937

4986

● He should then take this total and add the digits together (**4**). If he is left with two digits he should add these together until he is left with one digit (**5**).

4

7923
−2937

4986

4+9+8+6=27

5

7923
−2937

4986

4+9+8+6=27

2+7=9

● Continue "I know the number you've got. I got there before you." And saying this, ask the volunteer to get the spectator with the magazine to turn to that page. There, the audience will find your message and be suitably surprised.

Note: When the instructions for this trick are followed, the final number is always a 9. Interestingly, the two-digit number obtained beforehand, if there is one, will also be a multiple of 9.

MAGIC STAR

This trick employing the magic star can be repeated, to great effect, particularly with a young audience.

Effect

The performer gets a volunteer to throw two dice – the numbers obtained are kept secret from the performer. The volunteer then makes some simple mental calculations based on features of the magic star and the final total is written in the center of the star. From this total the performer correctly determines the two numbers shown by the dice.

Equipment

A marker pen and a ruler. A white card 6 x 4 in (15 x 10 cm). Two dice of different colors (for example, one white, the other black). A duster or a similar-sized piece of material. A pencil and paper.

Preparation

With the ruler and marker pen, carefully draw a five-pointed star of the dimensions shown (**1**).

You will need to memorize the directions to give to the spectator, but they are quite straightforward.

Performing

● Ask a spectator to throw one die, say the white, while your back is turned. Say he throws a 3. Ask him to note the number thrown but to keep the number from you. Get him to then cover the die with the duster. Give him the paper and pencil in case he wants to use them in the calculations which follow.

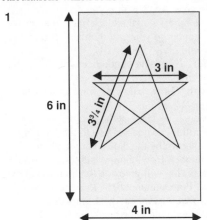

1

6 in

3 in

3¾ in

4 in

● Now bring out the magic star and explain that you will use it to help unravel the mystery of this trick. Point to the two horns (the downward-pointing arms of the star) and explain that these are significant. In a black magic star they point upwards, representing the horns of the devil, but in friendly or white magic, the horns point downwards.

● Continue advising the spectator, "The number 2 is important, so take the number you threw and multiply it by 2." In the example here, this would give 3 x 2 = 6.

● Now add, "The star has five points – this is significant – so add 5 to the number you have." This would give 6 + 5 = 11.

● "The star also has five angles between the points –
also significant – so, please multiply your last total by
5." This would give 11 x 5 = 55.

● "Now take the other die – the black one – and throw
that. Add this number to your last number." If the 6 is
thrown, this would give 55 + 6 = 61.

● Continue with, "Now cover both dice with the duster
so I can't see them."

● And finish with, "Now write your final total in the
center of the star."

● When this is done, a glance at the number and some
simple mental arithmetic enables you to work out not
only the values shown by the dice – but which die
shows which number. How? Simply subtract 25 from
the final number. That will give you the numbers shown
on the two dice. For example, 61 – 25 = 36 showing
that a 3 was thrown for the first die – the white one –
and a 6 for the second die – the black one.

Note: This trick works every time, and the magic star
can be used again and again if the center number is
rubbed out each time. But don't repeat the trick more
than once in a single performance, or the audience will
catch on how it is done.

BEAT THE CALCULATOR

The performer beats two challengers hands down.

Effect

The performer challenges two spectators to a
mathematical contest – the performer pitting his mental
arithmetic against the calculators of the spectators.
Performer and spectators perform the same calculation,
but the performer gets there before them.

Equipment

Three sheets of paper and three pencils. Two simple electronic calculators.

Preparation

Practice the trick several times, using different numbers, to convince yourself that it works each and every time.

Performing

● Start the trick by explaining that, in an age of high technology, there are still some calculations better done by the human brain, rather than a computer or calculator.

● Find two people from the audience who wish to take part in a simple mathematical challenge. Call one challenger A and the other challenger B.

● Give A and B a paper and pencil and get them to write the letters A and B separated by about an inch (**1**). You do the same.

1

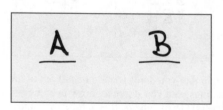

● Ask person A to provide a three-figure number composed of different digits; for example, 625. All three of you then write this number down under letters A and B (**2**).

2

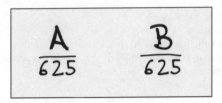

● Now get person B to think of a three-figure number made up of three different digits, say 784. You all put this number under 625 in column A (**3**).

3

A
625
784

B
625

● Explain that you don't want to be left out of the proceedings, and you'd like to throw in a three-figure number too. To the others, this number will appear random. In reality, you have decided on the number by mentally subtracting B's number, in this case 784, from your personal magic number, 999. This gives 999 − 784 = 215, and it is 215 which you and the others write in column B (**4**). Now for the challenge.

4

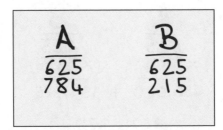

● Give A and B each a calculator. Explain you want them to multiply together the two numbers in their own column, and then get together with the other person and add their totals together. They have the calculators, you will do it in your head.

● Once they are clear what they have to do, say "Ready steady, go" and start. You will be able to do the calculation very quickly and here is the method. Subtract 1 from the first number, in this case giving 624, and write this down. Then subtract this number from the magic number 999, giving 999 – 624 = 375, and then write this down. The six-figure number, 624,375 is the right answer. It has taken you seconds. Meanwhile, the two challengers will still be working on their calculations (**5**) (see over). They should get the same answer as you, but you will have beaten them hands down.

● Don't repeat the trick with the same audience.

5

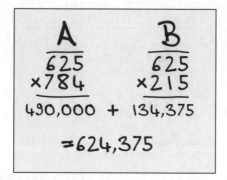

Note: The magic formula for the performer to remember is:

● Your number – to be put in column B – is the difference between the second (challenger B's) number and 999.

● To get the final total subtract 1 from the first number (challenger A's) and write this number down. This gives you the first three digits. Then subtract this three-digit number from 999. This gives you the second three digits.

7. Miscellaneous magic

This chapter contains a potpourri of tricks and novelties which use a variety of props. Some are more suitable for party tricks or stage magic, others for close-up performance.

WAND VANISHES HANDKERCHIEF

Effect

A handkerchief appears to vanish, having been pushed into a simple cone of newspaper.

Equipment

A silk handkerchief, a sheet of newspaper and a specially designed, hollow wand with a steel rod inside, obtainable from a magic shop.

Preparation

Check that the steel rod is free to slide out from inside the special wand.

Performing

● Roll a sheet of newspaper into a cone (**1**, see over). Show the audience the open end of the cone and use the wand as a pointer to push down into the cone to demonstrate that it is empty.

● While doing this, slide the steel rod out from the wand and grip it through the bottom of the cone (**2**, see over).

● Once this is done it is important to keep the cone upright so the steel rod cannot be seen by the audience.

● Next, place a handkerchief over the mouth of the

cone (**3**). Tell the audience that you are going to make the handkerchief disappear.

● Taking the wand, push the handkerchief down inside

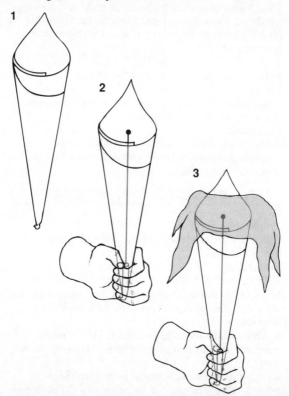

the cone (**4**). What you are really doing is placing the wand "case" back over the steel rod and, in doing so, forcing the handkerchief up into the wand (**5**).

● Place the wand on the table and, taking one corner of the newspaper, shake out the newspaper to show that the handkerchief has vanished!

BIG WAND FROM TINY PURSE

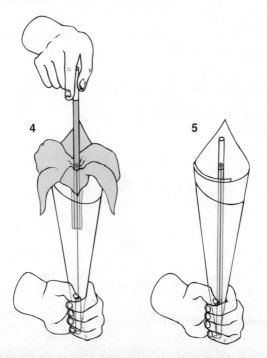

A trick in which the conjurer apparently produces a wand from a small purse into which it could not possibly fit.

Effect

The performer produces a small purse, opening it to show the audience that it is empty. The next moment he opens the purse and a 15 in (40 cm) wand is magically produced!

Equipment

A small purse, a magician's wand, a rubber band and a pair of scissors.

Preparation

Cut a 1½ in (4 cm) hole in one end of the purse (**1**). Place the purse in your *right* pocket. Insert the wand into your *left* sleeve and secure it by placing a rubber band not too tightly around your wrist (**2**).

Performing

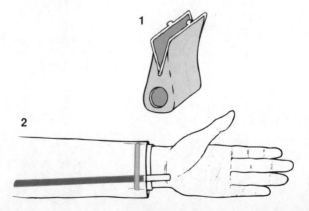

● Facing your audience, casually take the purse from your right pocket, using your right hand. Open it and show the audience that it is empty. Be careful to keep the hole in the purse hidden by having it next to your palm.

● Next, place the purse into your left hand with the hole nearest your wrist (**3**). Open the purse and pretend to feel about in it for the wand. As you do this, put your fingers through the hole and take hold of the wand that is still attached to your wrist.

● Slowly, pull the wand out of your sleeve, through the hole, and out of the purse (**4**). Show the wand to the audience so that they can check it is real. Meanwhile, return the purse to your pocket and begin the next trick.

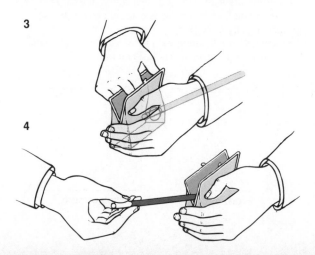

WHICH WAY?

A fast and funny trick with which to begin your performance. Use the patter described here, or make up your own story.

Effect

The performer tells a story about a journey and uses a card with arrows to describe her progress. It starts off clearly enough, but as she continues, the arrows seem to miraculously change direction, much to the amazement and confusion of the audience.

Equipment

A 10 x 10 in (25 x 25 cm) square of card. A marker pen and a ruler.

Preparation

Carefully draw an arrow on each side of the card (**1**). It is important that the arrows are at right angles to each other, exactly as shown.

Practice the trick, along with your accompanying patter, so that your performance is fast and funny.

1

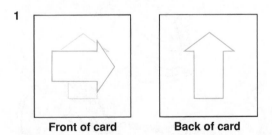

Front of card   **Back of card**

Performing

● Start the trick with the arrow on the back facing
upwards and with the front arrow (on the side toward
the audience) pointing from your right hand to your left
hand (**2**). Hold the card at the top left and bottom right.

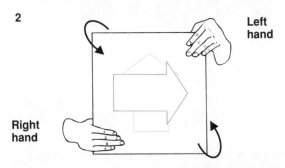

2

Left hand

Right hand

● Explain that on your journey here it was plain sailing
for the first few miles. As you say this, turn the card
over several times, pivoting it about your hands. As you
do this, the arrow will always point from your right
hand to your left.

● Continue, "But as I came nearer things got a bit more
complicated. I asked someone the way, but I think they
misdirected me. For the next few miles I seemed to be
turning right, then left, then right, zigzagging my way
here. It was really confusing!" Saying this, shift your
hands so that they are now holding the bottom left and

top right of the card. Turn the card over several times. Now the arrow will shift direction, first one way, and then the other (**3**).

3

Right hand

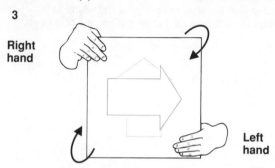

Left hand

● Stop turning when the arrow is pointing from your left hand to your right.

● Continue with, "Then I asked someone else, just to check I was on the right track. She didn't have a clue. I ended up going back the way I'd come." Saying this, move your hands so that they are holding the bottom right and top left again. Rotate the card as you talk, and the arrow will point from your left hand to your right (**4**).

● "By this time I was really fed up. I checked on the map and saw that I really needed to be going north." As you say this, turn the card over from top to bottom but keeping your hands in place on the card (**5**). Your right hand will now be at the top, your left hand at the bottom, and the front arrow (facing the audience) will now be pointing up.

4

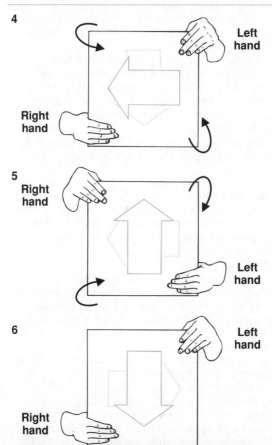

Left
hand

Right
hand

5

Right
hand

Left
hand

6

Left
hand

Right
hand

● When you now turn the card over several times, pivoting it between your hands, the arrow is always pointing upwards.

● "But that still wasn't it! I still hadn't got here. I'd overshot, and had to double back a mile or so, traveling south." And with that shift your right hand to the bottom and your left hand to the top. Turn over the card just once, and the arrow will be pointing down (**6**, see previous page).

● "But as you see, I got here in the end." And with that, toss the card aside and launch into your next trick.

LOSING YOUR SHIRT

None of the other tricks in this book rely on a secret stooge or confederate – a member of the audience who is in league with you. This is the one trick that does. Make sure you choose a stooge who will keep quiet about the secret of the trick.

Effect

The performer goes to a male member of the audience and asks whether he has ever lost his shirt at gambling. When the answer is "no" – the performer unbuttons the spectator's collar and cuffs and in one swift movement pulls the shirt off the spectator. A great party trick.

Equipment

The stooge needs to wear a shirt (preferably an old one) beneath a jacket or pullover.

Preparation

Get the stooge to take off his jacket or pullover and unbutton and take off his shirt. Lay the opened shirt across his back, and then button the cuffs around his wrists but without his arms inside the sleeves (**1**). Then put the collar around his neck and button two or three buttons at the front (two buttons if his shirt collar is open; three buttons if he is going to wear a tie) (**2**). Hold his jacket or pullover so he can get back into it

1

2

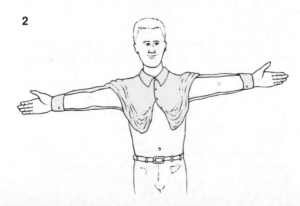

again. If he is wearing a tie, put that back on too. Make any final adjustments so that with his collar and cuffs visible, he looks as though he is wearing the shirt as normal.

Performing

● Look around the audience, as though you are searching for a likely candidate (in reality, of course, you have decided in advance who will be the other person in your trick).

● Go to your stooge and ask him, "Have you ever lost your shirt at gambling?" When he answers, apparently unsuspectingly, "No. Why?," reply with, "Well, let me show you."

● Proceed to unbutton his cuffs and then undo the two or three buttons at the front of the shirt (if he is wearing a tie undo that and remove it).

● Now count out loud, "One, two, three," and with that grasp the back of his shirt collar and pull the shirt up hard and fast so that the shirt comes clear of the pullover or jacket.

● Finish with, "And don't try that one at home, folks!" and take a bow. Oh yes, don't forget to give your helper his shirt back!

BALLOON CRAZY

A simple and effective balloon trick particularly suitable for a young, boisterous audience.

Effect

The performer takes an inflated party balloon and proceeds to stick a hatpin straight into it. Amazingly, the balloon does not burst. With the balloon still

impaled on the pin, the performer invites someone else
to stick another pin in. This time, the balloon bursts.

Equipment

Two or three large, patterned party balloons. Clear
adhesive tape and scissors. Two large, sharp hatpins.

Preparation

Inflate the balloon so that it is fairly taut and then knot
the neck of the balloon. Apply a square of clear
adhesive tape, about 1 x 1 in (2 x 2 cm), to one side of
the balloon (**1**).

1

Start the trick with the inflated balloon to hand, but
with the square of tape hidden from the audience's
view.

Prepare two or three balloons in advance, so that should
one burst before you do the trick you have another
ready on the table.

Performing

● Pick up the balloon and hand the two hatpins to a
spectator.

● Ask the spectator to check the pins and then hand one
back to you.

● Now continue, "Of course, balloons and pins don't mix very well. But this is a friendly balloon and if you ask it nicely . . ." On saying this, hold the balloon carefully in the crook of your left arm and proceed to stick the hatpin into the balloon through the center of the square of adhesive tape (**2**). Keep the pin away from the audience's direct view as you stick it into the balloon.

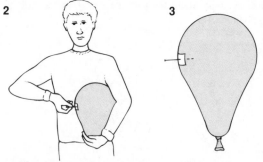

2

3

● Turn the balloon sideways on so that the audience can see the hatpin sticking out of the balloon (**3**).
● Now turn the balloon so that the hatpin is facing you and away from the audience. Hold on to the hatpin so that later, when the balloon bursts, it doesn't fly off and hurt someone. Walk up to the spectator who is holding the hatpin and ask her to stick the pin in, just as you did.
● When she tries this, the balloon will burst. Finish with, "Ah. You didn't ask it nicely!" Take back the spectator's hatpin and carefully dispose of the remains of the balloon. Then get on with the next trick.

STICKY FINGERS

A trick using a table knife. It works well with a young audience.

Effect

A knife appears to be stuck to the fingers. If anyone guesses the secret, the performer has another trick up his sleeve.

Equipment

A table knife, a pencil, and a wristwatch on your left wrist.

Preparation

Slip the pencil underneath your watchstrap and keep it hidden up your sleeve (**1**).

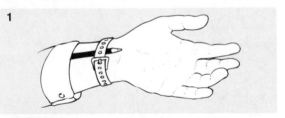

Performing

● Tell the audience, "This trick is called sticky fingers. Watch!" Saying this, hold the knife upright in the clenched fist of your left hand (**2**, see over).

● Now bring your right hand over and clasp it around your left wrist. Slowly open the fingers of your left hand and, as you do so, extend the first finger of your right hand to press the knife against your left hand (**3**, see over). Seen from the front, the knife appears to be stuck to your fingers (**4**, see over).

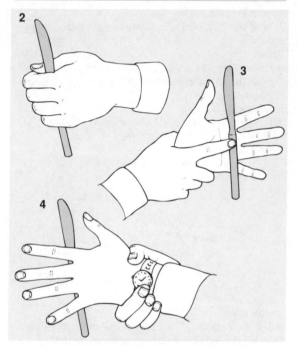

● At this stage, it is possible that someone correctly guesses the secret of the trick. If not, then the trick is over and you are free to move on to the next trick. If they do guess correctly, you are ready to move on to the next stage of the trick.

● Run through the trick again, just as before, but this time use your right hand to pull out the pencil from your left sleeve. You can position your right hand exactly as before, but with the pencil between your forefinger and the knife (**5**).

● Now when you remove your right hand – as you will be told to do – press the knife against the pencil using your left hand. The knife will stay miraculously stuck to your fingers, dumbfounding the audience (**6**).

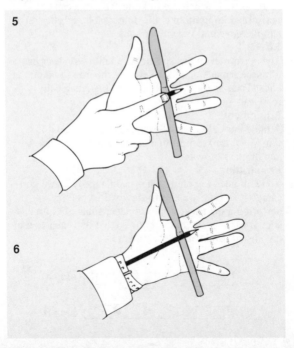

● To complete the trick, pull the knife away from the pencil and toss it on the table. As the audience goes to examine the knife, push the pencil back up your sleeve. You can now show your empty hand to the audience as well.

THE MAGIC KNIFE

Another trick which uses a knife. This one can be performed impromptu at the dinner table. It relies on a simple move and very few props.

Effect

The performer shows spectators a knife with four bits of tissue paper stuck to it – two on the front, two on the back. The papers are removed, and then magically reappear.

Equipment

A table knife. Four small squares of paper about ½ x ½ in (1 x 1 cm) torn from a paper napkin or tissue. A cup or glass of water.

Preparation

You will need to practice the "paddle move" until you can do it smoothly and effortlessly. Just before performing the trick, wet each paper square in turn and stick it to the blade of the knife so that two squares are on one side and two on the other (1).

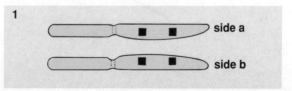

Performing

● Start with the knife held downward between the
thumb and first finger of your right hand (**2**).

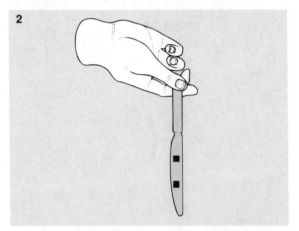

● Explain that this knife looks like an ordinary one but,
in fact, it is a magical one. Proceed to show the knife to
the audience using a method of presentation called the
"paddle move." This move gives the appearance that
you are showing both sides of the knife when, in fact,
you are showing only one side.

● The "paddle move" is performed as follows: Turn the
hand over and up, but as you do this, give the knife a
half-turn by rotating it between your thumb and first
finger (**3**, see over). On the way down, reverse the
movements to bring the knife back to its original
position.

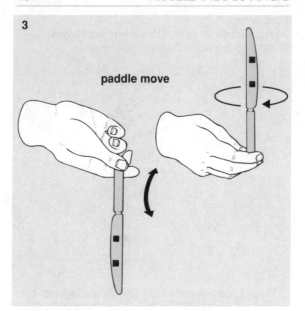

paddle move

● At this stage, show "both sides" of the knife using the paddle move (in reality you are showing only one side of the knife).

● With the left hand, remove one piece of paper from the knife and pretend to throw it away, but actually keep it in your hand (**4**).

● Now do the paddle move, raising the knife to pretend to show the other side, but as you do so, return your left hand to the knife. It looks as though you are removing the paper from the other side of the knife. Really, you

4

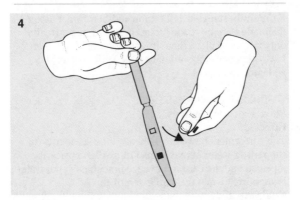

are simply returning the paper to its original location. Having done this, remove the paper again but now really throw it away.

● Do the paddle move again. To the audience the knife appears to have lost a piece of paper from both sides; in reality it has lost a paper from only one side.

● Repeat the above moves to take away the second piece of paper on that side.

● Do the paddle move once more. To the audience the knife appears to be blank on both sides. In fact, it is blank on one side and has two papers on the other side.

● Click the fingers of your left hand and with a quick upward sweep of the right hand, revolve the knife in your fingers to bring the paper side to the front. The paper squares have magically returned! Do the paddle move once more to show the audience that the squares have returned to both sides.

● Carefully run your left thumb and first finger along the blade to remove the "four" pieces of paper (really only two) and place them in your left pocket. You are left with a perfectly ordinary table knife to give the audience to inspect.

UPSIDE-DOWN MYSTERY
Make water defy gravity.

Effect
The performer shows the audience the classic trick of supporting water above a sheet of card. The trick is repeated and the card removed. Miraculously, the water is supported when the card is removed.

Equipment
A wine glass with mouth and foot of the same diameter (**1**). A disk of clear perspex of the same diameter as the foot of the glass. A piece of card 6 x 4 in (15 x 10 cm). A jug of water, a large plastic bowl and a towel.

Preparation
Wet the perspex disk and it will stick to the underside of the wine glass (**2**). The disk is now ready for use when needed.

Make sure the jug of water, the bowl, the towel and the card are all close at hand.

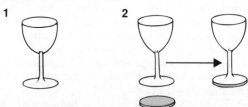

Performing

● Explain to the audience that you will demonstrate the classic trick where you can make water defy gravity, adding, "I'm sure many of you know the trick."

● Hold the wine glass upright in your right hand and over the bowl. Then carefully pour in water from the jug until the glass is absolutely full.

● With your left hand, place the sheet of card on top of the wine glass. Any water that might spill will fall into the bowl.

● With your left hand in place supporting the card, carefully turn over the glass (**3**).

● Take your hand away from under the card. The water is held in place by the card with no other support.

● Continue with, "The problem is, when you take the card away, the water falls" and, saying this, slide the card off the mouth of the glass. Of course, the water will cascade into the bowl (**4**).

3

4

● Add, "But there is an incantation I learned recently from an Oriental magician. Let's see how it works."

● Fill the glass as before but this time, just before you place the card on top of the glass, sit the glass on your left hand (**5**).

● Bring your left hand up from below the glass, taking with it the perspex disk that has been concealed under the glass. Place your hand over the glass and as you do so, place the perspex disk snuggly over the mouth of the glass (**6**).

5   **6**

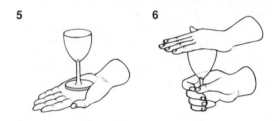

● Keep your hand over the glass, close your eyes and appear to concentrate hard while saying a secret magical incantation which no one can hear. Then remove your hand and place the card over the glass as before. Water may spill into the bowl.

● Holding the card in place with your left hand, turn the glass upside down as before. This time, however, when you slide the card across, the water will not fall into the bowl but will stay in the glass as if by magic (**7**).

● Allow the glass to stay like this for a few seconds, and then put your left hand over the mouth again, and turn the glass right way up.

7

● Move your left hand under the glass and, as you do so, bring the perspex disk below the glass again, where it will stick of its own accord.

● Now simply pour the water into the bowl. No one will see the perspex disk under the glass and the method you have used in the trick will remain a real mystery.

● Put the glass into the bowl of water, wipe your hands on the towel, and get on with the next trick.

HANG ABOUT

Another opportunity to defy gravity – this time using empty beakers.

Effect

The performer shows a handkerchief to the audience, places the handkerchief on a book, positions two tumblers on the handkerchief, and then proceeds to turn the book and the tumblers upside down. The tumblers are suspended in the air, apparently defying gravity!

Equipment

A large, colored linen handkerchief. Two ⅕ in (5 mm)

diameter colored beads and thread matched to the color
of the handkerchief. A sewing needle. Two lightweight
plastic tumblers. A medium-sized hardback book.

Preparation

Sew the two beads onto the handkerchief about 2 in
(5 cm) from the mid-fold (**1**). The distance between the
two beads should be about ¼ in (3 mm) more than the
width of your thumb.

1

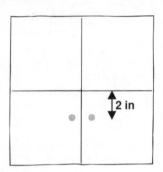

Place the handkerchief on a table with the book and the
glasses and you are ready to perform.

Performing

● Hold the handkerchief up to show the audience, but
keep the side with the sewn-on beads toward you so
they cannot be seen.

● Fold the handkerchief in half with the beads on the
inner surface of the upper half (**2**).

● Lay the handkerchief on the book and tuck three sides
of the handkerchief under the cover of the book to stop
the hankie hanging down later in the trick (**3**).

2

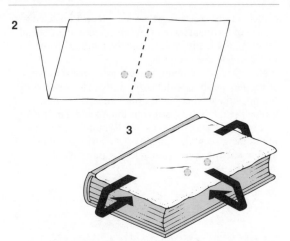

3

- Now hold the book, with the handkerchief on top, in your right hand with fingers underneath and thumb on top. The thumb must be carefully positioned between the two beads (**4**).

4

● Pick up one of the tumblers and place it upside down on top of the handkerchief; this is apparently a casual move, but in reality you wedge the tumbler's rim between one bead and your thumb (**5**).

● Now place the second tumbler, also upside down, alongside the first, with its rim wedged between your thumb and the other bead. Both tumblers are now trapped securely between your thumb and the beads.

● Now turn your hand over (**6**). The tumblers do not fall to the ground but remain apparently suspended underneath the book – much to the amazement of the audience.

5

6

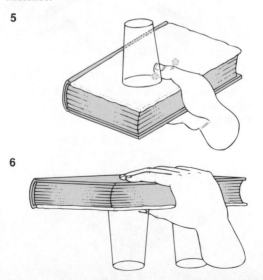

● Wave your left hand above and below the book to
show that there are no hidden supports – magic alone is
responsible for holding the tumblers in place.

● As the audience applauds, turn the book over and
remove the tumblers. Pull off the handkerchief and
place it in your pocket. Turn the book spine uppermost
and shake the book as if to see whether the secret will
come tumbling out from between the pages. Shrug your
shoulders and take a bow.

TEN DOLLARS TO A CENT

An economical trick which uses very few props and
depends on crafty presentation for its success.

Effect

The performer challenges a spectator to a friendly bet.
Having lulled the spectator into a false sense of
security, the performer turns the tables.

Equipment

A book of paper matches. Pencil and paper. An
electronic calculator.

Preparation

No special preparation is needed.

Performing

● Tear a match out of the book of paper matches and
challenge a member of the audience to a friendly
contest. Claim that when you flick the match in the air
you can control the flight of the match and make it land
on the side of your choosing. Saying this, mark one side
of the match with a pencil line (**1**, see over).

● Get ready to flick the match into the air, adding as
explanation to your challenger, "When the match is in
the air call out 'marked' or 'unmarked' and I'll make

1

sure the match lands with its other side face up. We'll try the best of three."

● Carry out the three tosses of the match.

Note: Which side is up when the match lands is largely a matter of chance, and in all probability you will win only one or two out of the three tries. Occasionally, you will win none out of the three, in which case you are well set up for the scam which follows. In a few cases, you will have won all three tosses, in which case, you can finish the trick there and then by saying, "You try it." Repeat the three tosses of the match, but with the other person tossing the match and you calling the side. The probability is small that he or she can repeat what you did.

● In most cases, you will have lost one or more times and the challenger is now set up for the last part of the trick. Continue with, "Look, this worked OK the other day. I'll tell you what, I'll bet you $10 that I make the match land on its edge. In fact, I'll make it easier. You bet a cent. If I win, you can pay me back over three weeks – a cent on the first day, two cents on the second, four cents on the third, and so on, doubling each day, up to 21 days. If you win, I'll give you $10 straight off."

● Having drawn the spectator into the challenge, just before you flick the match, bend it into a C-shape around your thumb (**2**).

● Flick the match into the air, and it is almost certain to

2

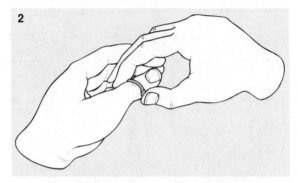

land on its edge. When it lands, add, "Well, I didn't say what condition the match would be in when it landed!"

● When the spectator and the audience roar in disapproval, finally back down and say, "All right, I'll give way on the bet. It's just as well. I'll show you what you owed me."

● With this, write out the four columns on the piece of paper and, using the calculator to help you add up, show just how much you would have won (**3**, see over).

● Finish with, "I could have retired early on that!"

3

Day	Payout each day (in cents)	Total payout (in cents)	Total payout (in dollars)
1	1	1	0.01
2	2	3	0.03
3	4	7	0.07
4	8	15	0.15
5	16	31	0.31
6	32	63	0.63
7	64	127	1.27
8	128	255	2.55
9	256	511	5.11
10	512	1023	10.23
11	1024	2047	20.47
12	2048	4095	40.95
13	4096	8191	81.91
14	8192	16383	163.83
15	16884	32767	327.67
16	32768	65535	655.35
17	65536	131071	1310.71
18	131072	262143	2621.43
19	262144	524287	5242.87
20	524288	1048575	10485.75
21	1048576	2097151	20971.51

GRAND TOTAL = **$20,971.51**

THE RING IS THE KEY

An astounding trick. This one will have your audience
truly perplexed.

Effect

The magician makes a borrowed ring disappear from a
wine glass. The ring is found attached to a clip inside a
key case. The case has been in the audience's view
throughout the trick.

Equipment

A wine glass. A thick linen handkerchief, a needle and
color-matched thread, and a metal ring about ½ in (15
mm) in diameter. A key case of the fold-over press-stud
type containing a row of clips (**1**). A jacket with top
pocket and side pockets.

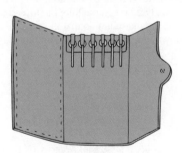

Preparation

Bend one of the key clips open so that a finger ring will
easily slip onto it (**2**, see over). Then attach three or
four keys onto the remaining clips.

2

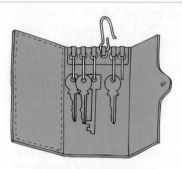

Close the key case so that the open clip hangs outside the case (**3**) and place the case in your left pocket. Prepare the handkerchief by knotting the metal ring onto the thread and then attaching the thread to the center of the handkerchief so that the ring, when hanging down, does not extend beyond the edge of the

3

handkerchief (**4**). Place the handkerchief in a top pocket with the ring well concealed.

4

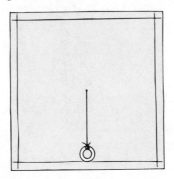

Performing

● Borrow a finger ring from a spectator and hold it in your left hand. With your right hand, take out your handkerchief and in full view of the audience place the ring under the handkerchief (**5**).

5

● As you do this, secretly palm the spectator's ring in your left hand (see p. 32).

● Bring the threaded ring up under the handkerchief (**6**).

6

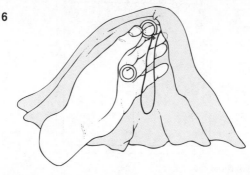

● Hold the threaded ring in your right hand through the material and give this to a second spectator to hold (**7**).

7

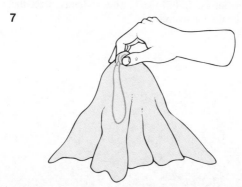

Put your left hand (containing the palmed ring) into your left pocket and quickly attach the ring to the open clip.

 Bring the case out of your pocket, making sure you conceal the clip and ring behind your hand (**8**).

8

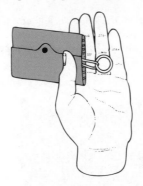

 Ask the spectator with the hankie to hold it over the glass and then to release the ring so that it drops into the glass (**9**).

9

● With your right hand reach across and whisk the handkerchief away and put it back in your top pocket (taking with it the threaded ring).

● Ask the first spectator to retrieve her ring from the glass. When she tries she will discover that the ring is no longer there.

● At this point, open the key case, and turn it to face the audience so that the keys are hanging down. There in the middle of the row of keys is a ring attached to a clip (**10**).

10

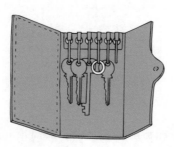

● Unhook the ring from the clip and hand it to the first spectator. She will verify it is hers. This should meet with appreciative applause – your audience will be genuinely baffled.

CUPS AND BALLS

A variation on the oldest known conjuring trick. This trick can be performed as a mime, i.e. in silence.

Effect

Using three beakers and three small paper balls, the magician makes a ball appear to pass through a stack of plastic beakers. This illusion is repeated once, and then once again. At the end, as if revealing the secret of the trick, the magician shows that he was using a fourth ball all along. When revealed, this fourth ball is much larger than the others and could not possibly have been used to perform the trick.

Equipment

Three opaque plastic beakers that nest (fit together). Four 2 x 2 in (5 x 5 cm) squares and a 10 x 10 in (25 x 25 cm) square of the same colored tissue paper. Table covered with a cloth. A jacket with side pockets.

Preparation

Roll the squares of tissue paper into four small balls and one large one. Place the large ball in your left pocket. Put one small ball in each cup and nest the cups together as shown (**1**, see over). Conceal the fourth small ball in your left hand using the palm technique (see Glossary).

Performing

● At the start of the trick pick up the three cups and hold them horizontally, with the fourth small paper ball still concealed in your hand (**2**).

● Now slide off the top cup and in one smooth movement place the cup in position on the tablecloth.

Done quickly and smoothly, the paper ball will remain inside the cup (**3**).

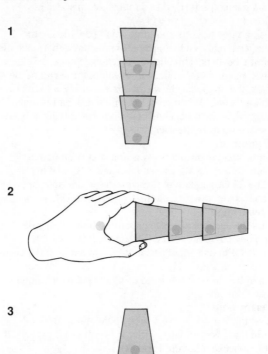

● Repeat this movement for the other two cups so that the three cups and their concealed balls are in position on the table (**4**).

● Tap each cup and lift the first to reveal a ball beneath it. Lift the cup with your right hand and casually place it into your left, its mouth over the concealed ball, as you direct the audience's attention to the ball on the table.

4

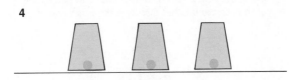

The second and third cups are lifted to reveal two more balls. As you pick up these cups nest them on top of the one in your left hand (**5**).

5

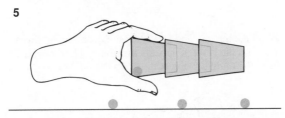

● Now place the three cups mouth down behind each of the balls. The first two cups are placed to the right and left positions and the third cup (containing the concealed ball) is placed in the center (**6**). The audience is unaware of the fourth ball.

6

● Pick up the center ball from the table and place it on top of the center cup, and then nest the other two cups on top (**7**).

7

● Tap the top cup and lift all three cups as one to reveal a ball on the table. It appears that the ball has moved from the middle to the bottom cup (**8**).

8

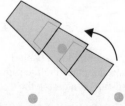

● Once again place all three cups on the table but place the middle cup (containing the extra ball) in position over the center ball on the table (**9**).

9

● Place the right-hand ball on top of this cup, then repeat your previous actions to make it apparently pass from the middle to the bottom cup – and reveal two balls on the table when you lift the three cups together.
● Repeat these actions once more but place the left-hand ball on top of the center cup and then, when all three cups are nested, get a member of the audience to tap the top cup. While this is happening you have ample opportunity to steal the large ball from your pocket and hold it concealed within your left hand.
● Lift all three cups as one to show that there are now three balls on the table. Casually place the nested cups into your left hand and over the concealed large ball (**10**).

10

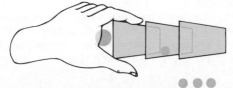

● Put all three cups on the table, with the large ball concealed beneath the bottom cup. The fourth ball remains hidden between the bottom and middle cup. This action should be done casually as if you have finished the trick.

● As if an afterthought, as you place the cups on the table pick up the three balls one at a time and say, "Sometimes people accuse me of using more than three balls when I do this trick. Who thinks this is the case?" Look around the audience and when you have found someone who thinks so, add, "You're right. In fact, I use four. This is the extra one." As you say this, lift all three cups as one to reveal the large ball on the table and take your bow.

● Dispose of the beakers carefully so that no one finds the hidden fourth small ball.

THE INDESTRUCTIBLE BALLOON

A baffling balloon trick, suitable for all age groups.

Effect

The performer inflates a long balloon, inserts it into a tube, and then proceeds to push several knitting needles through the tube and into the balloon. The needles are removed, and the tube then handed to a spectator. He takes out the balloon which, amazingly, is still intact.

Equipment

Several long, strong balloons. A cardboard or plastic tube about 3 in (7.5 cm) in diameter and about 5 in (12.5 cm) in length. A skewer or similar hole-punching device. Spray paint. Five smooth, slim, steel knitting needles.

Preparation

Take the tube and, with a skewer or similar device, punch ten holes around its middle (**1**) – five holes on one side of the tube and five holes on the other. The position of the holes is important. They should be staggered in two rows so that five knitting needles can be pushed through from one hole to another, leaving a central region inside the tube through which no needles pass (**2**).

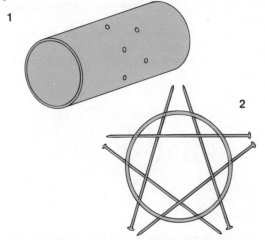

Once constructed, the tube can be decorated using spray paint. Check that the tube has no sharp edges which could puncture the balloon – any such defects must be removed.

Start the trick with the tube, the knitting needles and a selection of balloons on a table in full view of the audience.

Performing

● Ask a member of the audience to choose freely one balloon out of the several provided.

● Now show the tube to the audience and explain and show that there are several small holes around the center line of the tube.

● Hand the knitting needles to someone in the audience to inspect.

● Now take the chosen balloon, lower it into the tube, and start to inflate the balloon. Keep checking the balloon, so that it protrudes equally from either end of the tube (**3**).

3

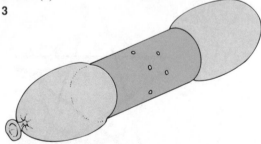

● Make sure you do not inflate the balloon too hard, but just enough for the balloon to be gripped securely by the tube. When you are satisfied, knot the neck of the balloon.

● The trick depends on you being able to twist the inflated balloon secretly so that a waist is introduced which effectively divides the balloon into two (**4**). Do this by distracting the audience momentarily, perhaps by asking for the return of the knitting needles. As you drop your hands to take back the needles, secretly twist one end of the balloon two complete turns away from you (**5**).

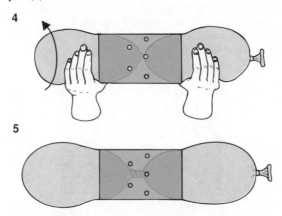

4

5

• Now take a needle in your right hand and hold up the tube in your left hand but with your thumb secretly inserted between the tube and the balloon (**6**, see over). The thumb allows you to check that the waist of the balloon is in the correct position, aligned with the holes. It also enables you to check that you are guiding the needles correctly from one hole to another and around the balloon.

• Now, carefully insert a needle from the back (your

side) through one hole so that it exits through a hole at
the front (the audience's side). Use your thumb to guide
the needle. When inserting or removing a needle, do so
slowly. Friction will cause the balloon to burst if the
needle is rubbed harshly along its side. Now hold up
the tube so that the audience can see the tube from all
sides and see that the needle does pass right through.
● Continue in this way, inserting one needle at a time,
until all five needles are in position (**7**). Hold up the
balloon and take a bow.

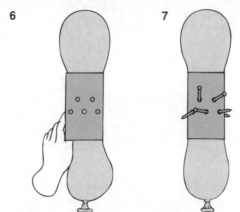

● Now, slowly and carefully, remove the needles one at
a time, again with your thumb in position.
● Just before removing the last needle, secretly untwist
the balloon so that the waist is removed.
● Now hand the balloon to a member of the audience
and get him to slowly remove the last needle.

● Take the intact balloon out of the tube and hand the balloon, tube and needles to the audience for them to inspect. Take a well-deserved bow.

SAYING GOODBYE

A magical way of saying goodbye at the end of your performance.

Effect

The performer folds a plain banner in half, inserts a length of red ribbon and then unfolds the banner. The word "Goodbye" is now magically revealed, written in red ribbon.

Equipment

Three pieces of soft, dark material, all the same color and size, about 16 x 12 in (40 x 30 cm). Two pieces of red ribbon about 3 ft (1 m) long. At least 15 ft (5 m) of color-matched sewing thread, a sewing needle and chalk. A ruler. Glue (optional).

Preparation

Place one piece of material on the table and lay a second piece on top of it. Sew the two pieces together along the top edge and exactly halfway down each side. Open out the two unsewn flaps and place these flaps against the third piece of material. Sew this third piece onto the other two pieces so that you now have a three-sided banner as shown (**1**, see over).

Across one side write, in chalk, "Goodbye." Then sew or glue one of the red ribbons over the chalk to form the word (**2**).

Performing

● Pick up the banner and hold it with the written side folded down as shown (**3**).

1

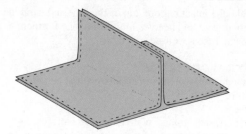

2

3

● Raise both bottom edges to the top, so forming two
pockets (**4**). Into the rear pocket place the length of red
ribbon.

● Now change hands, and as you do so, release your
grip on the outer fold (the one facing the audience). The
flap falls, revealing the message "Goodbye" (**5**).

● Take a bow and leave the stage, hopefully to well-
deserved applause.

4

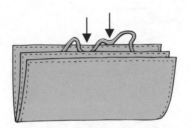

5

Glossary

The following is a list of some of the terms you will
need to know when performing tricks.

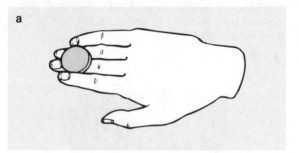

backpalm
A sleight that allows the hand to be shown empty while
concealing behind the fingers (**a**).

bight
A loop of rope, string or similar contained in a knot.

block of cards
A section of the pack kept together during shuffling,
cutting or dealing.

changing bag
A bag with two (or more) compartments, used for
exchanging one item for another.

close-up magic
Tricks designed to be performed close to the audience.

cut

Dividing the pack in two and putting the half that was on the bottom on the top. A deck can be also cut into several parts (see pp. 20–22).

deal

The method by which single cards are distributed from the top of the pack.

deck or pack

Playing cards used for a particular game. The standard deck is 52 cards, ie four suits of 13 cards each.

double lift

A SLEIGHT where two cards are lifted from the pack but the audience believes that only one card was removed (see pp. 25–27).

false count

A count of items which appears genuine but where the number of items is actually more or less than it seems to be.

false shuffle

An apparently fair shuffle that keeps all or some of the cards in a set order (see pp. 12–16).

fan

Spreading the cards to form a neat fan shape (see pp. 18–19).

finale

The finish to a trick or an act – usually the high point of the performance.

b

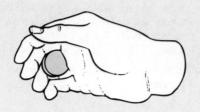

fingerpalm
Concealing an item between the fingers of a hand (**b**).

flourish
A dramatic way of turning a spread of cards face up in a wave-like motion (see p. 20).

force
To give a spectator an apparently free choice but really making him or her select an object of the performer's choice.

gimmick
A secret piece of equipment (sometimes called a **fake**).

glide
A SLEIGHT in which the performer retains the bottom card of the pack and deals the next card as if it were the bottom card (see pp. 22–23).

glimpse
To view an item secretly (see also pp. 24–25).

homing

The magical return of an object to its original place after it has seemingly disappeared.

key card

A known card which locates or marks the position of other cards.

lapping

The art of secretly dropping items on the lap while seated at a table.

mentalism

Using physical methods to give the appearance of mind-reading or clairvoyance.

misdirection

The art of drawing the spectator's attention away from a secret move.

move

The execution of a SLEIGHT or other secret maneuver.

one ahead

A principle of MENTALISM in which the performer is at least one move ahead of the audience.

overhand shuffle

The standard method of mixing a pack of cards (see pp. 10–12).

pack See DECK.

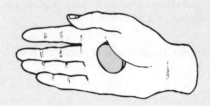

palming
Concealing an item in the palm of the hand (**c**) (see also pp. 29–31).

patter
The speech – story line, jokes, and so on – used by a performer during an act.

pile
A portion of the pack formed, for example, by cutting the cards.

production
Making objects appear from thin air or from an apparently empty container.

props
Objects used by a conjuror in performing a trick.

pull
A GIMMICK, often worked by elastic, that makes an item vanish by pulling it up the sleeve or beneath a jacket.

riffle

To flick the edge or corner of a pack to make a clicking noise.

riffle shuffle

An on-the-table shuffle in which the two halves of the pack are interwoven as the thumbs riffle and release the cards singly at speed (see pp. 16–17).

routine

The order of events that make up a trick or a series of tricks in a performance.

servante

A hidden shelf or suspended pocket, behind a table or chair or otherwise concealed, to receive items discarded or exchanged.

set up

The way props are arranged for a trick.

shuffle

To mix the cards, by hand.

sleight

A skillful movement of the fingers by which a trick effect is accomplished.

sleight of hand

The performing of SLEIGHTS.

spread

Cards in an overlapping arrangement which allows an individual to easily pick a card or – if the cards are face up – to see the values of the cards (see pp. 18–20).

squaring the pack
Neatly aligning the cards, eg by tapping their edges on a table.

stack
An arrangement of cards in a known or predetermined sequence.

steal
To remove something secretly from the place where it is concealed.

stooge
Also called a **confederate**. Someone from the audience posing as a volunteer, but who is actually working with the performer to make the trick work.

sucker trick
A trick in which the performer lets the audience believe that they have worked out how the trick is done or that they have seen a mistake. The performer then proves them wrong.

suits
Clubs, spades, hearts, and diamonds.

switch
To exchange one item for another secretly.

talk
The accidental sound made by something hidden, thus revealing its presence to the audience.

d

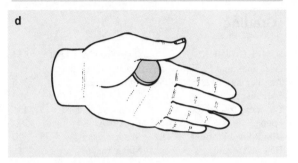

thumbpalm
Concealing an item by holding it at the base of the
thumb and first finger (**d**).

top
The part of the pack that is uppermost when the pack is
face down. The "top" of a face-up pack, therefore, is at
the bottom.

wand
Originally used to describe the stick claimed to be the
source of a magician's power. A wand in one hand is a
practical device which can, for example, be used to
conceal a small object in the palm or, by pointing, to
direct (or MISDIRECT) attention.

Grading

TRICKS REQUIRING SKILL AND PRACTICE

Index